Contemporary Indian Writing in English

Edited by
Charu Mehrotra

ATLANTIC
PUBLISHERS & DISTRIBUTORS (P) LTD

Published by

ATLANTIC

PUBLISHERS & DISTRIBUTORS (P) LTD

7/22, Ansari Road, Darya Ganj, New Delhi-110002
Phones : +91-11-40775252, 40775214, 23273880, 23275880
Fax : +91-11-23285873
Web : www.atlanticbooks.com
E-mail : orders@atlanticbooks.com

Branch Office: Chennai
Phones : +91-44-48531784, 28291383
E-mail : chennai@atlanticbooks.com

Reprint 2021

Printed & bound in India by Atlantic Print Services

Preface

Indian writing in English, which has unbounded appraisal both in India and abroad, is now in its full swing. It has paved a new path, a new vision that is full of an unswerving faith and hope, myths and traditions, customs and rites that our glorious country has enveloped in its bosom since time immemorial. A deep study of the works of great masters reveals that their works are not mere imitations but highly original and Indian in both theme and spirit. They have given a new dimension to English Literature in the same manner as the Australians, Canadians and Americans have evolved their own literature. Today, English is a heritage not only of England but is also gaining ground all over the world. Perhaps that is the reason it has assimilated a number of Indian words in the latest English dictionaries. Since Independence, several Indian writers have been published and won praise abroad. They have won awards in equal competition with writers whose mother tongue is English. The journey of Indian literature in English narrates India's long struggle from tradition to modernity. It is perhaps easier to detect the new changes in English than other literatures in India, because English is a global language. Our writers feel as comfortable in writing in English as in their mother tongue. They have been quite familiar with the important modern Western literary movements like post-modernism, post-colonialism, feminism, structuralism, etc. This has equipped them to realize the relative points of India and the West. It is remarkable that the spirit of the age is mirrored in various genres of literature, but it is more effectively seen in the fiction of the period. It does not mean that other genres of literature are not prospering; they are equally winning recognition at the international platform.

The post-independence period is a landmark in the development of the short story which deals with the intense inner feelings of individuals that are implanted in their very consciousness. Women writers are more concerned with feminist issues. Feminism in Indian writing in English followed the Western feminist movement. It has got support from our freedom struggle under the dynamic humanitarianism of Mahatma Gandhi, independence, spread of education, job opportunities, and laws for women's rights. These women novelists do not stand in the patriarchal circle of confinement. Instead, they come out and address the world from their vantage point. Indian women in 21st century have been presented as politically conscious, professionally qualified, and ready to prove themselves in men's world. Individual identity is the central theme of almost all feminist fiction. Shashi Deshpande, Rohinton Mistry, Upamanyu Chatterjee, Manju Kapur, Anita Nair, Chitra Banerjee, Amit Chaudhari, Namita Devidayal, and Rupa Bajwa are some of the prominent explorers of woman's heart.

The second coming of the twice born novel happened with the help of the diasporic community under the leadership of Salman Rushdie. Credit goes to this community that it continues to cultivate the genre of Indian English fiction in a commendable way. The diasporic novelists are constantly exploring answers to questions of identity, as they are pulled apart between their country of origin and the country of adoption. They remember their past through memories, fantasy and myth, and also write about their immigrant experience. Bharati Mukherjee, Jhumpa Lahiri, Chitra Banerjee, Anita Rau Badami, Boman Desai, Roswitha Joshi, Amulya Mulladi, and Amitabha Chatterjee deal with the multi-cultural family and problems of the Indian immigrants to the U.S. at the cultural level.

The first decade of the 21st century saw a revolution in the field of popular fiction which was lead by Chetan Bhagat, who has been welcomed as the largest selling Indian writer. The genre of popular novel is known by different names like metro reads, chick-lit, tech-lit, campus-lit, etc. Chetan Bhagat's *Five Point Someone* (campus novel), Suman Hossain's *A Guy Thing*, Abhijit Bhaduri's *Married But Available*, Soumya Bhattacharya's *If I Could Tell You,* Anuja Chauhan's *The Zoya Factor*, Varsha Dixit's *Right Fit Wrong Shoe*, Swati Kaushal's *Piece of Cake*, Jaishree Misra's *Secrets And Lies*, Advaita Kala's *Almost Single*, Anita Jain's *Marrying Anita*, and Tarun Tejpal's *Alchemy of Desire* are some of the names of the writers and books written in the popular genre in the contemporary time.

Science fiction does not have deep roots in Indian English Literature. Historical novels need not totally conform to the historical truth. Similarly, mythological, and supernatural novels do not do away with the writer's inventiveness. Novels like *The Return of Vaman* by Jayant Narlikar, *The Calcutta Chromosome* by Amitav Ghosh, and *Transmission* by Hari Kunzru are based on science. *Armies of Hanuman*, *Siege of Mithila,* and *Gods of War* are the examples of mythological novels, while *Fireproof* by Raj Kamal Jha, *Q and A* by Swarup, and *In Shadowland* by Chitra are the examples of supernatural novels. The mind-boggling process taking place in science and technology, social sciences, etc. has led to a fast pace of life, and literature too is being expected to move along.

In summing up, it can be said that contemporary Indian English Literature by and large is the monopoly of the city-bred middle class elite, the privileged public school-educated, or the foreign-educated people. Motivated by the success stories of the recent past, the novelists write for the English-reading privileged class within India or outside India. The diasporic writing mostly depends upon media reports which capture reality selectively and sensationally so that what comes to light may not be the entire truth. This class has been responsible for selling to the West a crooked, exotic India. In the name of reality what we get is only a re-affirmation of the Western suspicion of our ability to govern ourselves.

It is to note that fiction is getting popular but most of it falls in the category of kitsh or pulp fiction. It is a fact that the record sale of Chetan Bhagat's books has remained unbroken. It indicates widening of readership which is a welcome sign. The trends in popular fiction are also set by publishing houses just as it happens in the case of commercial films. But there is always scope for better works. The significant thing here is that the kitsh should not supplant serious literature.

The influence of the theoretical debates strongly prevalent in the Western academies is earnestly recorded in the literature produced in India. Therefore, the concept of nation, history, subjectivity, and society are sought to be problematized with abandon and without the least consideration for the context and the consequences. Deconstructing the concept of nation to underline its imaginary nature may be good theory but it is certainly bad in practical terms, as was the other utopian ideals of stateless society.

Indian English writers appear to be moving partially in a single direction by the spirit of post-modernism. Although they are ready to lend their ear to the narratives circulating in the public domain, their choice is dominated by political ideologies. It is still in question in this postmodern picture, what is the place and where do Indian culture and thought exist.

This collection of critical essays is an attempt to explore the dominant thematic and ideological concerns of contemporary Indian English Literature. The stylish experiments of the new-age authors shall also be an area of critical attention. Altogether the present work will evaluate the contribution of significant Indian English authors to their chosen genres.

Charu Mehrotra

Contents

Contributors

Rita Garg, Reader, Department of English, INPG College, Meerut.

Amrita Meharwal, Lecturer, RKGEG College, Ghaziabad.

S.V. Singh, Associate Prof. and HOD, English, S.R.K.P.G. College, Firozabad.

Kamni Kumar, Assist. Prof., English, Bareilly College, Bareilly.

Aparna Sharma, Lecturer, Department of Communicative Skills, Utkarsh College, Meerganj, Bareilly.

Shivali Singh, Assist. Prof. and HOD, Department of English, IFTM University, Moradabad.

Ravindra Kumar Singh, Assist. Prof., Department of English, K.K.P.G. College, Etawah.

Arun Kumar Yadav, Research Scholar, University of Lucknow.

Sanjay Johari, Assist. Prof., Department of English JSHPG College, Amroha.

Tripty Seth, Lecturer, Department of English, Bareilly College, Bareilly.

Darkhasha Azhar, Assist. Prof., English Govt. PG College, Bisalpur, Pilibhit.

Neha Vatsal, Academic Counsellor, IGNOU Study Centre, Mandi (H.P.).

Deepa Singh, Assist. Prof., English, Chamanlal Degree College, Landhaura, Haridwar (U.K.).

Ghanshyam Kumar, Research Scholar, LNMU, Dharbhanga (Bihar).

Faraha Naqvi, Research Scholar in the Department of English, Integral University, Lucknow.

Gunjan Saxena, Lecturer, Department of English, Bareilly College, Bareilly.

Jyoti Vishnoi, Lecturer, Abdul Razaq PG College, Joya, Uttar Pradesh.

Seema Srivastava, Lecturer, Department of English, Bareilly College, Bareilly.

Mirza Sibtain Beg, Assist. Prof., Shia PG College, Lucknow.

Charu Mehrotra, Associate Prof., Department of English, Bareilly College, Bareilly.

Suman Chauhan, Assist. Prof., English, Meerut College, Meerut.

Parul Rastogi, Assist. Prof., English, Government PG College, Badaun.

1

The Overshadowed Kaleidoscope of Kamala Das's Short Stories: *A Doll for the Child Prostitute*

Rita Garg

Her verse is renowned and brings her international fame but the stories are not much acclaimed. No doubt, with regard to her prose, autobiography, novel, and short stories also, she has carved a niche for self. The stories have—thematically and technically—the standard of the writer as proven through the better known genre poetry.

The critical approaches to the themes of her poetry are also applicable to the prose. The researchers on her poetic talent link the autobiographical element at large. Her emotions expressed are looked upon as the window to share her experiences. She is a well-read person also associated with such eminent journalists as Pritish Nandy. Her association with such poets as Meena Alexander, Eunice de Souza also plays a role in the fame achieved.

Research on Kamala Das brings her fame as a feminist also. She herself does not claim so. She composes as a woman and what she paints is possible but by a woman only; that too, with minute details, agony, perception and above all, that agony which be associated largely with others. This his suffices as a parameter of feministic delineations.

Rajeshwar Mittapalli and Pier Paolo Piciucco comment: "Kamala Das has been a unique literary phenomenon in India.

Frank, bold and controversial in life and literature. Kamala Das made enormous contribution to the growth of Indian Poetry in English. Although she sporadically ventured into the realms of fiction, she will be remembered primarily for her poetry, because it is as a poet that she excels herself" (Preface).

Her poetry reveals the poetess to various researchers as a split-self too. Sharda Iyer writes: "It describes an opposition women feel between essential aspects of the self, between what is socially prescribed on the basis of gender and what is defined on the basis of the self, between what a woman feels she should be and what she feels she is. Kamala Das has written a substantial number of poems exploring this duality, the pain and frustrations. She particularly identifies the two selves with the domestic gender role and the artist" (114).

Besides feminism, the relevance of the theme of love is also discernible. To be accurate, love is much cherished in her poems. This not only mesmerizes but also calls for much of analysis. This vision is not singular. Rather, that has Radha and Meera myths; single woman's feelings; or, the scene of emotion in general. K. Indra Sena Reddy observes: "Of all the Indian English women poets, Kamala Das has received maximum critical attention. More often than not, she has been acknowledged and acclaimed as an outstanding love-poet. Her poetry, in the main, deals with the various facets of love-experience" (123).

Kamala Das has poetry in her blood. Both her mother and grandfather being established poets in Malayalam. Besides the feminine sensibility, her works are filled with Indianness. K.V. Surendran opines: "The world of her poems is thoroughly Indian or a world of that she has made her own" (130).

In case of Kamala Das quality steals a march over quantity. It is by virtue of lyricism, openness, that she reigns the world of Indian Writing in English Poetry. No doubt, A.N. Dwivedi appropriately comments on her range: "Kamala Das moves in a narrow range in her poetry. Like Jane Austen in English fiction, her range of themes is limited. Very often there is witnessed repetition and consequent monotony, in the body of her poetical works. However, she moves in her circle with grace and skill. She does not try to transgress her self-imposed limitations, and this accounts for her success in poetical endeavours" (20).

The undercurrent of sympathy for the sufferer has dominance in verse as well as prose. The above applies to her prose with equal weightage. The sensibility of hers; the projection of patriarchy; the child's forbearance; the ill-treatment at the hands of parents; economic pressures; social demands; faithless spouses, etc. sustain that she has a wide understanding and ability to project in the right ethos. She expresses her views on all these as an observer as well as an insider. Broadly speaking, the themes have commonality in both the genres. Even then untarnished goes the attentiveness of the reader for her dealing with the subject. The title story depicts how the innocence of a child is looted.

Her story collection, *A Doll for the Child Prostitute* has touching short stories relating to those issues which are concerned with the aspects of life and society, unresolved till date. The sensibility; patriarchy; child's forbearance; or parental ignorance, are the root themes.

She expresses her views on all these as an observer as well as an insider. The themes have commonality in verse, autobiography, novel and short stories. Even then, untarnished goes the interest of the reader for her treatment of the subject. The title story depicts how the innocence of the child is cheated. Instead of being thrown into the trade of flesh at the immature age of thirteen, she should have been given a doll. The girl, Rukmani is physically assaulted by stepfather and later she is sold to Ayee. The seller is none other than poor, Anasuya, the mother.

The story has ironical style. Rukmani is ill-treated by parents but in the brothel of Ayee, she is protected by an Inspector Saheb. The Inspector calls Rukmani for pleasure but she starts yelling and calls him, 'Papa, Papa' (50) and this changes her attitude because he has a granddaughter living with parents at Poona. He assures her protection. In this story, the storyteller describes of one more inmate who elopes with a boy who is caught by the Inspector and beaten as well. On the one hand, the story tells of human nature, on the other it pertains to moral malpractices, and undeserving men working in uniformed services of a city like Bombay. To be true the story shatters the ethos of civilisation believed by in general. This is not only ironical but also capacitated to hammer the minds of those generally quiet on the miserable conditions of the lower class people.

The second story, "The Young Man with the Pitted Face" has the relevance because it is highly suggestive of community helping hand being extended for the strangers and for no gain of the helper. This was published in 1977 but its significance deepens now. A woman who is on death bed is looked after by a young, handsome boy who stops visiting after the recovery of the patient. Like the previous story, here too the writer is referring to the outsider's affection and sympathy. After the improvement of health, she waits for the supporter but he serves the purpose to vanish from the scene.

How the confidence of a woman suffering from disease is shattered, is the psychological dealing by the writer in the third story, "December". In a cold December night, a woman after recovery, has carnal satiation and tells the man that she would never be able to write again as she has the change of psychology to being 'sentimental' (63). She considers herself a weak person although she is physically fit.

In both the stories, the autobiographical part has a depiction but to be true, these apply to many persons and this way a realistic psychological picture has the portrayal. Other than this a strong feministic picture is also brought forth.

With the rise of space given to feminism, the next story "A Little Kitten" is based on the drudgery of a housewife who is alone at home and her husband is much involved with official duties. To be engaged, her desire expressed to rear a kitten and the refusal on the part of the husband shows the lack of understanding. Rather, joyfully enough, the spouse offers self as her kitten. With regard to carnal relations she has no choices and similarly, about the pet. The role of patriarchy has complexities as well. This is the theme to permeate through the creation. Even this affection of his comes to doldrums as the secretary of his carves space for self in his life. This coming to light brings forth the rebel in her and the step taken is of adultery. This crucial act is not described at length; rather hint is given of it. Not to let agony dominate the situation and infuse subtlety of expression is noticeable here with. No doubt, the drastic situation would have had no dearth of the dramatic descriptions.

In "Darjeeling", once again the delineation of familial scene with economic pressure is delineated. Raghvan, the central figure finds it difficult to spend much on the family. Even the critical moments in the family call for overdrafting. When his wife is in of hospitalization, he has to seek ₹ five hundred by overdrafting. The situation takes an ironical turn with this step of his as he is reminded by his son how his wife was always keen on visitation to the snow-capped Darjeeling hills. The constraints of a man with insufficient means are focussed in the story.

This is a direct narration of fiscal shortcomings which are sorted out after a casualty rather than prior to that. The writer pinpoints the middle class attitude that there is no amount for fun but only for emergencies.

"The Sign of the Lion" hits upon the old traditions of patriarchy. The fears and apprehensions of a newly-wed girl are based on the hearsay that she might be killed. Instead of being discouraged, she believes in giving birth to a little lion like baby. At the opportune moment, she delivers the news to her husband who does not show any inclination of joy. Thus it hampers the reader's mind if he is really going to be sincere to his wife. The reader is disgusted but also inquisitive as to what the situation is like. To mention that the bride would be killed is beyond imagination but Kamala Das makes it not so easy to disbelieve. His lack of enthusiasm is a prediction of some ill-will. Thus through ethos and inklings is conveyed the idea of negativity.

It is worth mentioning that a negative picture of woman is carefully drawn by Kamala Das in her story, "Sanatan Choudhary's Wife". The depiction of a woman as a disloyal figure to her husband is a conviction that Kamala Das does not necessarily appreciate woman. Her belief of man and woman appears balanced. Fault is of the individual and not necessarily of man or woman, in general. The fact is that greed is natural to many of human beings. It is self-discipline that helps it fight.

Here Gopi Menon's wife is not satisfied with the poor show of her sarees. Her husband cannot afford all the desired sarees for her. One day her husband develops doubts of her as he overhears her muttering in sleep, Sanatan. To check her, he returns home early and finds that she has gone to the house of Sanatan Choudhary. On reaching his place, Gopi Menon finds that she is served a stylish breakfast and also that Sanatan is free to fondle her. When he questions his wife, she says that there is someone befooling him. Out of sheer helplessness, Gopi returns.

Kamala Das is charged with the limited range but in the story, "The Coroner", this is refuted. The story depicts a scene of colonisers and their style of functioning. Here is Sylvester Louis Gomes who is a collector of rents working for an old man. Gomes's twenty-three-year old son, Richie and his friends go to the sea where he is drowned. In such an accidental death, the coroner is supposed to inquest but the master Gomes phones him and to hand over the body without official procedures. The coroner agrees as his grandfather and Gomes's master had studied together in London. Gomes narrates this story to a nice rent-paying pregnant young woman.

The poignancy of love unrequited is touched upon by the story writer in the next creation, 'Iqbal'. Here the writer describes how the poet takes a suicidal step. The reason is that his lady love is married to his friend. She is not aware of the fact. In hospital he is taken care of by his old room-mate. The beautiful wife of the friend also visits him. She is at the centre of his verse and this truth is not known to her. After improvement in his health, he visits the family of his friend but this does not continue long. He starts declining the offers. Getting to understand through the verse, she questions her husband who the poet's love is, but he evades the query. This also assures that she is the love of the poet. Later on, she blames the poet that he is jealous of her. No doubt, this story is also remarkable for the matured attitude of the husband and wife. They understand the situation but elude the complexities.

A familial scene of filial ingratitude is pictured in "The Tattered Blanket". The pains of a mother are painted here like Premchand. An officer in Delhi, Gopi is not willing to retain his ancestral property in Kerala. He comes to dispose it off. The occupants of the house are his widowed mother and sister. The latter are too reluctant to sell the house. Out of anxieties mother has become mentally crippled. She has a tattered blanket which does not suffice her needs. Even then her demand of a new red blanket is not paid heed. The officer is lost in his own world and these two family members bear no sense for him. How the man prefers to look after his own needs rather than of his mother and sister is an agonizing picture to disturb the reader.

'Leukaemia' too has a familial depiction of a less understanding mother. She sends her daughter to a boarding school where the daughter lives but reluctantly. The ultimate is that she develops leukaemia. Ironically, as the scene is, the calamity rids her of the boarding. Mother informs her that she would not be sent to boarding again and the daughter is very much pleased. She is also supplied with lots of toys. Ignorant of the severity of the disease the girl is overjoyed to see the toys and is relieved of the tension. The scene is entirely the much desired one.

The contemporary questions associated with patriarchy, eco-feminism, and community help, surfaced with human psyche and captivating projection mesmerize the reader.

How the characters are agonized for the lack of understanding. The agony, anxiety, pain, mortify impacts, financial seas city, life in a big city, unhealthy practices on the part of the spouse and familial discrepancies are the noteworthy features which make the story collection worth appreciation. It is the human sensibility that she basically hits upon.

WORKS CITED

Das, Kamala, *A Doll for the Child Prostitute*. New Delhi: India Paperbacks, 1977.

Dwivedi, A.N., "Main Themes of Das's Poetry" *Kamala Das and Her Poetry* (Second Revised and Enlarged Edition). New Delhi: Atlantic Publishers, 2000.

Iyer, Sharda, "Split-Self in the Poetry of Kamala Das", *Kamala Das: A Critical Spectrum*, Eds. Rajeshwar Mittapalli and Pier Piciucco. New Delhi: Atlantic Publishers, 2001, rpt. 2013.

Mittapalli, Rajeshwar and Piciucco Paolo (Eds.), "Preface", *Kamala Das: A Critical Spectrum*. New Delhi: Atlantic Publishers, 2001, rpt. 2013.

Reddy, K. Indra Sen, "Between the Fire and the Hungry Earth: A Note on Kamala Das", *Kamala Das: A Critical Spectrum*. New Delhi: Atlantic Publishers, 2001, rpt. 2013.

Surendran, K.V., "Suffering and Humiliation in Kamala Das' Poetry", *Kamala Das: A Critical Spectrum,* Eds. Rajeshwar Mittapalli and Pier Piciucco. New Delhi: Atlantic Publishers, 2001, rpt. 2013.

2

Haroun and the Sea of Stories: Search for Identity as an Individual

Amrita Meharwal

By the publication of this novel in 1990, Salman Rushdie had been established as a revolutionary writer in the world of literature. With this artistic fancy, Rushdie deals with the crises and problems of the contemporary world. His novel, *Haroun and the Sea of Stories* has the appeal for artistic freedom. In the novel, Rushdie raises the issues of creativity, artistic freedom or search for identity. The novel is about Rashid Khalifa, a storyteller and his son Haroun. It is a tale of artistic freedom, desire of free speech and true recognition also. Storytelling or speech is a medium to communicate with others and show the realities of the world. This novel comes out after the exile of Rushdie and the exile prohibited Rushdie's individual liberty and freedom of expression. This is the grief of a writer who has lost his communicative skill. Rushdie presents this fact with his imaginative power and visualize the artist's struggle for his happiness in *Imaginary Homelands* Rushdie stated that literature is an interim report from the consciousness of the artist, and so it can never be 'finished' or 'perfect'. Literature is made as the frontier between the self and the world and in the act of creation, the frontier softens, becomes permeable, allow the world to flow into the artist and the artist to flow into the world.

It is necessary that the values of artist must be free from the social and political statements. A writer wants freedom and without it he can never create best identity in this world. The novel, *Haroun and the Sea of Stories* comes out after the fatwa, a death sentence to the writer of *Satanic Verses* which was issued by Ayatollah Khomeini. During the period of fatwa imposition Rushdie wrote a book for his young son Zafar. The book began with some lines dedicated to his son and the first letter of each line spelling out the boy's name—Zembla, Zenda, Xanadu: All our dream worlds may come true but fairy lands are fearsome too. As I wonder far from view, read and bring them home to you.

Although this book is for his son and it is like a child story book but Rushdie connected it with the personal liberty and freedom of speech. According to a critic W.J. Weatherby this "...long fable for children...had been in his (Rushdie's) mind for the last three years as something he wanted to do next (after completing the *Satanic Verses*). It was a very long, very fantastic story that he found very pleasurable to write, perhaps because it had such obvious connections with the Arabian Nights stories of his boyhood and few reminders of the grim reality he was living through, i.e. the controversy over the *Satanic Verses*. He had originally planned the story for his young son, Zafar, and he used to read an early version to the boy in serialized form at the boy's bed time. "It was the part of the deal so I could finish *Satanic Verses*." Rushdie once said. He was asked "why all my books were for grown-ups and I did not have an answer" (27). But when Rushdie was deeper into the fable, he didn't find it so very different from writing his grown-ups novels. Once you set the tone of your voice and the idea for a fable going, you don't really have to write it in any different way than you normally would. You just tell the story, and you make it as interesting as you can, because, the thing about children is, if they're bored, they will tell you, they will shut the book.

Haroun and the Sea of Stories is Rushdie's creation for children, it begins like a fairy tale. In other words, the novel has harsh reality, it contains the feelings of a writer who suffers from exile and solitariness. It depicts the pain and eternal agony of an individual who losts everything, his family, country and his liberty during this exile. The story revolves around the master storyteller Rashid Khalifa and his only child Haroun. They lived in the country of Alifbay, a sad city and Rashid Khalifa was famous for his stories and cheerfulness, Rashid approves his identity as a storyteller in the society. He earned two nicknames, for his admires he was ocean of nation and for his rivals he was the Shah of Blah. The stories of Rashid fascinates Haroun and he thinks that his father is a juggler whose tricks bring stories together. Haroun is very curious to know that where the stories come from? And his father replies that 'from the great Story Sea'. He'd reply, "I drink the warm story waters and then I feel full of steam" (17).

The personality of Rashid is full of imagination and through this he creates new stories. Through the language and imagination an individual can elaborate his ideas and his attitude towards life. Generally, Rushdie writes his novels in social and political context, but *Haroun and the Sea of Stories* is an attempt to conduct a child story which relates with the search of identity with a touch of fancy. He creates a logical arena which makes an appeal to reader's heart and mind also. In the novel, Rushdie portrays the struggle of a person for his family and identity, Soraya has stopped singing but Rashid don't notice this. This is the sign of something going wrong. Haroun is very much fond of stories but Mr. Sengupta, neighbor of Rashid don't like the stories of Rashid. He lives upstairs with his wife Oneeta. Sengupta has a practical approach towards life and he criticises Rashid and his stories. Adiga's career in journalism began as a financial journalist as an intern at *Financial Times*, *Money* and the *Wall Street Journal*. His area of coverage was the stock market and investment. He's got his head stuck in the air and his feet off the ground. What are all these stories? Life is not a story book or joke shop. All this fun will come to no good. What's the use of stories that aren't event true?

One day *Soraya* runs off with Mr. Sengupta. The circumstances changed and Rashid lost his art of storytelling. After some days Haroun and Rashid Khalifa are invited by a political party from the town G in the valley of K. The politicians have planned to attract the crowd through the stories of Rashid. But unimaginable things happened:

> Then the thing happened, the unthinkable thing, Rashid went out on to the stage in front of that vast jungle of a crowd, and Haroun watched him from the wings—and the poor storyteller opened his mouth, and the crowd squealed in excitement and now Rashid Khalifa, standing there with his mouth hanging open, found that it was an empty as heart. 'Ark', That was all that come out, The Shah of Blah sounded like a stupid crow, Ark, ark, ark. (33)

Rashid Khalifa lost his power of imagination and identity as a master storyteller. Language is the best medium of expression; this expression defines the personality and the recognition. Identity means recognition; identity is recognition of a person in the society and provides social and religious authority. It is solid and fixed recognition of an individual and encourages people to take part in social activities. Every individual personality has their set rules and values. A.L. Epstein defines the identity: "Identity...is essentially a concept of synthesis. It represents the process by which person seeks to integrate his various statuses and roles, as well as his diverse experiences, into a coherent image of self" (21).

Every individual identity has its own limits and area. A person struggles with his boundaries and limitations and society or social institution provide the opportunities to prove the recognition of the self. In *Haroun and the Sea of Stories,* Rashid Khalifa presents his identity as a creative storyteller because of his imagination and creativity and proves his identity in the social context and gain popularity or happiness. An individual embodies emotions, desire and feelings in his identity. A man lived in this world-wide society and every person wants own identity and personal existence in this world. "Personal identity, according to the psycho-sociologist, Erik Erikson, is an individual's "subjective sense of a continuous existence and a coherent memory" (15).

Personal identity is individual's real presence in the world and its connection with world. Every personal identity has demerits and up and down but it has the qualities to make firm existence in this world. In the world an individual adopt identity from their parents and continues it to the next generation and adopt a social identity in a specific country or a culture. Personal identity is directly connected with the social identity because man makes family and family makes society. Social identity, by contrast is the identification of one individual with the other, be it a small group, a religious community, or a nation.

Every identity has its own set rules and values. A society which has no boundaries or restrictions is always stronger than a society that is bounded by the government policy. The entire world is in the grip of globalization and in this materialistic age an individual identity has been lost. The material age demolish the charm, expression and self-satisfaction of one's personality and every individual has struggle for identity and union of characters and soul. Rushdie submits about identity: "O eternal opposite of inside and outside! Because a human being, inside himself, is anything but a whole, anything but homogeneous, all kinds of everything are jumbled up inside him, and he is one person one minute and another person the next" (19).

Identity also includes the actions, emotions and action towards society. In Rushdie's novels migration is another aspect of lost identity. Most of the protagonists of Rushdie's novels are migrants. There is sense of loss and some urge to search for identity. Rushdie himself has analyzed the dilemma that an expatriate writer like him has to face at every step as he tries to create an imaginary home for himself and reconstruct his roots. "Our identity too is at once plural and partial. Sometimes we feel that we straddle two cultures; at other times, that we fall between two stools. But, however, ambiguous and shifting this ground may be, it is not an infertile territory for a writer to occupy" (12).

An individual is the part of the country and the world. Every person has the urge to search and prove the identity. For a writer his writings are the instrument to prove him and establish new values for the world and his own self. In the novel, Haroun and Rashid Khalifa struggle to gain his ability of storytelling. This struggle is full of adventures. Haroun thought that he has to do something for his father. Rashid tells about, the Khattam-Shud to Haroun.

He said: "Khattam-Shud, he said slowly, is the Arch Enemy of all stories, even of language itself. He is the Prince of Silence and the Foe of Speech. And because everything ends, because dreams end, stories end, life ends, at the finish of everything we use his name. It's finished; we tell one another, 'it is over Khattam-Shud:' The End" (22).

In the valley of K, Haroun and Rashid Khalifa are received by Mr. Snooty Buttoo and Haroun thought that he is the right person who is helping them. He accommodates Haroun and his father in a houseboat named Arabian Nights Plus One. Haroun is sleeping in the houseboat but his sleep is disturbed by some noise which is coming from bathroom. Here he sees a small ancient looking blue bearded man. His hair are also blue and he is wearing a huge purple turban on his head. He introduces himself, "I am the Water Genie Iff, from the Ocean of the Streams of Story...Supplier of story water from the Great Story Sea" (46).

Water Genie discontinued the water supply of his father from the Great Story Sea. Water Genie Iff shrugged 'P2C2E'. It is a process too complicated to explain. In this process, there is an advanced technology, it occurred the Thought Beams. Haroun makes clear to Iff that you can't cut off my father's water supply. But Iff tells him that this is the order of Grand Comptroller who lives at P2C2E House in Gup City, Kahani and whose name is Walrus. Water Genie Iff helps him to take a trip to Gup City. There is a bird Hoopoe for their journey. Hoopoe takes off them and flies into the sky for Gup City, city of freedom. Hoopoe is the medium of freedom for Haroun. So it was that Haroun Khalifa the storyteller's son soared into the night sky on the back of Butt, the Hoopoe with Iff, the Water Genie as his guide. The sun rose; and after a time Haroun spotted something in the distance, a heavenly body like a large asteroid, "That is Kahani, the Earth's second Moon, said Butt, the Hoopoe without moving its back" (9).

There is a sea of stories and Iff told him about the Ocean of Streams of story. "He looked into the water and saw that it was made up of a thousand, thousand, thousand—and one different currents, each one a different colour...and Iff explained that these were the Streams of Story, that each coloured strand represented and contained a single tale different parts of ocean contained different sorts of stories, and as all the stories that had ever been told and many that were still in the process of being invented could be found here, the Ocean of Streams of Story was in fact the biggest library in the universe" (81).

The Ocean of the Streams is the description of the creativity and imagination. In the novel, there is a struggle of a person who searches his identity in political and social arena. Rushdie quotes Kundera, "The struggle of man against the power, is the struggle of memory against forgetting, and observe writers and politicians are natural rivals. Both groups try to make the world of their own images; they fight for the same territory. And the novel is one way of denying the official, politicians' version of truth", he maintains (23).

In *Haroun and the Sea of Stories,* Rushdie deals with the struggle of identity crises, freedom of expression and right to express ideas and feelings of an individual. A human being has wish to express his desires and wants to achieve his purpose and throughout his life he struggles for that. Earth's other Moon Kahani has two aspects one is light named Gup City and other is dark called Chup City. Chup City allegorically represents the darkness, dictatorship and lost of freedom of speech on the other hand Gup City symbolizes the delight, freedom of expression and cheerfulness. In Gup City, the parliament called Chatterbox when the discussion runs on for weeks, months or even years also because Guppees were fond of conversation. Haroun has curiosity to know about the Guppees and he also notices the extraordinary things.

Iff told him, "...are the famous pages of Gup; that is to say the army, ordinary armies are made up of platoons and regiments and suchlike; our Page are organized into Chapters and Volumes; Each Volume is headed by a Front, Title, or Pages; and up there is the leader of the entire 'Library, which is our name for the army—General Kitab himself'" (67).

King Chattergy has a beautiful daughter Princess Batcheat who is engaged with Prince Bolo, a foolish fellow. The dark side of Moon called Chup City governed by the Cult master Khattam-Shud his fellow worshipped the Silent God Bezaban and Khattam-Shud and his followers want to pollute Ocean of the Streams of Story. There is a dispute between Guppees and Chupwalas because both of them want to capture the Ocean of Stories. The dispute is not only between Gup City and Chup City but the contradiction between imagination and censorship and between silence and creation or free speech. The Chupwalas abduct Princess Batcheat and in the meantime Rashid Khalifa caught by Prince Bolo and General Kitab when they were on search of Princess Batcheat. "The man standing and shivering on the palace balcony between Prince Bolo and General Kitab was Haroun's father, Rashid Khalifa the storyteller, the unhappy Shah of Blah" (59).

The Guppees consider Rashid a spy. But Haroun makes clear that he is not a spy but he is searching for his father's gift of storytelling. Then Rashid tells about Chup City and abduction of Princess Batcheat. Rashid says that he has seen bad things and a silence in Chupwalas army. The Land of Chup is ruled by power of the Mystery of Bezaban. His followers swear vows of lifelong silence. Because of silence laws in Chup City, every person lost his voice or expression. Silence laws and loss of expression represents the dictatorship and darkness. Khattam-Shud is the enemy of stories, dreams and freedom of expression. The Chupwalas want to offer Princess's sacrifice to their idol. Haroun reached Chup City with his friends and finds that Chupwalas are poisoning the colours of story streams and the water of Ocean of the streams of story were in worse condition; the ocean has lost its charm and warmth. In Chup City, Haroun saw a mock combat of Chupwalas. He saw a man who was fighting against his own shadow. Haroun thought it the war between two—Gup and Chup. He is marvelled: "Gup is bright and Chup is dark. Gup is warm and Chup is freezing cold. Gup is all chattering and noise, whereas Chup is silent as a shadow. Guppees love the ocean, Chupwalas, seems hate these things just strongly. It was a war between the lovers of the ocean or the Princess and Death which was what Cultmaster Khattam-Shud had in mind for the Ocean, and for the Princess too" (53).

The gestures of Shadow Warrior express that the silence is also beautiful and full of grace and the creation of darkness is as noble as aspect of light. Haroun has much interest in story or speeches but he realizes that sometimes silence is so graceful when he sees the silent language of Mudra. This silence has the power of attraction and expression. Shadow warrior has name Mudra and he introduced him through Abhinaya.

Khattam-Shud kept Princess Batcheat in the Citadel of Chup. Khattam-Shud sent a union of Zipped Lips on a Shadow Ship to the South Pole to destroy the Ocean of Stories and pouring a large number of poison in the Ocean. He wants to ruin stories and dreams.

Khattam-Shud was saying. "We must make a great many poison; because each and every story in the Ocean needs to be ruined in a different way. To ruin a happy story; you must make it sad. To ruin an action drama, you must make it move too slowly. To ruin a mystery you must make the criminal's identity obvious even to the most stupid audience. To ruin a love story you must turn it in to a tale of hate. To ruin a tragedy you must make it capable of inducing helpless laughter" (69).

Khattam-Shud and the land of Chup is symbol of darkness and Khattam-Shud, dictator of Chup City who repressed the world. His aim is to remove imagination, creativity and dreams from the world. Khattam-Shud hates stories so much and standing for silence or regimentation. He expresses his view when he answers the question of Haroun. But why do you hate stories so much? ...Stories are fun..."the world, however, is not for fun; Khattam-Shud replied; The world is for controlling." Which world? Haroun made himself ask. Your world? my world, all world, came the reply, "they are all there to be Ruled. And inside every single story, inside every stream in the ocean there lies a world a story world, that I cannot rule at all. And that is the reason why" (22).

Rushdie have the artistic perfection by which he amused his reader with the stories and charmed them intellectually, and emotionally. The characters have recognized through the victory and failures and manner of speech. In the novel, Haroun has the wish of freedom and happiness. For this he struggles much and achieves his aim. I wish thought Haroun Khalifa, squeezing his eyes tightly shut, wishing with every fiber of his being. "I wish it to this Moon, Kahani, to turn, so that it's no longer half in light and half in darkness...I wish it to turn, this very instant, in such a way that the sun shines down on the Dark Ship, the full, hot, noonday sun" (22).

Prince Bolo and Guppees want to save Batcheat from the grip of Chupwalas. Guppees and Chupwalas gathered in the battlefield of Bat-Mat-Karo. There is fight between the two forces between silence and freedom of expression. General Kitab, Prince Bolo, Mudra join the battlefield and Rashid Khalifa also, to translate the gestures of Mudra, including Pages and Blabbermouth to act as messengers and guards. The Chupwalas are unable to resist the force of Guppees. The Pages of Gup, now that they have talked through everything so fully, fight hard, remain united, supported each other when required to do so, and in general look like a force with a common purpose. On the other hand, Chupwalas, they have lack of unity and they fight for their own self, their vows of silence and their habits of secrecy have made them suspicious and distrustful of one another "...the upshot was that the Chupwalas did not stand shoulder to shoulder, but betrayed one another, stabbed one another in the back, mutinied, hid, deserted...and after shortest clash imaginable, simply threw down all their weapons and ran aways" (48).

The victory of Bat-Mat-Karo is a victory of originality and creative sense. It's victory of Rushdie's creation which establishes new values of freedom in the creative world, and defeat of a dictatorship and victory of democratic values. After the defeat of Khattam-Shud, Chup City, the dark side of Moon Kahani shines with brightness. The sun rises over the Chup City and Dark City receive sunlight and happiness. The new government of the Land of Chup, headed by Mudra, announces its desire for a long and lasting peace with Gup, a peace in which Night and Day, Speech and Silence would no longer be separated into Zones by Twilight Strips and Walls of Force.

Rashid Khalifa was given back his Story Water facilities and this is the limit of a victory that Shah of Blah achieves the freedom of expression. An individual has the limits and values and identity. All human beings in this world have urge for freedom and recognition. It is indeed a mission to search for freedom because the loss of freedom means loss of everything, loss of humanity and creativity. In *Imaginary Homelands,* Rushdie submit that "Art is a passion of the mind". And the imagination works best when it is most free. "The plea of free interaction of expression is related to groups, minority or the individuals. The individual is the part of entire world and the decision and expression reflect the society or a nation. *Haroun and the Sea of Stories* is also a challenge against the silence or brutal authorities. The worst impact of censorship is on the mind of a creative artist. "But the worst, most insidious effect of censorship is that, in the end, it can deaden the imagination of the people-is total" (28).

Rushdie presents the restraint of dictators and the agony of a person who is the victim of this repression and visualizes—the horror and sufferings of a son and his father who have the desire to search his freedom of expression. In true sense the novel Rushdie's voice for freedom of expression. In the novel after many adventures Rashid Khalifa regains his power of storytelling and Princess Batcheat is restored by Prince Bolo. Rashid Khalifa rejects to favour Buttoo and announces that choose the leader of your choice. Then he gives Haroun a real shock, because his first words are "Ladies and gentleman, the name of the tale I am going to tell is *Haroun and the Sea of Stories*" (83).

Rashid Khalifa and Haroun return home and discover that the country of Alifbay, sad city has transformed into a cheerful city. The people full of joy and laughter. One gentleman argues that it is because of rain. A policeman tells the reason of this happiness: "I tell you what to be happy about; said a policeman '...we remembered the city's name'; 'well out with it tells us quickly'. Rashid insisted, feeling very excited. 'Kahani', said the policeman brightly as he floated off down the flooded street. 'Isn't it a beautiful name for a city? It means 'Story', you know'" (82).

When Rashid and Haroun reach home, they find that Soraya is there and she begins to sing again. This is the happy ending of the novel *Haroun and the Sea of Stories*. It is a victory of a person against the censorship. Rashid Khalifa presents the identity as a creative storyteller, and gains popularity. It presents the emotions, desires and feelings of a writer who has lost his freedom of expression. After complication he regains the power and proves himself. It is evidence against fatwa or censorship. It deals majorly about the contrast of speech and silence also. He highlights the need of silence and the foolishness of useless chatter. He also points out the grace and beauty of darkness as opposed to sunlight.

The novel *Haroun and the Sea of Stories* is an extremely amusing, highly colorful and vivid account of a young boy's adventure into an unknown land to help his father regain his lost talent. The novel ridicules politicians, advocates freedom of speech, makes fun of foolish wars, admires the beauty of darkness and night, shows respect to silence and the language of silence and gestures, gives an insight into a child's mind.

WORKS CITED

Baral, Kailash, C. and Prafulla C. Kar (Eds.). "Identity and the Social Self", *Identities Local and Global* (Delhi: Pencraft International, 2003).

Rushdie, Salman. *Haroun and the Sea of Stories*. (Penguin, 1991).

———. 'Censorship'. *Imaginary Homelands*. (Great Britain: Granta Books, 1991).

———. "Is Nothing Sacred". *Imaginary Homelands* (Great Britain: Grant Book, 1991).

———. "Salman Rushdie's *Haroun and the Sea of Stories*: Fighting the Good Fight or knuckling under." *Journal of South Asian Literature*. Vol. 26, No. 182, Win-Spr-Sum-Fall.

3

Lesbian Relationship in Shobha De's *Strange Obsession*

S.V. Singh

With the publication of her first novel *Socialite Evenings* (1889), the best seller, Shobha De took the literary world by storm and invited both unqualified applause and strong denunciation by the critics. Succeeding novels appeared one by one rapidly in a decade and established her as one of the mainstream women writers in India owing to her profound writing skills and her extraordinary gift to discuss every sensitive aspects in her fiction. Even while writing on sex, she feels no hesitation and is not stopped by social sanctions. She does not think sex as a matter of shame or an activity to be concealed. She differs considerably from other Indian women novelists for her boldness, openness and frankness. Her bold and modern approach has made her famous the world over. Appreciating some significant features of her fiction, Paul W. Roberts observes:

> What emerges is what one reads in her work: enigmatic, straightforward, crude, erudite, girlish, wise and untimely contrived truth. She doesn't know how good a writer she is which is why she is so good a writer.[1]

With the advancement of civilization and an awakening among feminine world, the scenario has changed to a striking extent. The question of identify in the recent years has been related to the representation of lesbians in literature. Currently many Indian writers have boldly depicted lesbians in literature.

Currently many Indian writers have boldly depicted lesbian relations in their fiction. Lesbianism is not a new aspect of society but as a movement it has sprung up in India during the last decade and with a recent judgment of Delhi High Court decriminalizing homosexuality, a new era has begun. Shobha De's *Starry Nights* (1990), *Strange Obsession* (1992) and *Snap Shots* (1995). Manju Kapoor's *A Married Woman* (2002) and Rita Garg's *Precursor of Love* (2006) deal with the Lesbianism. Deepa Mehta has also focused on lesbian relationship in her film *Fire* (1998).

Lesbianism is an age-old phenomenon of society but as social norms looked upon it hatefully, lesbians did their best to keep such relationship as something top secret. Even in Manusmriti and Kamasutra it is clearly mentioned. In Manusmriti, punishment is mentioned for spoiling a young girl through lesbians contact or mutual sexual gratification:

> If an unmarried girl spoiled another raw girl and taught her the lesson of self-abuse or gratified with her fingers or other Counterfeit male organ or cylindrical substances, she was liable to pay fine of two hundred currency coins.[2]

In his *Kamasutra*, Vatsyayan has also depicted the physical activities of the lesbians:

> Some women of the harem
> When they are amorous
> Do the act of mouth caress
> On the yonis of one another[3]

Softness of female body is also an important feature in lesbian relationship. A male body can never be so soft and so woman's body is preferable in sexual advances: During late nineteenth century Pierre Louys has written in his novel *Aphrodite*.

> A woman is perfect instrument from head to toe. She is made solely and wonderfully for love. Therefore, if a couple is composed of two women, it is perfect: if it has only one woman, it is only half as good; if it has no woman at all, it's completely idiotic.[4]

These days, the steps of feminism are so rapid that the feminist writers are taking pains to liberate woman in every way. Every writer attempts to develop a theory out of his writings. As various feminist theories have been evolved by now like Liberal feminist theory, Radical feminist theory, Psycho analytical feminist theory, Existentialist feminist theory, Cultural feminist theory, Postmodern feminist theory and some more, Lesbianism is also a fast emerging theory of feminism.

Shobha De's *Strange Obsession* is a story of lesbian relationship between two girls, Meenakshi (Minx) and Amrita. Minx is the only daughter of a busy police officer. She did not get her mother's love. She gets all love and care from her father. It laid an adverse psychological impact on her and hinders her balanced psychological growth leaving her mentally weak, unstable, self-centred and vulnerable. She feels pity for her father's sexless life and therefore starts liking him sexually. She had also developed a feeling of hatred for men as a result of beatings she got from her father. This all turned her into a lesbian and she forces a lesbian relationship on an upcoming model Amrita. Minx becomes an obsessed crazy lover of Amrita and can do anything for her. She tells Amrita in a crazy way;

> What more do I have to do prove myself? Kill? I'll do that too.
> Just tell me—who? you want me to kill someone? Anyone?
> I'll do it, I'll kill for you.[5]

Minx's obsession for Amrita is so intense that she kills Lola—a competitor model of Amrita in order to prove herself true lover. She is so maddened in her love for Amrita that she undergoes surgery to remove her breasts for she wants to please Amrita and win her love at every cost. Minx is so over possessive of Amrita that she has a sharp eye on everybody who wishes to come closer to her. She gets Rover terribly beaten by police. She sets aside Karan, a director and a charming editor Partha who could be of great help to Amrita. She haunts Amrita like an evil spirit and Amrita is helpless before her madness. Gajendra Kumar has rightly observed:

> Minx is lesbian eccentric who behaves like a male. She is thoroughly deprived of womanliness. On the thematic plane there seems to be no question of power. But one

> the theoretical plane it is difficult to disagree with the basic questions of power pleasure as Foucault underlines.[6]

Amrita is full of abhorrence for Minx but there is no escape for her. Fortunately, she gets married to Rakesh, but to her extreme surprise, Minx gets her husband kidnapped and forces Amrita to leave him. Luckily both Amrita and Rakesh escape safely from her clutches. In a few years Minx dies and only then Amrita feels finally relieved from her. To quote Gajendra Kumar once again.

> Psychologically, Minx is case in study in psychoanalytical framework. Minx is a fit case to be treated as a pervert, obsessed and crazy who manipulates Amrita a young lady full of love, warmth and innocence.[7]

Thus, Minx is a strange creation of Shobha De. Her love for Amrita is an instance of offensive lesbianism as Amrita never shares it equally and happily. In others words, I may say that Minx is no better than a man who behaves his beloved at his own sweet will without caring for her sentiments. The discussion may be summed up with the statement of the Radical Lesbians;

> A lesbian is the rage of all women condensed to the point of explosions. She is the woman who often beginning at an extremely early age acts in accordance with her inner compulsions a more complete and free human being than her society...cares to allow her.[8]

NOTES

1. Paul W. Roberts, Toronto Review, qtd., Shooting from the Hip (New Delhi, 1996).
2. Prabhat Kumar Pandey, "Tender, Beautiful and Erotic: Lesbianism in Starry Nights", *The Fiction of Shobha De*, ed., Jay Dipsinh Dodiya, 208.
3. *Ibid.*, 200.
4. *Ibid.*, 205.
5. Shobha De, Strange Obsession in Shobha De, Omnibus: 6.
6. Gajendra Kumar, *Indian English Literature: A New Perspective*, New Delhi, Swaroop and Sons, 83.
7. *Ibid.*, 84.
8. The Woman Identified Woman, notes from the third year, 1971.

4

Nissim Ezekiel's Observation on Oddities in Human Life and Behaviour in Indian Panorama

Kamni Kumar

> At any rate, I feel that Indian English-Writing has come to stay as part of World Literature. I would like to believe that in the best writing in this language, the words soar in the imagination like a pigeon in flight, shrill when they are frightened, nervous and sensitive, often soft and soothing, somewhat heavy-footed but always compelled by the love of flight.
>
> —Mulk Raj Anand

Indian English Literature has received the attention of critics and scholars since last fifty years. Indian English Literature is seen as a continuing tradition since the nineteenth century and it is studied as a part of English literature. It has created its own interests which have sometimes tried to project it as the most significant Indian Literature, as it is widely accessible to audiences in India and abroad. It is not much different in kind and form from other Indian literatures, rather it is actually a form of other Indian literatures. It is a curious phenomenon with a fairly long history of more than one hundred and seventy years. The Indian English writing has an immense potential and appeal.

Due to the lack of a regular theatre, Indian English Drama could not register any noticeable gain during the post-independence period. Although regional language theatre was promoted with the establishment of National School of Drama. The theatre group in Bombay and some other agencies successfully produced plays in Indian English. During this period Indian English Drama moved away being in the hands of playwrights like G.V. Desani, Partap Sharma, Gurcharan Das, Girish Karnad, Nissim Ezekiel, Asif Currimbhoy.

Nissim Ezekiel was a man of varied interests. He is regarded as 'the barometer of modern India's literary atmosphere'. As an Indian English poet and playwright he has written plays on hollowness of urban middle class, futility of social modes and the institution of marriage. His *Three Plays* (1969) consists of *Nalini: A Comedy in Three Acts*, *Marriage Poem: A One-Act Tragi-Comedy* and *The Sleepwalkers: An Indo-American Farce.* His *Song of Deprivation* has dramatic value.

Ezekiel's *Three Plays* provides healthy social criticism through the theatre. He has used irony, wit and satire to expose variety of urban middle class. *Nalini*, a full length play, is based on personal experiences and observation. *Nalini* (sub-title a comedy), exposes the hollow life of Bharat and Raj, the two advertising executives. In order to take the favour and sympathy of Nalini, a young woman painter, Raj comes to Bharat to request him to organize publicity for her paintings. The play opens 'humorously and ironically'. Raj is busy listening to music but is disturbed by Bharat. He is sitting still. Bharat, full of affectations and pretensions, is ignorant of art but deceives people by his jugglery of words. *Nalini* is a social satire. Both appear 'modern, full of variety' but they are hollow from within. It shows that there is no inner worth, no seriousness, no thoughtfulness in the life of so-called modern middle class people. They suffer from false notion of superiority. So the playwright exposes the middle class snobbery and pretensions.

Ezekiel's *Marriage Poem* is a one act tragicomedy and is domestic in content. Naresh, the male character, pretends deep love for his wife Mala—who loves him sincerely. But he flirts with Leela. So their married life is an unhappy one, full of skirmishes and conflicts. Mala is upset. Her friend Mrs Lal suggests how to reform a husband who has gone astray.

The play shows that extra-marital affair brings sufferings in married life. Ezekiel ignores plot construction and emphasizes on discussion and characterization.

The Sleepwalker satirizes Indian middle class people's fascination for America. The programme of cultural and economic exchange between India and America is also satirized in *The Sleepwalkers*. Prof. Shah, a character in the play, thinks that India is culturally rich but economically backward. Ezekiel has successfully presented the depravity of so-called cities in India.

Song of Deprivation is a comic morality play in one act. Two lovers who are not able to meet in real life choose to make love on telephone. The heroine is depressed with senseless Indian society where the boys and girls are not permitted to mix from childhood.

His plays present the eccentricities, oddities in human life and behaviour. As a well-known poet he also mingles together contradictory concepts and tries to reconcile and harmonize them. His poetry is a battlefield where contrary concepts clash.

In 'Enterprise', he frankly tells that if one wants grace, he must accept life with all its art, quarrels and conflicts. In 'A Morning Walk' he describes Bombay (Mumbai) as

> Barbaric city sick with slums,
> Deprived of seasons, blessed with rains,
> A million purgatorial lanes,

But in another poem called 'Island' he portrays Bombay as Pleasure Island. The contradiction is seen when he says that Bombay has its glazing breezes but it fails to give him a single direction.

Ezekiel is a very Indian poet, writing in English. He is best when he writes poems about the most ordinary events and human behaviours. 'A Warning' and 'The Visitor' are a few examples where he describes the ordinary human relationships coping with the day-to-day situations of ordinary life.

Ezekiel is completely Indian in his sensibility, through his poetry he tried to reveal Indian culture. Ezekiel is hopeful that everything in India is coming gradually—'Regeneration,

Remuneration and Contraception'. His poem 'Very Indian Poem in Indian English' deals with the ordinary Indian attitude towards drinking so the speakers prefer a glass of 'Lassi' to the glass of wine. Ezekiel firmly believes in national integration. As an Indian he does not believe in any particular system of thought and religion but is always content to be a Man of God.

Nissim is a great playwright and Indian English poet in modern age. He has attained a very high place in the world as a poet of International standard. He may be truly called "the barometer of modern India's literary atmosphere". As a poet, as a critic, as a playwright he is a trend setter. He symbolizes in his poetry the modern Indian urban life with all its complexities.

His plays deal with typical Indian themes and a true reflection of Indian attitude. His plays are also a mirror of contemporary Indian society in certain respects. The struggle for individual human beings for a space in the society is uppermost in his mind. He occupies a distinguished place in post-independence dramatic literature. He is addressed as 'playwright and critic of attitude, sensibility and behaviour of Indian society'. He has certainly enriched Indian English Drama by his plays. His achievement is commendable.

Nissim is acclaimed as the father of post-independence Indian-English verse. He started modernism in Indian English poetry. Not only in style but also in the selection of themes we find the influence of Ezekiel in the contemporary Indian English poets. The major themes of Ezekiel are love, loneliness, lust, creativity and political pomposity of urban dissonance. As the poetic muse of Ezekiel flew higher and higher in the course of years, his attitude also changed.

Modern writers have a tendency to justify the complexity of their writing on the ground that modern life is complex. However complexity can be presented in deceptively simple form as sometimes the profoundest philosophical truths are presented. Ezekiel wants simplicity of thought and language in modern poetry. He extends the concept of simplicity.

Ezekiel always felt a sense of belonging to India. India always was his motherland to which he was much attached. Though belonging to Jewish community, Ezekiel was primarily an Indian. What Ezekiel did was to satirize the evil practices, superstitions and ignorance of the Indian people in a humorous way as Pope and Dryden did in their novels. Ezekiel's preoccupation has always been with the avoidance of both 'the sophistication of the rootless' and 'the parochialism of the native'. Ezekiel is of opinion that a writer should be a man of convictions upholding human values.

Ezekiel is totally committed to India as he has no place to go. He understands that he cannot get rid of his sense of being an Indian. The homogenous, imperialistic nativism is forced to provide space for another culture, another ideology and another subjectivity. He underlines the heterogeneity of local identity and strongly censures the nativist chauvinism with its inherent imperialistic design.

Ezekiel brought a sense of discipline, self-criticism and mastery to Indian English poetry. He is unique in terms of craftsmanship. His poems show his desire to be away from distraction and obsessions of worldly life, but it's grounded in the physical and social reality. The major concern is how to live calmly and ethically by avoiding all personal difficulties and depressions.

'Night of the Scorpion' is one of Ezekiel's poems which is very favourite to the westerners as it reinforces some myths about India. The tension between two clashing attitudes has also brought out effectively, the attitudes of traditional world of superstition and the modern scientific scepticism and rationalism.

A good satire on the English language of the urban Indians is reflected in the form of a farewell speech in 'Goodbye Party for Miss Pushpa T.S.'. The occasion is Miss Pushpa 'is departing for foreign'. English being the second language to Indians, it is quite natural that English of the majority in India is ungrammatical. Their English has the influence of their mother tongue. As language is for communication, the speaker serves his purpose of conveying his message. Ezekiel has no reluctance to tell the world that his compatriot's English is not pure. As he does not claim to be a master of English language, after all how many percent of the Englishmen speak correct English.

To sum up, Ezekiel is not only a good poet in post-independence India but also a cause of good poetry in others. He has opened a new era and trend in Indian English poetry. He has observed well the human behaviour and complexities in Indian society. He became the pioneer of 'New Poetry' by his greater variety and depth than any other poet of the post-independence period.

5

Justifying Chetan Bhagat's Novels as Reflection of Contemporary India

Aparna Sharma

At present, Indian English literature is enjoying the equal status with the literatures of the other languages and Indian fiction writers have displayed their interest with confidence in dealing with new themes and experiments with new techniques and approaches to handle those themes. "Post Modern English writers focus on the burning issues of contemporary society and their subject matters have been revolving around the changing scenario of modern age. Indian English fiction has come forward with new hopes, new dimensions and new aspirations because of the diversity of themes related to different aspects of life as observed by these emerging novelists."[1] One of such novelists is Chetan Bhagat who has been very innovative in dealing with the hopes, and aspirations and failures and frustrations of the young generation. "There is a bulk of characters who attempt to define their relationship with society in a different manner and consequently fall into alienation from their true identity. This rootless sense is a subject for several psychological, sociological, literary and philosophical researches. Fiction has always been responsive to the changes in material reality and theoretical perspective that have impacted and governed its study since the time of its inception."[2]

At a crucial point of time, Bhagat merges on the literary scenario as a practical thinker and it becomes really very difficult to introduce a novelist whose literary works are read virtually by everyone in small towns as well as in Metropolitan cities. There is something about equilibrium that the universe tends to be quite calm about. It is reflective in every facet of creation itself, with an intimate entanglement of opposites. So, to make up for the classy hard back editions of coffee table books are Chetan Bhagat's paperback editions. "As a novelist, columnist, motivational Guru, screen-writer and a television personality Chetan Bhagat has touched almost every fringe of contemporary India and his central focus is always on Indian youth of urban middle class. The *New York Times* has cited him as "the biggest selling English language novelist in India's history".[3] Since his novels have sold over a total of seven million copies. The *Times of India* has mentioned him as a rock star of Indian publishing. The tremendous success of Bhagat as a novelist is a miracle of rare device and for that the credit goes to his management skills. He is tapping a market, the non-English, first time English fiction reader marked. Somewhere, somehow he is clear in saying: "I know you, rural, non-English type. I feel your pain."[4]

There are only a number of writers who have attempted to highlight true Indian spirit, its culture and its people in the light of existing set up of the new found opportunities and materialism without being prejudiced from local, provincial or national ideas. The present as well as the next generation is at the crisis of culture because the youth of present age searching a new identity and thus finds himself standing at the cross roads of individuality, culture and society. At such a crucial point of time Chetan Bhagat appears on the scene and tries to bring this crisis in the mind of his characters that are in fact reflective of its generation. As we all know literature is mirror to social life, his characters are realistic and representative of contemporary age. They are often frustrated with the system but at the same time they are optimistic to bring about the change as in Revolution 2020. Raghav, the protagonist jumps into the fray to clean up the country. Gradually, he gets in sync with what was later to follow like the Civil Movement of Anna Hazare and Arvind Kejriwal. He has in fact very beautifully drawn the picture of the present day India where people are more manipulative and play their cards for relations. "Ambitions get prioritized at the risk of morality. With the new found materialism and the change in the way of living brings with it the eternal fears of losing it, too. Man is torn between the self and the morality."[5] Thus, it is crystal clear that his novels are mostly inhabited by urban India's youth who are trying to fulfill their ambitions while studying at Engineering Colleges or Management Schools or working in Call Centers finding love along the way and for this the credit goes to his management skills, his mastery over simple past tense, his justification of immoral instinctive human acts in the garb of new age realism.

Now, the question arises what is there in Bhagat's works which has touched the fringe of human emotions especially the emotions of the youth of present age. After *Five-Point Someone*, *One Night at the Call Center*, *The Three Mistakes of My Life* and *2 States*, came his novel *Half Girlfriend* which was dedicated to the "non-English types". This novel touches on serious topics including the role that English language skills play in succeeding modern India. In this novel, his English language forms the basis of a class divide anymore. It narrates the story of a boy from rural Bihar who cannot speak English fluently and due to this reason is ditched by a city-bred girl in one of Delhi's elite colleges. His lack of English proficiency becomes the reason for her refusal. In this novel, Bhagat has tried to explain the anguish of millions of Indians who can't get better job opportunities, who can't get into university or good colleges and those who are underestimated and considered not cool enough just because of their broken English. He has very aptly pointed out the middle-class Indian society where English has become the new class system.

Since the phrase, the bestseller English language author has become the synonymous for Chetan, the legend deserves some critical attention and evaluation as the master of sentiments of young generation, a name and place, both in the hearts of his readers and in the society. Bhagat himself has admitted that he is not competing with the literary greats of India especially when it comes to fiction, but it is also true that he has revamped the concept of "best-sellers" just because his stories are written for Indians. He says, "When in 2004 his first novel *Five-Point Someone* came, there was a different literary landscape in India. It was the time when many young people were learning to speak English for better job prospects." He has always emphasized to be more adaptive in life because "brilliance is not just enough to survive in this world. One has to realize that adapting is winning. Being smarter or intelligent is not enough in this world. These days people are associating language with intelligence and this is creating a social caste system which he is always trying to stop."[6] Now, this is not surprising from a popular Indian author who is known to attract first time readers to English language books in his home country. His way of narration is simple and easy-perfect for those who otherwise might never pick up an English language book.

Many writers are successful at expressing what's in their hearts or articulating a particular point of view. Chetan Bhagat's books do both and more. He has written one after another gripping tales from the heartland of India and has hit first generation English readers and has always picked those subjects that work for that class of readers. He caught something of the tech hostel atmosphere with its skewed gender ratios and its tunnel-vision bright kids. One interesting factor pre...Call Center, the concept of reading simply for pleasure and fluency didn't exist. The average aspiration of middle class kid would have been discouraged from wasting their time and energy in reading story-books. "Post...Call Center, there's a host of kids who have twigged that the fluency has a direct co-relation to getting a decent job".[7] So it can be said that his strength lies in his connection with the youth. His 'straight from the heart' style reaches straight to the heart of the adolescents. It is the youth of New India which has enthroned Chetan on the acme of glory so they were on the tender hooks as to what would be served by Chetan this time. He has explored the vitality of human life through his plays and thus he has embellished the tradition of Indian English novel with his creative innovations. He has written focusing on youth and national developmental issues. A noted public intellectual, Bhagat also writes columns about the youth, and their career development and current affairs.

Chetan Bhagat is a different deal altogether. His mediocre works are often welcomed by simpletons as path-breaking master-pieces. He is revered by many and to us that's blasphemous. He never confined his literary talents to just writing novels. As a responsible social person, he also cites and dwells on various social and national issues. Many of his columns were noticed by parliamentarians and triggered issues like corruption by sending an opening letter to Sonia Gandhi and also has spoken about the political issues that revolved around Baba Ramdev. It would really be helpful for Indian readers to reach a stage of understanding with his writing where he has projected himself as the spokesperson for Indian youth. Issues against which he has talked about are corruption and discrimination based on caste and religion and these are the issues that will gain him the credibility as a writer. He writes, "We don't have to become a society where nothing bothers us. Bad roads, corruption, inefficiency, mediocrity and poverty should bother us. However, in these areas we seem to be quite tolerant. We often elect corrupt or inept leaders. Even on the issues of intolerance he wrote, "I don't care how much you dislike this government or how intolerant you think India is, if you don't let Parliament function today you are harming India".

He is often criticized but he almost remains untouched by all this. He says that he is amused by his critics. Even on being tagged as the Rakhi Sawant of English Literature, he retaliated calmly and called it a kind of lazy criticism and finds himself amused after being criticized in this way. To him people are unable to understand what he is doing. Bhagat has been a brand now. In an Interview to *The Times of India*, he said:

His books about the middle-class Indians and their daily struggle to climb to prosperity have made him a publishing phenomenon. He has helped in popularizing the risk of inexpensive mass-appeal, by writing novels in a country where the publishing industry is growing and paperbacks are more popular than smart phones and e-readers. Mohit Kumar, an engineering student who reads Bhagat says, "He may be not a literary genius but he connects with us. He is our favorite author."[8] After going through all this, it is not surprising that Chetan Bhagat has come in for a barrage of criticism for his overtly simplistic views and his unabashed attempts at prompting himself. Bhagat is not a thinker. He is our great unthinker, as sure a representative of headless 'New India' as the Khadi-clad politician is of 'Old India'. He in several ways has touched the aching nerve of young Indian readers. In his own words, "instead of writing about complex subjects, he preferred to write about ordinary life".[9] That is the reason why his subject matters differ from that of the India's other writers.

A thorough study of his novels reveals that his management skills to a great extent are responsible for his tremendous success as a novelist. His point of view is practical and different altogether. Asserting his views on the privatization of education he says that the privatization of education would be beneficial for the society. His novel *Revolution 2020* encapsulates a serious concern for education where the story of Gopal obliquely becomes a scathing attack on education being increasingly used as a profit-making business venture. Here, not only a horrid and gloomy picture of the present educational scenario is drawn but also directed to make it beautiful. The novel narrates a romantic love story which tosses between Gopal, Aarti and Raghav. In this novel, Bhagat not only raises the question, but comes with remedial ways. *Revolution* 2020 displays that there is "The mushrooming of private colleges in India is conspicuous. From the hoarding to the full page advertisement and the wall stickers, a mortal soul will find it difficult to divert his mind from the lucrative scheme they offer. The business tycoons, the local shop owners and the leisurely housewives all find the business of teaching convenient."[10]

In *Revolution 2020*, there is a new emerging system where one may easily find two schools of thoughts going parallel. One side there is Gopal who tries hard to crack engineering entrance test to get a secure future. In his own words: "My dad is not in the IAS. My grandfather was not a minister. We are from a simple Indian Family. We don't ask questions. We want to make a living. Engineering gives us that."[11] On the other side, we have Raghav an engineer turned firebrand journalist who has a quest for understanding of his self.

To convey his messages effectively he has used perfect blend of the American slang which is very common to the modern student. He has given place to swear words starting from "crap" to the four letter "f" word. Apart from these words, there are some other commonly found words like "dude", "buzz of" and "heck" etc. Surprisingly all this is done to show the change in the vocabulary of English, especially with the college boys who have developed a taste for swearing and American English. Chetan should be praised for his humor elements which exist through all his novels and it is quite obvious with his writings. There is a touch of black humor which he made to bring out the stark reality of life and that is the reason there is not always a happy ending in his works. It is appreciable to bring a touch of reality with pointing out the thinking of next generation about religion. Young generation might be funky, funny and may take things lightly, but when it comes to taking decisions they prove their mettle.

Metropolitan cities have a number of issues to deal with and Bhagat has taken all the issues in his works. His *Five-Point Someone*, *The 3 Mistakes of My Life* and *Revolution 2020* portray pre-marital sex that seems to be very common at present and the novelist has put this issue with ease and everyone has accepted it as natural phenomena. He has made constant use of the booze and drugs also find a place in *Five-Point Someone* and *Revolution 2020*. But the author cannot be accused as that is the reality of present time. We find a crisis of religious identity in *The 3 Mistakes of My Life* as the central focus of the novel. Chetan Bhagat takes the incidents of Babri Masjid and the Godhara riots in this novel. Though the incidents were more political and less religious, it had drastically changed the thinking of the youth at that point of time. In the same way *The 3 Mistakes of My Life* brings out exactly that Govind, the hero of the story and his friend Ishaan and Omi and their relationship with Ali is the main concern of the novel because the 'mamaji' of Govind who is a Hindu fundamentalist instigates their allegiance to their religion. On the contrary, we realize one more and relevant issue, i.e. the concern of modern parents for the CGPA of their wards, this issue was raised by Bhagat in his *Five-Point Someone* where he has pointed out that a 10-pointer (CGPA) is labeled as intelligent and all 5 pointers are dumb is a myth that is broken now. In the novel, three friends are considered to be five pointers and they are always at the target of the teachers and their classmates as well. But at last making their mark in the project brings out the effectiveness of the evaluation system in the country. In the novel, it is showcased that IIT has the best of intellects in the country, but nobody thinks about the so-called low achievers of the institute. Even the title is also sarcastic. If your CGPA is not 10, you are someone. Ryan's rebellion against the established rule of IIT in the name of adventure brings in only the reality of the institute where students are just made only to score high CGPA.

All the novels of Bhagat follow first person narration and it surely has an autobiographical element. His stories are set in such a way as the central character is narrating the story. The tone of the novels is always maintained as that of a jolly good college going boy who does not care about the issues of day-to-day life. On the other hand in portraying the picture of present-day India, he becomes a detached spectator and observed that the people are now more manipulative and play their cards for relations. Ambitions get prioritized at the risk of morality.

Besides writing novels he has adopted other genres also to convey his meaning like columns, extracts and essays. Publishing open ended columns in *Dainik Bhaskar*, a large Hindi newspaper and another at *The Times of India*, he asserts, "The main purpose of the books and films is to entertain, but the columns allow me to give my views on how the nation should be run."[12] He also published a collection of essays and newspaper columns titled, "What Young India Wants" in which he has mentioned rural people, "Just because they live in rural areas doesn't mean they're extremely different. They're also exposed to the same media, the same TV. The same Internet is reaching there. They also aspire to get a good job, learn English, and have a girl friend. They're people at the end of the day."[13] He views himself as a "bridge" across India's deep socioeconomic divides as he says, "My approach to change is different. My approach is more mainstream...." One may observe that his collection of essays, *What India Wants* is based on Chetan Bhagat's vast experience as a blockbuster writer and motivational speaker. In clear, simple prose and with great insight, he analyses some of the complex issues facing modern India, offers solutions and invites discussions on them. And, at the end, he asks this important question: Unless are all in agreement on what it is going to take to make our country better, how will things ever change? If you want to understand contemporary India, the problems that face it, and want to be a part of the solution, here lies the answer in this book. His articles are written in simple English to achieve mass appeal.

As William Golding's *Lord of the Flies* represents the predicament of the human race under the influence of cold war with the possibility of devastating Nuclear war. In the same constraint, *One Night at the Call Center* by Chetan Bhagat represents the predicament of the man-kind in the post-modern social set up. This novel showcases the real value of human kind in general, shorn off all its artificial embellishments. Thus, we see him as a writer who speaks from the heart and raises valid points voicing out the mind of new generation. India has undergone several changes Post-Independence in a very appreciable way, Indian attitude of bestial kind needs to be changed very seriously, because Indian mentality is governed by emotions not by practical wisdom and Chetan Bhagat loves to see the spark in the people around him: "I see students like you, and I still see some spark. When I see older people, the spark is difficult to find. That means as we age, the spark fades."[14] At present the older people and the younger generation complain of generation gap and of breaking down the communication between these two groups. This generation gap leads to misunderstanding and clashes. But who is to blame for this? Degradation of values is seen everywhere because the experience of elders is not given preference and young generation wants to live free at its own will.

Being a supporter of Gay Rights and empowering women, he wants men to support their 'wives' careers' the way as Mary Kom's husband Onler Kom did. He very often has dealt with troubling, niggling and irritating subjects. He writes, "If our nation doesn't come across having a basic level of common sense, it leaves terrible impression on outsiders."[15] His statement in a column on Women's Day highlights his suggestion that a man must see woman as people, not objects. Men must realize and truly believe that women are talented, capable as men and sometimes even more so. However, the stubborn, fragile and pampered Indian male ego is tough nut to crack. But Bhagat believes in believing in yourself and your heart. Knowing what you want and sticking to your decision is most important and he himself did just that. He fell in love, knew what he was doing and followed his heart firmly. Believing strongly that the function of literature is to reflect society and by means of his novels, he is causing some change in a large part of India, which is far more satisfying.

NOTES

1. "Reflections on Contemporary Indian English Fiction" Ed. by Kulbhushan Kushal, N.K. Neb. Nirman Publications, Jalandhar (53).
2. Shougat Dasgupta in Tehelka.
3. A.R. Rahman, in *TIME* Magazine, on Chetan's inclusion in the "TIME 100 Most Influential People in the World" (17).
4. Speech by Chetan at Symbiosis, Pune.
5. Chetan Bhagat. *Revolution 2020*. New Delhi: Rupa & Co., 2011: (77). Print.
6. Chetan Bhagat in Kathmandu Rejuvenates Youth Potential. Ekendraonline.com (20 July, 2010) Retrieved: 2012-06-19.
7. Siddhartha; Chetan Bhagat: A Ripped-Apart Author Review. June 21, 2011.
8. Winnowed: Book Review: Making India Awesome, by Chetan Bhagat, (39): Friday, on Oct. 2015.
9. Speech by Chetan at Symbiosis, Pune.

10. Chetan Bhagat (19 Aug. 2011). "Anna Hazare's Fight for Change Has Inspired Millions of Indians". *The Guardian* (London). Retrieved 17 Aug. 2011: 44.
11. Chetan Bhagat. *Revolution 2020*, New Delhi: Rupa & Co., 2011: 49. Print.
12. Columns. Chetan Bhagat. Retrieved 2012-06-19. 25 Nov. 2015 (Twitter).
13. Chetan Bhagat, Oct. 26, 2014: *The Hans India* (67).
14. Devangshu Datta (Dec. 16, 2015). "The Writer's Community on Chetan Bhagat." Forbes India (22).
15. Shanoor Seervai and Raymond Zhong, Chetan Bhagat on India's Youth, and His High Profile Writing on Gay Rights, 17: Jan. 25, 2015.

6

Arun Joshi: *Shadows of His Times*

Shivali Singh and *Ravindra Kumar Singh*

The age in which Arun Joshi lived and worked for the expression of artistic genius was marked by rapid changes in economic, social, cultural, educational and political set up of the country. Arun Joshi began his literary career in the fifties, just after the independence of India. His life covers the two important ages after independence—the age of Jawaharlal Nehru and the age of Indira Gandhi. The period from 1950 to 1984 was dominated largely by Jawaharlal Nehru and Indira Gandhi since Arun Joshi was the product of his age, he has successfully incorporated all the, political, social, cultural, educational and economic events taking place in the country from 1950 to 1990. All his novels from *The Foreigner* to *The City and The River* represent a period of nearly forty years. All the important historical, political, economic and cultural events of this period have been taken up by the author and used as raw materials for his novels.

The period from 1950 to 1864 was Nehruvian era known for its scientism, democratic socialism, industrialism and mechanization. After independence, Nehru was conscious of India's role in the world countries under one banner and became the leader of the Non-Aligned countries during the Cold War between the two books of the world. He was the man who propounded the principle of Panchsheel for maintaining world peace and emphasized the need of having good relations with neighbouring like China, Pakistan and Sri Lanka.

Nehru drew his inspiration from Marxism and Democratic Socialism, and stood for anti-imperialism, anti-apartheid, nationalism and socialism. Though leftist in his sentiments were tried by a silken thread to the right under the influence of Gandhi. As far as the general spectrum of ideologies for the regeneration of Indian society which was badly dislocated after the partition. At one end were the Gandhian who believed in a decentralization, relatively self-sufficient village communities without an artificial proliferation of wants minimal resource to modern technology. The socialists both within and outside the Congress argued that the removal of inequalities was an important as growth and stood for the land reforms, greater public ownership and strict regulation of the private sectors a means of achieving greater equality.

After independence, the Congress party under the leadership of Jawaharlal Nehru attempted a compromise between the above-mentioned viewpoints—a compromise which leaned towards socialism in declared intent but afforded the conservation ample opportunities to resist implementation of Socialist policies.

The partition of India adversely affected the economy of India, particularly in the matter of food grains and agricultural products. Sixty-eight per cent of irrigated areas of wheat and rice as of undivided India went to Pakistan. The divided India experienced an unprecedented situation prevailed in regard to livestock since the better milk yielding cattle was in Sind and West Punjab. The cotton textile industry in India also forced a very unhappy situation as most of the textile mills were situated in India and the raw material was produced in Pakistan.

As far as the general industry was concerned, India's resources largely unimpaired. Almost all the resources like coal, iron ore, manganese and mica and all the heavy chemical plants, all paper mills, glass factories, cement, paint and matches factories were located in India. The shortage of food stuff was big problem before the government of free India, the extensive imports of food stuff created a serious problem of balance of payments in the trade.

The problems which India faced after independence were not absolutely new. They had grown during the British rule. Jawaharlal Nehru wrote in 1946:

> Nearly all our problems today have grown during British rule and as a direct result of British policy, the prices, the minority problems, various vested interests, foreign, and Indian, the lack of industry and the neglect of agriculture, the extreme backwardness in the social services and above all, the tragic poverty of the people.[1]

For the rapid economic regeneration of India and up-gradation of national defense, and the elimination of poverty and unemployment, the need for rapid industrialization with a special emphasis on the development of basic and heavy industries was felt without ignoring agriculture which was the mainstay of the people.

After independence, India faced three major problems—rehabilitation of refugees, service food shortage and inflationary pressure on economy. The First Five-Year Plan (1951–56) accorded the highest priority to agriculture including irrigation and power projects. During this period, the Bhakra-Nangal Dam, Project of Damodar Valley and Hirakund Valley were started. A special emphasis was laid on the development of basic industries, not ignoring the small scale industries and the cottage industries.

During the Nehruvian era, the Indo-Pak and Indo-China relations became hostile. During this period, Kashmir became an apple of discord between India and Pakistan. In 1950, China gave a jolt to India by forcible occupying Tibet.

Both India and China had suffered from imperial rule. Hence, Jawaharlal Nehru believed that both the countries with common experience of exploitation at the hands of colonial powers and common problems of underdevelopment and poverty would join hands to earn a respectable place in the world. Both the countries subscribes to the policy of Non-Alignment and Non-aggression. When Nehru visited China in 1954, he not only recognized China's sovereignty over Tibet but also signed the Panchsheel, i.e. five principles of co-existence. But Nehru's ambition of Asian leadership and world reputation collapsed when in October, 1962 China launched an attack and over ran many Indian posts in NEFA.

All the major economic, political, military and social events taking place during Nehruvian era have been reflected in the first four novels of Arun Joshi in one way or the other. *The Foreigner* was written by Arun Joshi against the economic background prevailing in India in the fifties during the first and second Five-Year Plans. It was during this period that Nehru laid special emphasis on the development of basic industries and setting up of institutions of engineering and technology in public sector all over India. The Government of Indian encouraged students to go to abroad for the study of engineering and technology.

In *The Foreigner*, Khemka and his son, Balbir projected the very image of the fifties of India. Mr. Khemka who was the Managing Director of his company manufactured air-conditioner in New Delhi and had collaboration with an American company. He had been to New York. After coming back from there, he decided to send his son, Balbir to America to make a man of him. His training in engineering and technology would have been of great help to him but his son died in a car accident in America leaving a wide vacuum for his father and his sister, Shiela who were responsible for running their factory. When Sindi Oberai came to Delhi, he was offered a job as an assistant manager in Khemka's company. But an income-tax petty official who was a trade unionist and leftist was very much against Khemka because they thought that Mr. Khemka was a tax-invader and an enemy of the proletariat. Following is a very interesting dialogue between Sindi Oberai and his income-tax man:

> "Don't pretend that the rich people are the only honest people in the world," the income-tax man said darkly, "I know a thing or two about them. If I were the minister, this whole office would be wound up and handed over to the proletariat."[2]

The tax-man further said:

> India is working toward a new age, Mr. Oberai.... An age in which each man will be equal to mother.... It is only people like you and Mr. Khemka who are holding revolutions.[3]

The income-tax man called Mr. Oberai a "bourgeois" and the enemy of the "proletariat". The leftists and the trade unionists divided the society of those days in two parts—the bourgeois and the proletariat under the impact of Marxist ideology. The struggle between the capital and labour began. The capitalists were charged of exploiting the labour. The income-tax man labeled charges against Mr. Khemka saying:

> It is you have swindled those miserable wretches in rage who push carts on your streets and die at twenty-five. It is you who have been telling lies and fabricating documents just so that you could on-condition this ostentation house and throw gigantic parties for the horde of jackals who masquerade as your friends.[4]

Some troubles are developed in Mr. Khemka's company. There was no sale for months. The money transaction was almost choked off. The creditors began to queue up for their payments. Khemka's employee's got worried when they heard that Mr. Khemka was put under arrest and there was no chance for his acquittal and his company would be taken up by some banker sooner or later.

Billy Biswas in Joshi's second novel *The Strange Case of Billy Biswas* was also sent to the United States to study engineering but he soon have gave up engineering in favour of his choice of Anthropology and was already halfway through Ph.D. The novel is set against the background of cultural and educational exchanges taking place in India and the U.S.A. Billy Biswas belonged to a high sophisticated family. The author writes about his ancestry:

> Billy's family had originally come from Bengal. His grandfather had one time been the Prime Minister of a famous princely state in Orissa. His father after completing his law studies at Inner Temple, had mostly

> practiced law at Allahabad and Delhi. At the Time when we were in America, he was a judge of India's Supreme Court.[5]

Based on the local colour of Bundelkhand region, the novel is a story of horror, suspense, mystery and romance. It highlights a clash between the West and the East with regard to their civilization and cultures. Billy is seen first in New York attending a mid-Western University for a summer course at Colombia. Though he comes of a very high family, he is crazy by temperament. In America, he lives in slums with Indian and Negros. Though he was educated in England speaks English with a British accent, he has deep roots in the wild culture and association with the Negros in America. The author writes about Billy's Interest in the primitive mass:

> What impressed me even more was his passionate involvement with his subject. It was gradually dawned upon me that it was around his interest in the primitive man that his entire life had been organized.[6]

When Billy was asked why he was drawn to Anthropology, he replied that he was wanted to read the books of Anthropology and visit the places described on them. He said: "All I want to do in life is to visit the place they describe, meet the people who live—there, find out about the aboriginals of the world."[7]

Billy had a vague feeling which made him uncomfortable. Tulla once said: "Billy feels something inside him, but he is not yet sure. Sometimes he is afraid of it and tries to suppress it."[8]

It was a great force—a primitive force. He was afraid of it and tried to suppress it. But it was stronger in him than in any other person. It could explode any time. It was on account of the dominance of this force in him that he was not cut off from his roots in spite of his long stay in America. The narrator tells us about his alienation from his own culture:

> In spite of a somewhat longish stay in America, neither of us had lost our roots in India, or in the city of Delhi, nor did we suffer much, except for passing spells of loneliness, from that to be burdened with.[9]

Billy come in contact with Meena Chatterjee who belonged to a Bengali family and got marries to her but neither his parents nor his wife could please him. He could not find peace in the surroundings in which he lived. The letters he had written to Tulla revealed the abnormal state of his mind arising out of the cultural clashes in his mind. He found peace in the woods of Maikala Hills and among the tribal's there. He lived there as a primitive pilgrim and renamed a stranger to the civilized world.

Thus, in spite of the beginning of industrialization and mechanization in India during the Nehruvian period, India and her culture still retained their virginity and primitiveness. Dr. Mohan rightly remarks about Billy's journey from Boston to the Satpura Hills:

> From Boston to Delhi has been journey from alienation to arrival, from selfishness to sacrifice, from an anomic responsible to himself to a member of mankind, from being to becoming.[10]

The Apprentice which is the third novel of Arun Joshi is focused on the shameful defeat of India in the Indo-China War of 1962 and disillusionment with freedom and corruption in high offices rampant in the age of Jawaharlal Nehru. In spite of the treaty of non-aggression, peaceful existence and Panchsheel, China invaded India in NEFA in 1962 and occupied the frontier posts causing humiliation and shame to India. Ratan Rathore who is the protagonist of the novel tells the boy that during the Chinese aggression, people talk of Chinese betrayal and the honour lose by India after her defeat in the war:

> I imagine they spoke of Chinese perfidy, and of honour. The government, I understand, is determined to defend our honour.... What I learnt was that it was difficult to retrieve honour, once it is lost.[11]

India lost the war with China in 1962 on account of corruption in the government departments. Ratan Rathore after taking bribes from Sheikh alias Himmat Singh cleared the purchase of defective weapons for the army stores. He tells the boy: "The Sheikh had a big pile of military materials lying in Bombay which I had rejected because they were no good. He wanted the Minister and the Secretary to look into the case. They sent him to me. I refused to pass them. The Sheikh, then, offered me cut, a bribe. This bribe, for some obscure reasons, I accepted."[12]

Ratan Rathore, the Protagonist of the novel has learned from his experience that his father's sacrifice and martyrdom for the sake of his country's freedom were of no practical value for him and his mother. What his father had left for him after his martyrdom was starvation, a sick widow and patriotic favour with no funds. What the mother of Ratan Rathore had learned was not patriotism but the importance of money:

> It was not patriotism but money, she said, that brought respect and brought security. Money made friends. Money succeeds where all else failed. There were money laws, she said, but money was the law into itself.[13]

Ratan Rathore recalls how his father was forgotten after a tear from his death and how he was humiliated, rejected and jeered at in hunting jobs. He felt, that even after independence, people were not free, what the people of India had inherited from Englishmen which were a new kind of slavery: "We thought we were free. What we had in fact, was a new slavery. Yes a new slavery with new masters, politicians, officials, the rich, the old and the new. Swindlers in fancy cars."[14]

Ratan Rathore presents a picture of Delhi after independence in the Nehruvian era: "They are all the same, these governments' colonies. Acres of mortar, an occasional park. Box upon box of identical flats, yellow by day, colourless at night. Trees that die as samplings, a dispensary short of medicines, library without books...."[15]

In the post-independence period, the high-ups got more interested in deals than in the reconstruction of their country. Money became their prime motto, not the service of the people. Ratan Rathore tells the boy:

> Deals, deals, deals, my friend, that is what the world runs on.... It is not the atom or the sun or God or sex that lies at the heart of the universe, it Deals, Deal.[16]

Thus the social, political and military events taking place in the post-independence India during the Nehruvian era from the core of the novel.

The Labyrinth, the fourth novel of Arun Joshi is once again set in the period when India was on the way of industrialization and mechanization. The protagonist of the novel Som Bhasker is no different from Sindi Oberai, Babu Rao Khemka and Billy Biswas. Like Sindi and Billy, he got education in the foreign universities and learnt the way of modern life. His father himself was a great scientist and industrialist. After the death of his father, he became a millionaire overnight at the age twenty-five. After returning from Harvard, he became the Managing Director in his plastic factory. He was none to reckon with in the industrial world of Bombay. His primary work was to grab and annex failing industries to his industrial empire. But in spite of having wealth, good education and family life, he felt some want in his life. His urge to have a new experience in every walk of life misled him and deviated him from the right back. His sudden encounters with Anuradha bewildered him and he felt a victim to her magical charm. Aftab Rai, who was Som's double, was a plastic manufacturer but not good at handling business. Under the bewitching fascination of Anuradha, Som started neglecting his family and business and was drawn by suicidal impulse. Som's wavering mind adversely affected his business.

The City and The River, which was the fifth and last novel of Arun Joshi is a political fable. This is a novel that is truly a parable of the times. It startlingly presents a real vision of every day politics. The novel unfolds the story of the Grand Masters who rules the city by the river and is determined to become an unchallenged King. Things move smoothly till a strange prophecy is made by the palace Astrologer. They learned man predicts the crowning of a new king in place of Grand Master. The appeal of the novel lies in the skilful handling of the course plotted by intrigues and corruption in high places.

The City and The River is of a great historical and political interest because it is set against the background of Internal Emergency imposed by Mrs. Indira Gandhi in 1975 to save her throne from the wrath of people. The doctorial and autocratic policies of Mrs. Indira Gandhi led to the people's rebellion against her rule. Rallies and demonstrations organized by Jai Prakash Narayan forced Mrs. Indira Gandhi to declare a state of Internal Emergency in the country. Consequently the fundamental rights of citizens were suspended, the press was gagged, the freedom of thought and speech was withdrawn, the leaders of the political parties were thrown behind the bars, the family planning was imposed on the people against their wish, and atmosphere of terror and fear was generated in the country. Mrs. Indira Gandhi led by her son, Sanjay Gandhi and Yogi, Dhirendra Brahmchari. In General Elections of 1977, Mrs. Indira Gandhi was thrown out of power by the people of India and democracy was restored in the country. Indira Bhatta and Suja Alexander write about the political nature of the theme of the novel:

> The novel indirectly pictures the events of the emergency regime in India and the malpractices restored to by the political powers of the time. In the novel, the Grand Masters and his subordinated employ malpractices in order to reach the apex of political powers.[17]

Indira Bhatta and Suja Alexander further writes: "Arun Joshi satirises the way in which the political leaders struggle and make use of wrong means in order to guard the seat of power and position through the novel. He pictures the malpractices employed by Grand Master for the safe keeping of his power by taking the aid of guns, lacer weapons, police and army."[18]

Thus, *The City and The River* offers a powerful comment and satire on the social and political scenario of the seventies during the rule of Mrs. Indira Gandhi with a prophecy that oppression would continue and the oppressed would continue to struggle against it.

A close study of all the five novels of Arun Joshi unfolds the facts that these novels cover a span of about forty years from 1950 to 1990. It was a period when Congress party was led by Jawaharlal Nehru and her daughter Mrs. Indira Gandhi. Both Pandit Nehru and Mrs. Indira Gandhi ruled the country for about thirty-seven years with exception of about two years when Janta Party came in power after 1977.

The notable features of the regime of Jawaharlal Nehru were inefficient and corruption in high offices, the Indo-China War and rapid industrialization of the country with an emphasis on the development of basic and heavy industries. The regime of Mrs. Indira Gandhi was marked by the imposition of internal emergency and political totalitarianism. The happenings and tendencies of those regimes have been artistically reflected in the novels of Arun Joshi. The socio-political milieu of the age of Arun Joshi has been instrumental in bringing out his novels. Thus, Arun Joshi was the product of the age in which he lived and worked. In fact, his novels are the shadows of his times chequered with various hires. Though they belong to a certain segment of history, yet they have been presented in such a way that they have become universal and timeless.

NOTES

1. Jawaharlal Nehru. *The Discovery of India,* 284.
2. Arun Joshi. *The Foreigner.* New Delhi: Orient Paperbacks, 2010, 38.
3. *Ibid.,* 39.
4. *Ibid.,* 180.
5. Arun Joshi. *The Strange Case of Billy Biswas*. New Delhi: Orient Paperbacks, 2003, 11.
6. *Ibid.,* 12.
7. *Ibid.*
8. *Ibid.,* 18
9. *Ibid.,* 20.
10. Birendra Pandey. *The Novels of Arun Joshi: A Critical Evaluation,* New Delhi: Atlantic Publishers and Distributors, 2000, 17 (quoted).
11. Arun Joshi. *The Apprentice*. New Delhi: Orient Paperbacks, 1998, 60.
12. *Ibid.,* 97.
13. *Ibid.,* 19.
14. *Ibid.,* 61.
15. *Ibid.,* 06-07.
16. *Ibid.,* 48.
17. Indira Bhatta and Suja Alexander. *Arun Joshi's Fiction: A Critique,* ed. New Delhi: Creative Books, 2002, 80.
18. *Ibid.,* 82.

7

Anuradha Marwah's *Dirty Picture*: Negotiating the Cursed Body

Arun Kumar Yadav

Anuradha Marwah was born in the year 1962 in Ajmer, Rajasthan. Anuradha Marwah has written few short and some full-length plays. Her full-length plays are *Margins*, *Sarkari Feminism*, *A Pipe Dream in Delhi*, and *Danger Zones*.

Marwah has written articles and reviews for fiction, poetry and criticism. Her novels are *The Higher Education of Geetika Mehendiratta*, *Idol Love* and *Dirty Picture* (2007).

Unlike Marwah's first two novels: *The Higher Education of Geetika Mehendiratta* and *Idol Love*, which negotiates the space between the personal and the political life without locating a concrete political centre, her third novel *Dirty Picture* is honest, brave and candid. She fleshes out each character—even the 'villains' so non-judgmentally that they could be any of us. The indifferent prose disallows prejudice, as reader's judgments too are suspended and postponed or pushed towards a desire for deeper analysis.

Presently, Anuradha Marwah is a lecturer of English Literature and Creative Writing at Zakir Husain College, Delhi University. She is an evolving contemporary Indian Woman English novelist. She speaks about the source of *Dirty Picture*:

> Like many fictions, this novel too is based partially on facts, some of which may already be known to the reader

> via media coverage. My novel, however, is intensely personal. The characters took birth instantaneously when the nude photograph of a young girl crashed into my life—on May 16, 1992 by way of 'Dainik Navjyoti'—a local Hindi paper published from Ajmer. Her eyes were blotted out. Fully dressed men with lascivious eyes flanked her on either side, fondling a breast each. Her hair was plaited into neat braids. Dirty Picture is about that girl; the eyes I created for her; the two men in the photograph; what I read in their expressions; and other imaginary characters. Some events described in the novel did take place. In April 1992 'Dainik Navjyoti' broke the story of a 'sex scandal' in Ajmer. (Blog)

She was so much shocked with the scandal that she planned to write a novel on it. In this process she started investigating the scandal. She visited different places and people. She tells about her effort at one place:

> I tried to investigate. In 1996 I met the journalist who had broken the story in the Hindi language paper. I went through the statements the girls had submitted in court. I watched a video-clip. I spoke to one of the lawyers who had represented the accused. I had a conversation with my reluctant mother who was the Vice Principal of Savitri Girls College, Ajmer at the time of the scandal. I interviewed a police constable. I read all the articles in the press I could lay my hands on. (Blog)

Irbil Hasan's painting of a young woman sitting on a chair with an older woman standing beside her makes for the cover of Anuradha Marwah's *Dirty Picture*. She immediately identified it as one of several painted by the artist to document the lives of prostitutes in this area. Most locals are shy of admitting to the existence of prostitution in the city. For them, the red light area in the forted city still has certain *mujra* performances by 'artists' and *nothing else*. The painting illustrates in brush strokes what Anuradha Marwah documents in words in *Dirty Picture* exploitation of women and the lower classes through a deep-rooted mechanism of inequitable gender constructions often obfuscated by ill-disguised hypocrisy. However, *Dirty Picture* tracing the personal narratives of two girls Reena and Bharti uses the incident as a site of critique to critique exploitation at the levels of gender and class. Reena and Bharti live very difficult lives yet their narratives absurdly merge into each other's forthright question about notions of love and consent.

The society depicted in *Dirty Picture* is hugely patriarchal which acts as the manifestation and institutionalisation of male dominance over women and children in the family and the extension of male dominance over women in the society in general. It implies that men hold power in all the important institutions of society and that women are deprived of access to such power. It is a world in which women are defined as submissive, passive and virtually inert. Their sexual definition is one of 'masochistic passivity': 'masochistic' because even men recognise their systematic sadism against women; 'passivity' not because women are naturally passive, but because their chains are very heavy and as a result, they cannot move.

In this society, the norm of masculinity is phallic aggression. Male sexuality is by definition, intensely and rigidly phallic. A man's identity is located in his conception of himself, as the possessor of a phallus; a man's worth is located in his pride in phallic identity is that worth is located in his pride in phallic identity. The main characteristic of phallic identity is that worth is entirely contingent on the possession of a phallus. Since men have no other criteria for worth and identity, those who do not have phalluses are not recognised as fully human.

The story of *Dirty Picture* is about two sisters; Bharti and Reena. Bharti is neither a good girl nor bad girl. She looks at the all pervasive world of patriarchy from a progressivist's perspective. Bharti also says this "I want to do something for our family, in fact for the whole of Ajmer. The world is moving into the twenty-first century whereas here there is no movement except backward: our roads, civic facilities, and above all people's mind seem to be regressing to the nineteenth century" (*Dirty Picture,* 25).

Bharti knows that entering the realms of public sphere in a hugely paternalistic world is easy and rewarding. In Ajmer

Bharti lives a life driven by idealism and a desire to make a difference to the parochial town and its regressive outlook. Bharti understands this harsh reality about a daughter as she thinks over. To gain clout in college politics, she befriends local politicos Anees and Sarosh. But, Reena, her elder sister understands the masculine order very well and decides to protect Bharti from the onslaught of masculinity. Bharti was still young and unschooled in the way of the world. It was her duty to prevent those politicos from taking advantage of her sister's innocence.

> "Who are these men you've been seeing?" Reena asked
>
> "Sarosh and Anees." Sarosh's father has an export business. Anees is doing full-time politics.
>
> In school I got elected as Vice Captain of the Red house even though some teachers wanted Nisha Sharma" (24), Bharti said.

But Reena replied that one of them Anees is a muslim boy, and is dangerous to have a friendship with a muslim boy. So she suggests Bharti to keep herself away from such people. Their conversation goes on thus:

> "It's rather strange that you, of all people, are ticking me off for meeting Muslim men," she was saying.
>
> Reena began to feel a little tearful, "Bharti, it's because you are so young. I didn't say they're unsuitable because they're Muslim. I don't want politicos taking advantage of you." (25)

In an interview Marwah tells herself:

> In *Dirty Picture* it is clear that the sex scandal didn't take place only because of a handful of criminal men-majority of who happened to be Muslim; it took place also because society imposes an unrealistic code of sexual conduct on women and allows too much leeway to privileged men. As I understand it, the real story of the Ajmer sex scandal is neither about communal prejudice nor sexual perversions; it is about gender iniquity and class exploitation. (India Writes interview with Nair)

Bharti was too young to understand that men are always out to take advantage of women. She now understands that being a woman in a socio-cultural context where women are sexually objectified and treated as an object to be valued for its use by others is a greater challenge than her aspirations. Sarosh confesses to the strange 'unusualness' in Bharti's attitude. She was unusual girl and it was impossible to predict what she would do. She spoke of masculine things like rising prices, elections, and party politics. Her plans for the future sounded androgynous as though she expected to step into her father's shoes. Sarosh felt it was shameful the way her father was projecting her into the male world.

> On their way back, Anees put an arm around Sarosh's shoulder.
>
> "Seems to me, Miyan, you have forgotten the purpose of this exercise."
>
> "Which exercise, Anees Bhai?" Sarosh asked, still inebriated by wine and women.
>
> "That purpose of seducing Bharti." Anees replied.
>
> "The purpose?"
>
> "Yes, remember we are doing all this for the furtherance of our careers." (67)

Bharti does not learn the harsh realities of the paternalistic world until she is subjected to its horrendous face. She is date-raped by acquaintance Sarosh who, along with Anees, has lured her into the world of masculine enterprises. Sarosh was sitting on the bed. He was examining a huge knife moodily, running his finger along its edge.

> "I knew you wouldn't reject me just because I am a Muslim."
>
> He began kissing her face, arms, neck. Bharti was feeling desperate. "Please take me home," she said.
>
> He stroked her arms and breasts. His hands began to descend towards her salwaar.
>
> "No, don't do that to me again," he said angrily and knocked her back. In a moment he was on her. She shrieked but he was deaf to her.

> When it was finally over, she collapsed on the pillow sobbing. (33-34)

Now Bharti realises with a shudder that the entry into the world of masculine world, the public sphere demands a huge ransom from a woman. Woman needs space to articulate her conditioning in the society that space can be achieved through her presence in the public domain. Public sphere creates the environment in which a woman does not feel comfortable to respond/convey her views. Hence, she creates her own zone of articulation of language and speech.

Elaine Showalter has given a name to this zone and that is "wild zone". We call this place wild zone for its privacy as well as exclusiveness. Through this zone, she can realize herself with confidence and full independence. She can touch her bodily organs as well as emotive expressions. She is very close to herself. This private place can be of her closet, washroom or cosy and comfortable space.

'The Personal is Political': this feminist (but not only feminist) slogan from the seventies marked the crisis in a conception of political commitment and opened the way to rethinking agency and politics. The subject chosen and thoughts woven be viewed in the light of the shifting paradigms of women from private to public sphere where sometimes, they fail to recognise themselves, but, still they struggle for their movement. It may be because of her unrecognised positioning in public sphere or she is considered nothing, but as role player only in social discourse. A woman finds her comfortable in private sphere which is closet or private space.

In the span of public sphere and private sphere, a woman does not respond in the same manner as she was interfaced consequently, she is silent in the public domain. Public and private domain is created through political agency to undermine or control the behaviour of a woman through cultural scripts and language. The undergoing agency creates such a binary opposition, hierarchy of relationships between man and woman behaviour through language as well as negotiation of environment.

After this incident slowly and slowly she entered into the world of scandals. Sarosh falsely said to her that he is in love with her. Bharti thought it true without knowing that he is the member of the gang. Now they were planning to make a videotape of Bharti, secretly. At first Sarosh found the idea of videotaping their sexual congress repugnant. But Bharti was proud and headstrong. She could turn hostile; she could leave him.

> "If she's had so many rehearsals, what's the problem with the performance?"
>
> Anees Bhai, "she's young and shy. She'll never-never agree."
>
> "You've not trained her well yaar," Anees complained.
>
> They had emasculated him. Of course, "Bharti had been filmed-probably enough." (112)

Once, when Bharti was sitting in a hotel with Mukesh, he secretly talked with his friend about photographs. "Bharti was almost out of earshot when she heard Mukesh add softly, "You will come back to see the picture, won't you?" She didn't stop to question them about the 'picture' or what they meant." (177). They were fed up with the same sexual partner so they want a new girl from the college, they plan to convince Bharti for it. If she denies they have something to show her.

"Bharti might not agree. She's a very stubborn girl," Sarosh said, in the voice of a villain (184).

"Besides," Anees said, "we could take photographs. There is a market for such photos in Dubai. They love Indian woman" (184). When Bharti gets to know all about it, she was shocked and surprised. Anita was the girl, whom those rascals have kept to convince Bharti. Bharti weeps and says that if photographs went viral my father will die. Ever since she received a massage via Sarosh's driver asking her to get Maina to the farmhouse, she had been feeling nauseous. After all she planned to murder herself:

> She rushed into the kitchen and bolted the door. The kerosene canister stood in a corner. Even since Sarosh

> had got them the second gas cylinder they had not had to use the kerosene stove.
>
> There was enough in the canister to soak her clothes.
>
> But Papa, she must tell Papa. She must apologise. Bharti tore a Page from the calendar and wrote with the stub of a pencil that hung by a string over it.
>
> Somebody was ringing the bell insistently. It must be the driver, the charioteer of Death.
>
> Bharti struck a match and lit up. (265)

The patriarchal world never accepted her radical and transformative ideologies, for these are the prerogatives men enjoy. *Dirty Picture* narrates the ugly realities of paternalistic societies which operate through strategic exploitation of women.

On the other hand, the story of Reena is different. She got divorce from a man who was struggling with substance abuse. She lives seemingly a comfortable life in the cosmopolitan city of Mumbai weaving dreams of a married life with her boss, Suhas, a middle aged man drunk by the power she wields. In Suhas, a promising businessman, she finds an emotional man who offers her with dreams of a new and settled life. Suhas, who does not get along with her wife, turns to Reena for an emotional and 'physical' recourse. Reena is flooded with promises of a wonderful life by Suhas. She was so much in love and faith of Suhas Mehta that she answers calmly to her sister if divorce doesn't take place then we will have live-in-relationship:

> "We are going to have a live-in-relationship—you know, openly living together. For all principal purposes it would be a marriage."
>
> "Has he said this to you Didi?"
>
> "Yes, of course. He has given me his word, Bharti, and his ring." (156)

Marwah says at one place:

> I do perceive a weakening of ethical standards in sexual matters but this decline is in piece with the opportunism

> evident in—say—the economic sphere. Our society is in transition and often the globe whirls too fast for us. We're definitely more confused now than we were before. The Mumbai portions of Dirty Picture where a CEO makes false promises to a young woman who works for him are indicative of hypocrisy and what is made to pass in the name of liberalism. (India Writes interview with Nair)

All this seems to be heading towards a happy and satisfying ending until Reena discovers the harsh realities of patriarchal world. But slowly and slowly she feels change in the behaviour of Suhas, and their frequent meeting shrinked, so she questions to him:

> "Suhas, you don't love me any more," she said.
>
> "I love you much more than you think,"
>
> "Tell me why haven't we met for a long?"
>
> "Do you want the truth and nothing but the truth?"
>
> "Yes," she said with her eyes wide. (231)

After that she insisted every time whenever she met Suhas, to give divorce to her wife. She suggests her by saying:

> Your divorce will be much simpler. We'll only need a good lawyer and some money. But Meenakshi with Meera's help can create much more trouble than your husband probably can. Hindu divorce law is weighted in favour of women. Adultery is a criminal offence for a man, by the way. She can have me put behind bars. (232)

Slowly and slowly their relation feebled and reached to the matter of break up. The day came when he broke his relations with her:

> "But darling, what if she doesn't give you a divorce?"
>
> "We can still be together. It's the combination of the cow-scandal and the personal problem that is giving me trouble. I can tackle them quiet efficiently one at a time."

She was crying

> "You know what the ring means, don't you?" Suhas asked her.
>
> She did not reply. Then she whispered, "Eternity...." (236)

At last they left each other. "Take care" (236) he said alighting and walked away. Suhas immediately returned to the flat, changed the key of the house, and threw away all the belongings of Reena.

Pornography is not defined by sexual explicitness, but rather by its fusion of sexuality with male dominance and female submission. It is a general problem for oppressed people, not specific to women's oppression because oppression silences, fighting oppression requires developing voices, languages, and cultural and interpretive matrices for the articulation of women's experiences. It is difficult for both Bharti and Reena to name their experiences and describe their worlds, for oppression puts them in a double bind. If they tell how things seem to them, they will be viewed as either complicit or crazy.

Bharti's loss of voice and her inability to narrate traumatic experiences can be attributed to the fear of being singled out by men, their agents and their culture as a troublemaker. Her isolation is real and in this she is avoided, or ignored, or chastised, or denounced. Her victimization leads to her silence and she puts an end to her life. Both Bharti and Reena are victims of intimate partner rape which spells disaster for them. Bharti fails to raise her voice, but being raped does grant Reena a voice—the voice of the victim. Bharti's unspeakable truth finds an alternative voice in Reena as her speech becomes much more verbose and wandering as she ponders the consequences of her victimisation. Reena is not silenced as her speech shows an example of how charged female language can challenge gender power relations in a very political manner. When she meets Suhas, she replies to his 'love' saying:

> Not anymore. Not since I found out that Bharti, my sister, was one of the girls caught in the sex scandal. The man who took her there must have also told her

> he loved her. By the way, her clothes didn't catch fire, Suhas....
>
> "She didn't understand, Suhas. My sister went away because of the shame she felt. But now I am confused. It all seems shameful to me too: love, marriage, sex! I can't distinguish between love and lust. You who betrayed me, are you a rapist too? (280)

The words that appeared on Bharti's suicide note are the only and the most powerful instance when she reclaimed her voice. Though she puts an end to her life before her voice reverberated and pounded the walls of patriarchy, she does find the alternative voice in Reena who gets the voice translated into action through her crusade against the outrage. Reena's decision to join a newspaper and write life stories gives her access to media and an opportunity to challenge hetero-normative power relations. Reena's writings at the individual level can be linked to her embodiment, stressing that her writing also involves allowing her voice to be heard, 'seizing' the ability to speak outside of masculine discourse. When Reena 'laughed' on Suhas' face she embodies female self-assertion and distinction.

Reena uses the power of media to cut across the protected wall of patriarchal power relations and to disrupt and shift away from problematic discourse, attempting to create a community on media-escape where women can freely speak on their own terms. While even this act which breaks the silence technically silences the ability of sexists to express their sexism, overall this silencing aims for a world where ultimately more women can speak without being centralized around the subjugating language and institutions problematically imposed by a group of people upon others. Bharti's alternative voice potentially serves as a war machine by shifting the scripts of patriarchal discourse such that women can speak on their own terms. This practice can be seen in action through her 'life stories,' involving a refusal to engage with a climate of sexism through the deployment of speech and the creation of a space where marginalised women can speak outside of oppressive discourse.

In *Dirty Picture*, particularly Marwah has managed to bring all her interests together in a narrative that is both disturbing and persuasive. This is a story that needs to be told, but because of its complexity, it is not an easy story to tell. But Anuradha persisted, and we all owe her a debt of gratitude that she did. This particular incident at least will not be covered by the dust of ages. While most contemporary feminist writers see no reason to transcend their comfortable urban locations to engage with poverty, male domination and issues that trap middle class women in India's forgotten, small dusty towns. To weave, in fact, a fiction, biographical and imaginative elements and structure a story that would hold the readers' interest could not have been an easy task. There is ambition, desire, politics and much more in this novel about small town India, an interesting reading. Well crafted narrative and perfectly moulded incidents make this novel a must read. She says at one place:

> Frankly, deciding to tell the story of a sex scandal is to leave notions of 'sharam' (shame!) behind. Any censorship—especially self-censorship—would have falsified the story. Of course, it is not easy to write about sex. There are also obvious discouragements. For instance, in England there is 'bad sex award'—awarded annually by 'Literary Review'—that is given 'on the most pretentious, tasteless, embarrassing, otiose, self-infatuated or redundant description of the sexual act'. There may not be a similar award in India but the literary establishment doesn't take too kindly to sexual themes. (India Writes interview with Nair)

In *Dirty Pictures*, the author uses a foundation of solid fact to create her most believable scenario. She empathises so entirely that the most memorable segments consist of the use of stream of consciousness as a literary device to mentally box Bharti in so completely that she is helpless in the face of the circumstances that overwhelm her. Left with no option, fire becomes a way out. Even so, when it happens, it is a shock. Ultimately, private agendas had to be addressed. The book itself is worth a read. And while it may not be one that can be easily re-read, it can be allowed permanent space on one's bookshelf because, after all, it is telling the story of a modern

India trying to come to grips with the fact that nobody and nothing is ever perfect, whether in towns or cities.

Anuradha's writing is serious, responsible, yet funny and ironic. A false criticism is levelled all the time against women's writing that tends to be internal and domestic. I think in that sense Anuradha is not a woman—the larger world is her domain. So that she unites in her writing two kinds of sensibility—one that is intimate and personal, and the other that deals for example with politicised religion and socially disruptive forces. It is not easy to write about such things, and in a way that will induce people to be concerned about them, but I think she succeeds brilliantly.

Novelist Anuradha Marwah is no stranger to desire and its daemons. If *Idol Love*, her second novel, was about the suicidal sadness of unreciprocated love in an India that was becoming vulnerable to seductions of religious zealots, her latest novel *Dirty Picture* is an unflinching look at soul sickness that underlies sexual exploitation in an increasingly promiscuous society.

Anuradha Marwah presents an unflinching picture of two sisters 'who become a victim of their own mindset' to weave the fact and fiction, biographical and imaginative elements and structure a story that would hold the readers' interest could not have been an easy task. There is ambition, desire, politics and much more in this novel about small town India. Well crafted narrative and perfectly moulded incidents make this novel a must read. Blame it on the novel being sufficiently disturbing or on the fact that the lives of the protagonists in the novel could be. She used it well in her first book, she employed 'authority' in her second, and the fact that her own background is very different proves no obstacle at all in fleshing out the characters of Bharti and Reena, two sisters who are exploited in different ways.

Marwah described her book as certainly very dark, but not desperate. Why not, since there is no halfway happy ending for any of the protagonists, except perhaps Reena, and even for her; it's just the triumph of hard lessons learned and a sort of self-awareness achieved. Because, she says, the book focuses upon the real, the fact that life is tough, and with the rallying cries of liberalisation, globalisation and change ringing in everyone's ears, it is just going to get tougher. "Mores are changing and the lessons women are expected to learn can be very cruel," she declares, what could help, in her opinion, is developing greater degrees of self-awareness.

But the ending of *Dirty Picture* was far from satisfactory, even though the law did step in. Ultimately, private agendas had to be addressed. The book itself is worth a read. And while it may not be one that can be easily re-read, it can be allowed permanent space on one's bookshelf because, after all, it is telling the story of a modern India trying to come to grips with the fact that nobody and nothing—is ever perfect, whether in towns or cities. At best, we come to grips with the stresses that unhinge us and ensure that they become part of an urban legend that is recognisable without being terrifying.

While most contemporary feminist writers see no reason to transcend their comfortable urban locations to engage with poverty, male domination and issues that trap middle-class women in India's forgotten, small dusty towns, Anuradha Marwah presents an unflinching picture of two sisters who become a victim of their own mindset in her third novel *Dirty Picture*.

However, in *Dirty Picture*, Marwah goes off in another direction and she does it with equal felicity, if such a word may be used about what is essentially a most unpleasant subject—the sexual exploitation of young women by politicians and the law in small towns. As she has done in her first two books, in writing about what is essentially an 'underwritten' subject in Indian fiction writing. She writes from the perspective of the insider, at home in the small town milieu, an environment that you usually carry with you when relocating to the metropolis. She used it well in her first book, she employed 'authority' in her second, and the fact that her own background is very different proves no obstacle at all in fleshing out the characters of Bharti and Reena, two sisters who are exploited in different ways.

Because, she says, the book focuses upon the real, the fact that life is tough, and with the rallying cries of liberalisation, globalisation and change ringing in everyone's ears, it is just going to get tougher. "Mores are changing and the lessons women are expected to learn can be very cruel," she declares, what could help, in her opinion, is developing greater degrees of self-awareness.

While most contemporary feminist writers see no reason to transcend their comfortable urban locations to engage with poverty, male domination and issues that trap middle class women in India's forgotten, small dusty towns, Anuradha Marwah presents an unflinching picture of two sisters "who become a victim of their own mindset" in her third novel *Dirty Picture*. Novelist Anuradha Marwah is no stranger to desire and its daemons. If *Idol Love*, her second novel, was about the suicidal sadness of unreciprocated love in an India that was becoming vulnerable to seductions of religious zealots, her latest novel *Dirty Picture* is an unflinching look at soul sickness that underlies sexual exploitation in an increasingly promiscuous society.

She talks about the creative challenges of transforming a real life sex scandal in small town India into the redemptive fiction of her new novel, choices faced by her in exploring themes of sexuality and pornography and the liberating impulse that animates a writer in a society awash with consumerist distractions. Anuradha Marwah's *Dirty Picture* is a promising script of feminist resistance, allows a woman to shift oppressive scripts of discourse that discourages women from speaking to a context where they can speak on their own terms.

Thus, well crafted narrative and perfectly moulded incidents make the novel interesting. Sometimes it is hard to differentiate between imagination and reality. Anuradha has such a sharp ability to entwine reality and imagination that we don't realise when the line between imagination and reality blurs. So I call it reality re-imagined.

NOTE

All references have been taken from Anuradha Marwah's *Dirty Picture*, Indialog Publications Pvt. Ltd., 2007 and the page numbers are given along with the quotation.

WORKS CITED

Anand, T.S., L.S. Bedi, and Hargunjot Kaur. *Modern Indian English Fiction*. New Delhi: Creative Books, 2002. Print.

Bai, K. Meera. "Tradition and Modernity: The Portrayal of Women by Women Writers." *Indian Women Novelists*. Ed. R.K. Dhawan. New Delhi: Prestige (1991): 35. Print.

Ghadially, Rehana, ed. *Woman in Indian Society: A Reader*. New Delhi: Sage Publications, 1988. Print.

Hooks, Bell. *Feminist Theory: From Margin to Centre*. London: Pluto Press, 2000. Print.

Khan, M.Q. and A.G. Khan, eds. *Changing Faces of Women in Indian Writings in English*. New Delhi: Creative Books, 1995. Print.

Marwah, Anuradha. *The Higher Education of Geetika Mehendiratta*. New Delhi: Ravi Dayal Publishers, 1997. Print.

———. *Idol Love*. New Delhi: Ravi Dayal Publisher, 1999. Print.

———. *Dirty Picture*. Delhi: Indialog Publishers, 2007. Print.

Myles, Anita. *Feminism and The Post-Modern Indian Women Novelists in English*. New Delhi: Sarup and Sons, 2006. Print.

Sivapriya, M. "A Seamless Transition from the Fictional to the Real in Anuradha Marwah's A Pipe Dream in Delhi." *The Criterion: An International Journal in English* 5.2 (April 2014): 538-46. Print.

http://www.thehindu.com/thehindu/lr/2001/12/02/stories/2001120200180300.htm 1/3 25/06/2015

http://www.anuradhamarwah.com/2007/09/born-to-academic-middle-class-familyin.html

8

Gender Identity of Women in Mahesh Dattani's Play *Tara*

Sanjay Johari

Mahesh Dattani is an unorthodox and multifarious dramatist of contemporary Indian English Drama. He has written plays for the stage. To stage his plays Dattani moulds his characters in such a way that speak both of linguistic and cultural boundaries. Dattani himself says in an interview, "Personal Agenda", "The love of my life is drama and I want to write more plays" (26). He does not choose the subject on history, myths and puran but he raises his voice for the contemporary Urban Indian Society and the facts changing scenario of the Modern Society. John M.C. Rae says about his plays—

> They are the plays of today, sometimes as actual as to cause controversy, but the same time they are the plays which embody many of the classic concern for world Drama.[1]

He has written plays for the stage. He thinks that as poetry is meant to be read in order to enjoy, the plays are meant to be staged. In fact his plays generate the 'fresh arrival' in the realm of Indian English Dramas. Dattani like Shakespeare writes for the theatre. Shakespeare wrote plays for the stage and Dattani also believes that the realistic picture of Indian Society can be realized only through the performance on the stage. Rightly Shakespeare has remarked in his drama, *As You Like It*:

> "All the world is a stage and all the men and women merely players,
> They have their exits and their entrances;
> And one man in his time plays many parts. (available on http;//www.williamshakespeare)

In one of his interviews, he favours drama in comparison of any other art and says, "I think of all arts and of all writing genres, theatre perhaps is the most dynamic because no other art form is a vibrant." Thus he has depicted the vibrant Indian English and also presented the themes and the characters of middle class and upper middle class Indians in his plays. Alyque Padamsee calls him one of the "most serious contemporary playwrights," when he won the Sahitya Akademi Award for his book of play *Final Solution and Other Plays*. The Sahitya Akademi Award citation says "[Dattani's Work] probes tangled attitudes in contemporary India towards communal differences, consumerism and gender...a brilliant contribution to Indian Drama in English."[2] He knows very well the apathy for Indian languages. He admits, "You have got to be true to your expressions also. English is for me a sort of given. It's my language as it is to a lot of Indians here and abroad."[3] Dattani's characters struggle for some kind of freedom and pleasure under the burden of tradition, gender culture and pressed desires. He has sketched the realistic picture of marginalized society and its people who struggle hard to face the situation. He thinks, "Every individual wants to be part of society, of the main stream but we must acknowledge that it is a forced harmony."[4] He presents the multi-facets of contemporary Indian Society who compel to marginalized people to live drudgery life. Dattani's plays emerge different themes such as love, sexual fulfilment and the problem of gender issues.

No doubt he is considered among the great problem writers on the line of Ibsen and Shaw. His plays are so realistic that sometimes they produced a hot discussion and controversy. In fact, he has a mission to communicate with his readers the profound meaning through his plays so that he may produce their keen awareness for the downtrodden society. There is another technique that Dattani uses for the purpose of his plays. This is "Flash Back" technique and he splits scene device. Through this device Dattani's aim to realize that all the events take place here. He states, "The function of drama in my opinion is not merely to reflect malfunctions of society but to act like 'Freak Mirrors' in a carnival and to project grotesque images of all passes for normal in our world, it is ugly but funny."[5] He is a versatile writer who tries to present the reality as it exits. That is why his characters are deep-rooted in the urban cosmopolitan setting of contemporary middle class India.

There is no face of human life that is not traced by Dattani in his plays. This is his belief that his mission will complete when his plays have been performed before the audience. No doubt his voice for the subaltern is unconventional. It is said that it is a preface to the tradition of unconventional popular Indian Theatre. Through his plays he presents the several current social problems on the stage. He admits that drama is the more potent medium to create social awareness. He confesses:

> My Malicious theatre. You can't operate in.... I do want a theatre movement to happen. The major block for that is lack of sound training and professionalism. We have the talent but theatre is more than that, is a craft communicating through language of action.[6]

No doubt Dattani is radical and dynamic dramatist of today. He gives his readers a new hope to look better. He enlarges the Indian drama by presenting diverse themes like homosexuality, gender issues, the dynamic man and woman relationship, their frustrations in life and nothingness in the middle class life and tradition. He has presented the realistic face of human society on the stage. He is the true spokesman of all the marginalized people, whatever he wants to present before the audience, what he sees around the world. He is a versatile artist. He deals problems which are emerged by the educated Urban Society. This is the quality of Dattani that he handles every problem through his skill. It does not matter whether the problem of gender issues or sexuality.

The problem of gender issue can be seen easily in his play *Tara*. The theme of the play revolves round the central character, Tara. She is the victim of social norms that male is more valuable than female. The play related with the life of Tara. She is born congenial twin one girl and one boy who are joined together at the hip. They can be separated through a surgical operation which creates danger to the life of one of them. Mrs. and Mr. Patel become anxious. Mrs. Patel who is rooted with tradition, prefers her son Chandan to be saved and she does not bother about Tara. This operation was conducted in such a manner that the life of Chandan should be saved and Tara was left miserable. The play shows a pathetic condition of human society where the children of same womb are treated in two different ways. This is very shocking that injustice was done by their own mother who gave preference to male child. Tara becomes disable. Bharti, the mother of Tara becomes insane but she cannot resist the suggestion of her father. But the question emerges here how can she ignore the identity of Tara and she is too blind to see the consequences involving the risk of life of Tara. Dattani tries to realize us the gender prejudice which is seen in Indian Society. "Dattani plays with the idea of female infanticide that is prevalent among Gujrati's through the various intimations that Roopa makes and also suggests Patel's hegemonic patriarchy when he insists that 'proper' division in the gender roles be made with different sets or plans for the boys and the girls."[7]

Tara and Chandan are separated through a major surgery. But the mother, Bharti and Chandan suffers from the conscious injustice done to Tara. Chandan thinks that he is responsible for the suffering of Tara. Dattani presents emotional crisis of Chandan in different levels. Dattani does not ignore this view that it is not only the matter of Tara but it is the issues of 'self' and 'society'. In the introduction of the play Erin Mee points out.... Tara and Chandan are two sides of the self rather than two separated entries and that Dan is trying to write the story of his own childhood, has to write Tara's story to rediscover the neglected half of himself, as a means of becoming whole (*CP* 320).

Chandan does not ready to reconcile the situation. He realizes that he is the only responsible person for Tara's suffering.

So he leaves to London in a new identity 'Dan'. He wants to involve in his career and tries to withdraw from this external world. But this is too difficult for him to tolerate with injustice done to his sister. He thinks that Tara is an inseparable part of his inner-self. When Tara dies he accepts: Moving in a forced harmony. Those who survive are those who do not defy the gravity of others. And those who desire even a moment of freedom find themselves hurled in to space, doomed to crush with some unknown force. I no longer desire that freedom. I move, just move without meaning, I forget Tara, I forget I had a sister—with whom, I shared my body in one comfortable womb till we were forced out and separated (*CP* 378-79).

The play can be analyzed through the relationship of man and woman. Dattani tries to show the poignant situation of disabled children who struggle hard against a variety of odds which have been come in their life by chance or nature or accident of their birth. Dattani also presents the miserable condition of a girl child in Indian culture and society. The situation of man-woman relationship can be seen through the interactions between Mr. Patel and his wife Bharti. The situation becomes critical when Tara becomes crippled. Mrs. and Mr. Patel become depressed. They are unable to handle the critical situation. Mr. Patel cannot prove himself a caring husband. He says about Bharti: "May be I'm expecting the worst. It may never happen—no. Things are getting out of hand, I must worry about her. Yes. I am worried—about my life."[8]

On the other hand, Bharti feels guilty conscious. She thinks she has committed a sin. She is in depression so she wants to confess her sin to Tara. But Mr. Patel deprives Bharti to do this act. She suffers a nervous breakdown. She wants to recover this situation. She becomes over conscious for Tara. She tries her best to call young girls in the neighborhood to play with Tara and talk to her. She tries to recover her sin to Tara but no avail. Tara has no power how to express her desires or her demands. No doubt Bharti is a pathetic victim of patriarchy. Tara's disability becomes an uncontrollable anguish in the life of Chandan, Chandan and Tara's relationship is to establish the fact that the fabric of different relations with the norms and female concern may not be absolute and ultimate end of the relations.

In fact, Tara is not the story of the narrator of the drama, *Tara* but it is the story of every female child who is born in this contemporary Indian family whether urban or rural. This is true that in Indian family every girl child has to suffer if there is a boy child born.

Dattani give a glimpse of Indian Political Society. We come to know that Chandan and Tara's maternal grandfather was a wealthy man. He was a great politician and was about to become the Chief Minister. His conviction about male child in Indian society is highly embarrassing. Mr. Patel and Chandan are talking together:

Patel : He (grandfather) left a lot of money.
Chandan : And Tara?
Patel : Nothing.
Chandan : Why?
Patel : It was his money. He could do what he wanted with it. (360)

This is very surprising that this conversation is taken place when Tara is present. Nobody cares for the miserable plight of Tara. Dattani's aim is here to present the role of collective society in India. In Indian society girls like Tara, have to undergo the heinous ordeal to testify their place. Dattani's aim is to present the realistic position of Indian women. Throughout the play we find in Tara that she has some kind of hatred against the society. Her parents and her brother are the whole world for her because she is very close to them. Tara's internal anguish and her attachment to her brother can be seen in her conversation with her brother, Chandan in the speech when she says, "May be we still a like we have always been, Inseparable. The way we started life, two lives and one body, in one comfortable womb, till we were forced out...and separated" (325).

Dattani exposes here the reality of woman playing second fiddle to man. The play turns a twist. Chandan anguish is so much that he changed in to Dan so that he may recover himself from the guilt of killing his sister. He is scorched under the brunt of his grandfather's and mother's cruelty. In wordly he thinks that he is responsible for his sister's death. For that reason he leaves for London and changes his name from Chandan to Dan. On the other hand, this is very regretting how can educate parents like Patel and Bharti, take a wrong step. Bharti becomes more conscious in her daughter's matter. She shows her maternal love and takes care of her daughter. She behaves kindly to her daughter. She tries throughout her life to make up for the damage done.

No doubt Tara was very bold and courageous and she has high aspiration to fulfil her dreams but her dreams were shattered by her maternal relations. She could not fulfil them because she became handicapped. She had to compromise her pathetic situation. But the question is that why a girl cannot use an 'artificial leg'? it would be helpful for her to work properly if it is attached to her body. But she denied. Why? What is its reason? Only this that she is a girl. It is the curse of her? But who is responsible for this—the society? Is women the thing of mockery nothing else? In fact, the ratio of women, if it is compared to man, is really much less in our country. This is the root cause of women that they could not survive. Tara had to struggle hard because she was a girl and she was not given any right by the society to live better life than her brother. Dattani also points out here that there are numerous cases of female feticides. They are still common these days. This is very shocking and degrading that people do not like to be born a female child so they kill the foetus of the female child even before it takes shape in the uterus. Dattani focuses here the injustices which is done to women and also injustice to men like Chandan in our society. Though he has no fault still he has to live a life of guilt. But now this is acceptable in our society that a girl child is sacrificed than a handicapped male child.

This is true that male is always taken greater freedom and opportunities than female in the contemporary society. Mr. Patel has no feeling for Tara's education. He always makes planning for Chandan's education and makes his career secure in life. Dattani shows here gender patriarchy in which the adult males hold power over the family. For this Dan feels regretting in the end of the play and says, "Forgive me Tara. Forgive me for making it my tragedy." Mahesh Dattani expressed his view that male and female are not separated beings, they are domination and subordination parts of society. In an interview with Lakshmi Subramanyam, Dattani said: "I see Tara as a play about the male self and female self. The male self is being preferred in all cultures. The play is about the separation of self and the resultant angst."[9]

Dattani's women characters show the mirror of contemporary life. His women are also the part of suffering. No doubt they are the sufferers in the society but they are sensitive to perceive their identity and self-respect.

Dattani says himself:

> ...He seems to be fighting for my feminine self. And since I have the male self which is equipped to fight as well, it is a proportionate battle. The feminine self is not a victim in my plays. It's subsumed yes! It is marginalized but it fights back.[10]

Like a conscious mother, Bharti always tries to make a suitable atmosphere to Tara, but we cannot ignore that she is bound to the conventional society. It is her desire that a girl like Tara should be attained a least opportunity for self-development. So she struggles hard for the welfare of Tara but she is too attached to get rid of the myth. In fact, Tara becomes the smile of her life. She is entangled between herself and social conventions. Though she bears irritation from her husband, Mr. Patel, still she is not disheartened and in the end of the play she makes compromise with the reality of life. She sees real vision of life and says:

> The emancipation is not in repudiating the claims of her family but in drawing upon untapped inner reserves of strength. The wife in the end is not a rebel—but a redeemed wife...one who is no longer afraid of the dark.[11]

Dattani writes plays for a certain purpose. He wants that the play should be seen and heard not only for reading. He presents two sold purposes in his play *Tara*. First, he wants to expose the modern education urban family who adheres to the conventional trends of favouring only the masculine. Secondly, he wants to expose the corruption prevalent in the bureaucracy society and the ethical deterioration of the medical profession. All these situations can be seen clearly in the conversation between Mr. Patel and his children: "A scan showed that a major part of the blood supply to the third leg was provided by the girl.... The chances were slightly better that the leg would survive...on the girl. Your grandfather and your mother had a private meeting with Dr. Thakkar. I wasn't asked to come.... I couldn't believe what she told me that they would risk giving both legs to the boy.... The doctor had agreed.... It was later I came to know of his intention of starting a large nursing home—the largest in Bangalore. He had acquired three acres of prime land—in the heart of the city—from the state. Your grandfather's political influence had been used.... Chandan had two legs for two days. It does not take them very long to realize what a grave mistake they had made. The leg was amputated. A piece of dead flesh which could have—might have—been Tara" (378).

This speech points out the orthodox conception in the contemporary life. Tara and Chandan are physically separated but their emotional separation joined both. This is pathetic in modern urban society that people prefer male child more than the female one. This is regretting. Dattani also tells us that the tragic events of Tara's life and Chandan's is not really the tragedy of both of them but the tragic events of every day life of human being.

Tara is a challenging character of Dattani. She shows that physical deficiency has no mean and it cannot interrupt in the life of a girl. She made for her physically deficiency strength and fought with society at every stage. That is why she was energetic and enthusiastic. She possessed all the qualities of a normal girl. She is a modern girl who proves her strength and fervour in the world of supremacy.

Thus, Dattani focuses gender identity of women in this play. No doubt Dattani presents a mirror to the Indian Society. He shows the true face of human society. This is a curse to human society where male child has more important than the female child. This is much regretting and shocking, nobody cares for the crisis of a girl who becomes handicapped or cripple in the midst of male-dominant society. Dattani is a new innovator in real sense. Whatever he sees around him, it impacts on him too much that he cannot resist showing in his plays. He painted his imagination on his wide canvas by drawing predicament of human society. Through his plays Dattani makes an authentic representation of the several social matters and also expresses his own concern for the gender issues. John McRae, Director at the Abelians theatre attributes of him, "Mahesh Dattani always adventure in his ways of using the theatrical space at his disposal multiple levels, breaking the bonds of the proscenium, wondrously inventive use of lighting to give height, breadth and depth."

NOTES

1. McRae John. "A Note on the Play" in the Mahesh Dattani's *Collected Plays*.
2. Mahesh Dattani. *Collected Plays* (New Delhi: Penguin India, 2000), Cover Page.
3. Rajiv Menon and K.S. Prakash. "Theatre to Morning Raga", *The Hindu*, Hyderabad, 2nd July, 2003.
4. Mahesh Dattani, interview to indianexpress.com.
5. Elizabeth Roy. "Freak Mirrors and Grotesque Images", *The Hindu*, 15th March, 2002.
6. Das Gupta, Uma Mahadevan. "The Minute I Write a Play, I Want to Direct It", 2001.
7. Asha Kuthari Chaudhari. *Mahesh Dattani*, 89.
8. Mahesh Dattani, *Tara in Collected Plays* (New Delhi: Penguin, 2000), 330.
9. Lakshmi Subramanyam (ed.), *Muffled Voices: Women in Modern Indian Theatre*, New Delhi: Shakti, 2002, 134.
10. Anjum Katayal. "Of Page and Stage", An interview with Mahesh Dattani, *Seagull Theatre Quarterly*, 24th January, 2000.
11. Kamini Dinesh, "Movingout of the Cloistered Self: Shashi Deshpandey's Protagonists", *Margins of Erasure: Purdah in the Subcontinental Novel in English* (ed.), Jasbir Jain and Amina Amin, New Delhi: Sterling, 1995, 204.

9

Vikram Seth's *An Equal Music*—A Melodic Tale of Love and Music

Tripty Seth

Vikram Seth's fiction polarizes critics and readers. Gore Vidal praised *The Golden Gate*, Seth's novel in verse, as "The Great Californian Novel"[1] while Evan Jones deplored it as "a pastiche".[2] Since the publication of *A Suitable Boy*, Seth has been applauded as "the best writer of his generation"[3] who "ought to have won the Booker Prize in 1993".[4] *An Equal Music* has been praised as "a love story"[5] and denigrated as a "romantic tosh".[6] As a novel about music, it has been admired as the best of its kind and glossed over a "non-starter".[7] Music, in a wider perspective, is the essence of all living things in nature. All natural things, most of the time, are rhythmical and regular. Thus, the novelists use musicians and music as a medium to express their viewpoint because they represent a living tradition and provide a kaleidoscopic view of the social and cultural life of the particular period under study. The last decade of the twentieth century witnessed a proliferation of novels dealing with the subject of music. Like other writers, Seth also used music as a plot for the first time in *A Suitable Boy*.

If one recalls the whole Saeeda Bai thread in *A Suitable Boy*, with its multiple evocations of North Indian classical music, one way of reading *An Equal Music* might then be to see this novel as Seth following up the exploration of his own national musical tradition with a parallel voyage into the music of a completely different culture. When Seth was writing *A Suitable Boy*, he became more and more interested in Western classical singing. He says, "There were a lot of Indian musical characters in the novel. In the evening, when I wanted to be myself, I found that the moment I started playing an Indian musical instrument or singing an Indian song, I was drawn back into world of my novel. It wasn't a form of relaxation, but work by other means. That's when I began singing Schubert's songs. I didn't know them well then, but I love them now. They're wonderful melodies."[8] This love for Western music resulted in the form of Seth's next novel *An Equal Music*.

An Equal Music is a fraction of the size of *A Suitable Boy*, but is still deliciously expansive. Seth says, "I did realize that if I were to write another novel equally long, it would take up another decade of my life."[9] Thus he decided to write a novel comparatively shorter than *A Suitable Boy*. *An Equal Music* was conceived one wintry day, while Seth was walking across Hyde Park in Kensington Gardens in London with his friend Philippe Honore, to whom he has dedicated the novel later on. Seth recalls that as they were walking, he visualized in his mind's eye someone, European or American by race, who was looking very intently at the water of the lake in the park.[10] He turned to his friend and asked him of what profession he thought this imaginary man might be. His friend Honore, who is a violinist, decided that this person was a musician too and played violin like him. Seth realized that the image of this imaginary person stirred him and had something to do with not a short story, probably a novel he was going to write. That's how the opening scene of the novel was formed. Thus the muse here was this fanciful, imaginary person staring intensely at the water. As Seth says, "It's a very visual inspiration for a very aural novel."[11]

After the overly hyped *A Suitable Boy*, Seth offered *An Equal Music*, a novel, 381 pages long, a repertoire by virtue of it being stunningly different from all his previous works. In some ways, *An Equal Music* presents a kind of anti-thesis to *A Suitable Boy*. The difference is apparent not only in the sheer volume of the work but also in the intensity with which feelings are portrayed. In *A Suitable Boy*, Seth articulates life from a distance, firmly shunning any intense emotions and thus the novel echoes with a genuine, laid-back serenity. By contrast, *An Equal Music* deals with the darker passions—gloominess, unhappiness, obsession and reflects difficult issues about love and life in the process. In Seth's conception of the novel as a *raag*, a *banyan tree* and a *river* which appears in *A Suitable Boy*, a pattern of harmony is discernible as the frame for the novel *An Equal Music*. Again, unlike the romantic saga of *A Suitable Boy*, *An Equal Music* is a sad love story, involving a man, a woman, a quartet, a violin, and the cities of London, Venice and Vienna.

Love and music are the two operating themes in *An Equal Music* which runs simultaneously and sometimes merge with each other, yielding a perfect equilibrium. The subject matter is suggested by Julia when she says, "Making music and making love—it's a bit too easy an equation." It is a book about the love of a woman lost, found, and lost again. It is a highly readable tale about a pair of young lovers—Michael, a butcher's son, and Julia, the daughter of an Oxford professor of History, and their doomed romance. The structure of the novel—it is divided into eight parts and several subparts—is based on a musical pattern that demands a thorough knowledge of the history, range and structure of music. And the eight parts of the novel may correspond to the eight tones in the octave.

This novel is a first person narrative, which interweaves music, love and life using Seth's imaginative, delicate vocabulary. The plot, a staple of romantic fiction, involves the rekindling of a decade old first love, with the woman now a married mother. The protagonist of the novel is a violinist, Michael Holme who is born in a butcher's family in a Northern English town Rochdale. His mother wanted a good career for her son. Thus he was sent to an old Grammar School with the hope that he would go for university education. No one in the family had ever dreamt of going to university, and their only son Michael was refusing to try. He somehow manages to escape humble beginnings through his love of music. He finds a patron in an eccentric neighbour Mrs. Cecilia Formby who spots Michael's talent and lends him a cherished Tononi violin. He studies music in England and later in Vienna. When he left for Vienna, his mother died and his father did not object any more.

The novel opens with the protagonist Michael, the second violinist of Maggiore String Quartet, living in London as a fugitive from Vienna. By the time novel starts, he had left his student years in Vienna behind him, where he was fallen deeply in love with a talented pianist, Julia McNicholl who was his fellow music student in an institution, under the instruction of Carl Kall. Julia's beauty was as mesmerizing as her musical genius, and whom Michael loved with an intensity he never found again. Both were passionately devoted to each other and to the music. They realized that their music complemented each other very well and formed a trio with another musician. A sudden disruption is caused by Michael's distaste for his stern teacher, Carl Kall, because of an incompatible war of wills with him. He could not tolerate the despotic manner of his teacher in teaching music. His beloved Julia, who was lovable and sensitive by temperament, disagreed with Michael's impressions and advised him not to push the matter to a point of no return. But Michael had a nervous breakdown because of the tensions with his teacher and he abruptly left Vienna, and unintentionally Julia, without any warning. Julia was emotionally shattered by Michael's unsteady temperamental behaviour. By the time Michael recovered from his distress two months had elapsed and there was no communication between the duo. Michael's telephonic calls to Julia go unresponded by her as she felt the manner of his departure too shocking and irreconcilable.

Ten years later, as the novel opens, Michael is living in a flat near the Hyde Park in London and earning his living as a second violinist in a string quartet, the Maggiore, a musical group comprising Michael, Piers, Helen, and Billy. In these ten years, Julia gets married to an American banker of Boston named James Hansen and gives birth to a son, Luke. Though playing with a string quartet, Michael spends his days only with music which provide meaning to his life, yet he is still haunted by the memories of Julia whom he had left behind, and subsequently never heard from her again. He has a French girlfriend Virginie, but his mind is constantly drawn to his first and only love, Julia. Seth reflects Michael's loneliness from the opening paragraphs of the novel, the loneliness that attracts Michael to the dark water and the wind which is blowing at him:

> The branches are bare, the sky tonight a milky violet. It is not quiet here, but it is peaceful. The wind ruffles the black water towards me.
>
> There is no one about. The birds are still. The traffic slashes through Hyde Park. It comes to my ears as white noise.
>
> I test the bench but do not sit down. As yesterday, as the day before, I stand until I have lost my thoughts. I look at the water of the Serpentine.[12]

Michael is easily irritated by his girlfriend Virginie and by his colleagues in the Maggiore String Quartet. In short, he's fed up with playing second fiddle in life and art. His depressed words clearly show that a decade of separation does not dull his nostalgic memories of his lost love for Julia.

Into this chaotic world, Julia steps in again and they get a sudden glimpse of each other in a moving double decker bus passing in the other direction on the Oxford street. Such a chance encounter brings a sudden bliss to Michael and redevelops his desire and passion for Julia. Like a maniac, he runs after the bus but is unable to catch her and his world ceases to turn. This chance sighting of each other in the London traffic is followed by a purposeful meeting when Julia goes backstage after a Maggiore performance at Wigmore Hall. By now, Julia has settled down in London along with her family after the death of her father, but she is no longer the woman Michael left behind, not least because she now has a husband and a son, but also because she is almost totally deaf due to an auto-immune disease. A series of random events brings her back into Michael's life and he summons all his energy in an effort to resurrect their relationship and come alive once more. During some frequent visits, the love between them is revived.

Michael and Julia, both struggle awkwardly to find a new way of loving one another and communicating through music, even bringing Julia as a pianist into Michael's group for a performance of Schubert Trout Quintet. Michael feels hurt when Julia tells him that this quintet performance will be her last concert as it causes a strain for her because of her deafness. In desperation, Michael falls ill due to a sudden attack of nervousness. The premonition of losing Julia makes him unsteady with shivering fingers. Seth expresses the disturbance on Michael's mental equilibrium in his words, "It is a death, a passing; for will she ever?—she will not ever—play with anyone again."[13] He regains normalcy only after Julia's assurance to be a part of the music. She can't oppose Michael and both of them try to continue where they left off. Luckily, the Maggiore has to proceed to Vienna and then to Venice for performing musical concerts at these places. Julia, still playing the piano despite of her hearing loss, agrees to join Michael and the Maggiore as a pianist for the concerts of Venice and Vienna, where they were together as students an age earlier.

Michael and Julia travel to Vienna with the quartet and perform there. Against the magical atmosphere of concert halls and canals, they realize the revival of their love and ultimately, the perfection that they achieve in making music together somehow eludes them in their love. In Venice, they come in a full circle and spend four heavenly days together by living in an apartment which is spared for them by Julia's friend, Jenny. There both of them are haunted by the past and enjoy a brief magical time in which everything seems possible. Julia finds herself torn between two loves—her old love Michael, and her love for her family. The love of her husband James and her son Luke overpowers her. She refers her son as 'my poor baby' and the hopelessness of their relationship is reflected in Michael's words, "I feel a sudden surge of resentment against this poor baby. How can I ever compete with him? How could I even think of drawing them apart?"[14] Trapped between divided loyalties, Julia finds her real happiness with her family, her choice comes as no surprise. Like Seth's other heroines, she realizes that life does not require a companion, but a soul mate and returns to

London. This incident decreases the depth of their love and it comes to an abrupt end. Julia does not want to keep any more this extra-marital relationship with Michael because she suspects that her husband has smelt a rat. Michael also returns to London where he attends a solo piano performance of Bach's 'Art of Fugue' by Julia at the Wigmore Hall. The quality of her music heals Michael and gives him inner strength. Finally, he seems to get salvation from the obsession of the physical love of Julia by listening her charming and liberating music. Seth reflects Michael's reconciliation to the inevitable in his last words, "Music, such music, is a sufficient gift. Why ask for happiness; why hope not to grieve? It is enough, it is to be blessed enough, to live from day-to-day and to hear such music—not too much, or the soul could not sustain it—from time to time."[15]

A very interesting factor regarding the novel, is the ease with which Seth has dealt with a non-Indian theme. Seth has portrayed his characters, Helen, Michael, Julia, Billy, who are living in London and perform in Europe. He has worked hard to depict the culture of Europe in his characters as well as in his plot. He says, "I have to live in the place (Europe) for a while to write and unfold its culture, traditions and ethos while telling my story."[16] And then he would be able to introduce the tradition of European expressionist art music—the music of Bach, Beethoven, Mozart, Schubert and Vivaldi throughout the text and made *An Equal Music* a deeply moving love story set against the musical world of Europe. Vikram Seth's credit lies in leading the readers to the realm of music, and in acquainting them with the specific language of music which may have been known to them.

A tour de force of poetic, impassioned writing, *An Equal Music* is an unforgettable tale and its events are unfolding in the dramatic settings of contemporary London, Vienna, and Venice.

Here Seth has presented various milieus of Michael. He manages to give a sense of places which shows his skill to conjure up visual spaces through aural cues. His uniqueness is in what the place sounds like. Michael's hometown Rochdale is represented by a lark's song, his Bayswater flat by its deep silence, London is represented by the songs of robins in winter and black-birds in summer, Vienna is portrayed by the sound of nightingales, and Venice by the music of Vivaldi which is played by Julia and Michael in the composer's church. Seth's ability to translate the sounds of music into the written word is astounding. He portrays an enchanting picture of the contemporary life of the wonderful cities of London, Vienna and Venice.

The story shows the two dimensional love. On the one hand, Seth portrays the love of a woman, and the other thematic strand moves upon the love of music. It is a love story, woven around a musical backdrop. The suitable boy, Michael Holme, though racked by the memory of his lost love Julia McNicholl, yet spends his days with the intense passion for music which provides him the only solace. His remembrance is entangled in the very music he hears, plays, and breaths. It is through music that the emotions of their years together are revived as strong as ever. Though Michael and Julia both have a genuine passion for their vocation, yet Seth takes this much deeper with Michael's relationship to music, to his teachers and fellow musicians, to the composers whose music he plays, and to his beloved violin. In this novel, Seth uses music as a kind of metaphor for love. In fact, music dominates love's place as the driving force that pulls the reader along irresistibility.

An Equal Music successfully captures Seth's self-proclaimed love for music. His penchant for music began while learning *khayal*, the traditional form of classical music, in India. He admits "I am very close to music—in some ways, closer than to words. If I had to choose whether to have music on a desert isle or words—no question, I would choose music."[17] Blake writes about Seth's love of music, "This writer is a servant of music, like his creations."[18] Seth's intention of writing a novel about music is candidly stated in the authorial note annexed after the end of the narration. He has written, "Music to me is dearer even than speech. When I realised that I would be writing about it I was gripped with anxiety. Only slowly did I reconcile myself to the thought of it."[19] There is some kind of music on every page, and it provides the celestial framework over which the delicate gossamer threads of the love story are woven.

Seth believes that writing about an artist is incomplete without learning his art. Thus he has made himself highly knowledgeable about the great chamber-music classics of the Viennese school and then introduced various forms of musical compositions like a trio, a quartet, a quintet, the 'Art of Fugue' etc. His artistic goal seems to mirror those of the Maggiore Quartet who spurn modern music in favour of the classic repertoire. The sublimity of the music is reflected in Michael's words. He says, "We play in an energised trance—I only have to realise on the strings what is already real to me."[20] By the mingling of this kind of description and emotion, Seth enables to seize the inexpressible essence of music.

The whole firmament of the novel is resounded with the Western musical instruments like violin, piano, viola, bass and cello, etc. Seth candidly delves into the international music scene and into the souls of musicians. He shows that the instrument each member plays suited to his or her temperament. In his world of music, the musical instruments are not treated as lifeless objects. They express their happiness, they grumble and even purr at some suggestions. *An Equal Music* shows that each piece of music has a life of its own, just as each instrument has a soul. All the members of the Maggiore seem to involve in the musical compositions of classical music composers, such as Beethoven, Mozart, Schubert, Haydn, Bach and others. Seth writes so well of Haydn's Forellen Quintet, introduces so subtly Schubert's Trout Quintet and Bach's 'Art of Fugue' matters deeply, and the discovery of little known Beethoven opus is a miracle.

The highly engrossing and highly soothing masters, Beethoven, Schubert, Mozart and Bach, drench the love of Michael and Julia in the shower of music. Their love-affair is interwoven with the pursuit of music as both of them like each other by the force of their common, deep, ever-living interest in music. Though Julia is married, yet she discards to wear her wedding ring and says to Michael, "It distracts me when I play the piano. I look at it and I can't concentrate on the music."[21] The realization that the power of music elevates and lightens the gloom of a failed love affair, dawns upon Michael in the concluding part of the novel. After getting healed by Julia's solo piano performance, he says about the quality of her music, "There is no forced gravitas in her playing. It is a beauty beyond imagining—clear, lovely, inexorable, phrase across phrase, phrase echoing phrase, the incomplete, the unending 'Art of Fugue'. It is an equal music."[22]

Thus music and love are the two inseparable themes in the novel. Music is a powerful unifying and binding force which makes a natural corollary in the events unfolded. The ardour and consuming fire of failure in human love-affair are doused and made bearable by the divine, sublimating nature of celestial music.[23] Seth perfectly weaves both the themes together to create a canvas on which passions are depicted with a deep consummation. He shows that the music is more than a professional interest for the characters in the novel, they make sense of their surroundings through sound and music. Especially for Michael and Julia, music is not only a vocation, but their avocation and it has the intensity to bind them together beyond the boundaries of the world. Michael feels that Julia is not only his love of a lifetime, but also the very essence of his craft.

An Equal Music is not only a love story of two musicians, but it also shows the affection of a musician for his instrument that can't love back. Michael's relationship with his violin Tononi has been realized with a rare insight. He loves the violin which he had lent from his neighbour Mrs. Formby. He treats the instrument as a living companion. But unfortunately as Michael can't hope to possess Julia, he can't even dream of owning his beloved Tononi which he has long had only on loan. He feels depressed by the shadow of the thought that the violin will be demanded back by heirs of Mrs. Formby after her death. The fear of losing his another love is reflected in his words which he has said for his piano, "We have grown to know each other—We have been together for twelve years. Its sound is my sound. I can't bear to part with it."[24]

The most genuine aspect of Michael's character is revealed in his affair with Julia. Both of them are proven soul-mates. After losing Julia, Michael tries to control his life by the essence of music. They again come together by the strength of their music. He feels that their love will find its consummation only in music that they will play. Through music that he hears, and recalls playing with Julia, Michael is never allowed to forget their time together. For him, it is a substitute of love. It is music which takes him out of selfishness, out of himself. Though Michael himself sees the darker aspect of his own personality, yet it is the creativity of Seth's genius that the reader sympathizes with Michael's pain and accepts him the rare. Like Michael, Julia is also devoted to music, but she is also concerned for her family. After the departure of Michael to Vienna, she is deeply heartbroken but gathers all the pieces of her life. She is not depressed even because of her deafness but because of her loss of hearing music. She realizes that music, her lifeblood, is slipping away from her. She reveals the story of a musician under the threat of losing music from his life that is dedicated to music. All of Seth's efforts are reflected in Julia's character as she always tries to cope her deafness and allows the musical impulses to guide her back into proper musical functioning.

An Equal Music thus reveals a world of music where the people are supersensitive and are guided by intense emotion, often unaware of the loss and gain in the world of matters. One of the books joys lies in his creation of musical extremes. And one of the glories of the novel is its sheer sensuousness as it engages the reader in a journey of love. The same themes of music and love are used by Salman Rushdie in his novel *The Ground Beneath Her Feet*. But Seth did not know about Rushdie's intention. He says, "I had no idea that Salman Rushdie was also writing a novel with music as one of its themes, but music is a huge subject, so it's not much of a coincidence."[25] Like Rushdie, Seth himself is the immigrant connoisseur who has mastered a world alien to him. In contrast to Rushdie, Seth does not portray the life of musician in a fog of magic realism, rather he makes his characters nearer to reality. His writing is close to the bone, the private and public life of musicians in a string quartet. Seth's genius shines through this exploration that he makes reader accessible to the lifelong immersion and the maintenance of a craft that is the foundation of all serious music making.

The novel provides a real understanding of the connection between the humanity of the performers and the making of music along with the development of harmony in performance. Dazzling musicianship and astute knowledge of the music are evinced in this moving novel. On the whole, music is at the very heart of the novel. Seth's treatment of the essentially inexpressible power of music, a theme that runs like a vein through literature, is sensitive and thoughtful. The reader is deeply impressed with the opulence and accuracy of music expounded by the author. Seth's intimate look at the ardent and passionate world of classical music is a real treat. He succeeds admirably in representing the fragile and delicate portrait of the world of chamber music. Despite of some technical difficulties of a string quartet, Seth successfully captures the delicate balance of emotions and portrays the novel as an evocative one.

Apart from showing all the divine qualities about music and love, *An Equal Music* also exposes a certain inner darkness. It has a melancholic strain that reveals itself in the alienation of the characters, in Michael's obsessions, and in Julia's deafness. But the conclusion of the novel is as bright as ever when Michael agrees to hold the shared memories of Julia and finds that the final union of his love is in music. Though at the end, Michael is as alone as in the beginning, yet there is one remarkable difference, his thoughts have reached a resolution and he has learned acceptance which has brought him tranquility.

The epigraph from a sermon by John Donne with which the novel begins and from which the title is taken has the word "equal" repeated five times; "one equal light", "one equal music", "one equal possession", "one equal communion and identity", "one equal serenity". Setting the tone for the music of the novel, this sense of equanimity or harmony is used as a major trope. The title *An Equal Music* aptly suits with the spirit of the novel because the music of great masters is 'an equal music' for Michael which provides a serenity to his soul. Seth has also portrayed the love as 'an equal love', a perfect one, which is beyond the boundaries of this world. The idea of the novel is that in love there is no failure and the broken arches of the earth shall form a perfect circle in heaven.

Thus, *An Equal Music* shows Seth to be at the top of his form. It is a classy novel, told with keen intelligence and sensitivity, embodying a brave attempt to fathom the high strung world of performing artists. It is a story about the efforts to create a balance between personal and artistic milieus. The novel provides a fit stage for the unfurling of a love tale to the music of Beethoven and Bach. Seth writes it with a sense of poetry, which again, is almost musical to read. It is a work not only about music on a number of relative levels, but also tries to invoke musical effects and to incorporate musical form in its own structure. The novel is beautifully written, and extremely evocative and melancholic which is wrapped up in melody. The Baltimore Sun states that *An Equal Music* is "a beautifully written novel of music, romance, and the endless search for transcendent passion—A joy to read". The novel proves that Seth is a master wizard who has produced a world inhabited with living personalities and breathing for the ethereal impulse of music. It is a deeply affecting story about the strands of passion which masterfully confirms Seth as one of the world's finest novelists.

NOTES

1. Vikram Seth, *The Golden Gate* (London: Faber and Faber, 1986).
2. Evan Jones, "All That Glitters...", Scription 4.3 (1987), 173.
3. Eugene Robinson, "A Tolstoy—On His First Try", *The Washington Post.* <http:/www.washingtonpost.com>
4. Caroline Moore, "Among The Members of a Quartel", *Literary Review.* <http:/www.litreview.com>
5. Khushwant Singh.
6. Tim Parks.
7. Adam Mars-Jones, "Unequal to the Task", *Daily Mail* and *Guardian.* <http:/www.mg.co.za>

8. Vikram Seth, Bold Type Interview. *Loc. cit.*
9. *Ibid.*
10. Vikram Seth (Apr. 5, 1999), Interview with *India Today.*
11. Vikram Seth, Writers on Writing. Radio Series Transcript. *Australian Broadcasting Corporation.*
12. Vikram Seth (1999), *An Equal Music*, 3.
13. *Ibid.*, 239.
14. *Ibid.*, 276.
15. *Ibid.*, 381.
16. Firdaus Ali (May 30, 2000), For Better and Verse. *rediff.com.*
17. Cynthia Haven (May/June, 1999), Poetic License. *Stanford Magazine*: *USA.*
18. David Blake (Sep. 9–15, 1999), Me and My Fiddle. *Al-Ahram Weekly.*
19. Vikram Seth (1999), *An Equal Music*, p. 385.
20. *Ibid.*, 89-90.
21. *Ibid.*, 109.
22. *Ibid.*, 380.
23. K.K. Gaur (Winter, 2000), *An Equal Music*—A Critique. *Points of View.* 7(2): 83-88.
24. Vikram Seth (1999), *An Equal Music*, 69.
25. Brendan Bernhard (Apr. 30–May 6, 1999), Interview with Vikram Seth, *LA Weekly.* Online.

10

Moral Vision in Arundhati Roy's Writings

Darkhasha Azhar

Arundhati Roy is the name that has gained repute in the field of English literary writings. Ever since she has barged into this elite arena, she has surfaced as the brightest star among the cluster of stars. Speaking of her write-ups, there are varied hues that bring gleam to her scripts whether "fiction or non-fiction". She proudly confirms herself the citizen of the World and the title proves appropriate because we find her utter concerned and pained whenever there's a reigning problem, anywhere on the earth. It can very aptly be quoted about her charisma that "Roy's writings carry weight in this morally confusing time."

Roy's writing skill surpasses all biased norms and excels in quality. She, being the 'world's citizen', is not focused at a particular nation, sect, society or gender rather she is there where the problem is, anywhere in the world. Free from all the formal shackles and hurdles, she hasn't learnt to surrender to the assaults and violence of the world, accepting it as a destiny's sport. She has the guts to erase the wrong and engrave the right, with loud confident voice. For this unique quality, she's faced many charges, i.e. the charge of court's contempt, the sedition charge for her speech on Kashmir's Azadi and recently she is being targeted for her concern towards Maoists. Roy's first venture into the field of literature began in 1997. With a loud bang, she stepped in and achieved the most coveted award. The novel was extensively criticised for its bold theme, *the touchable-untouchable affair*, and Roy was framed up for scandalous writing. Before the situations had deflated she came up with her memorable non-fiction essay "The End of Imagination" scripted after the nuclear testing in Pokhran. And ever since, has been in focus due to her off-track writings, speeches and quotes. She is a daring writer, undoubtedly, but what's uniquely distinct about her persona is the touch of morality in her write-ups. Not anyone and everyone would dare to or care to do what she has been doing so boldly and yes, so dangerously. My research paper dwells on this aspect of the author, in particular, which due to heavy controversy, is often overlooked. Had she not been humane she would not have proven deep into human insight and surfaced with the novel *The God of Small Things* purely based on human relationships in this conflicting world.

The moral vision that she has is not acquired but is inherent. She's there where the problem is, and is found suffering with the sufferers and moaning with the moaners. Arundhati Roy is a true humanitarian, a human being with a golden heart. The heart that accepts the downtrodden and yearns to heal the wounds of the maimed. *The God of Small Things* is the novel based on simple love story. Love between two, the neglected and the accepted, which attains a sad destiny at the hands of the rulers of the society, the hands that know only to crush and crumble and compress and the hands that haven't learnt the art of shaping and moulding. The Ammu-Velutha episode resembles the Adam-Eve episode in Eden. Ammu is the Eve who is seduced by the Satan, here Satan is the situation in which she finds herself, abject and all sullen, automatically dragged to surrender to her all time lover; Velutha. Untouchable Velutha is the Charmer Adam, who readily accepts her like a ripened fruit bestowed on him by almighty himself. Unknowing and unaware of the consequence, they fall for each other, the most unaccepted relation in the highly rigid Indian society, and commit the heinous crime of making love to each other. Like a lightening, it struck the entire village and carried all, directly concerned, in its fold to justify the quantum of punishment on the offenders.

Ammu and Velutha, the prime convectors had the lion's share of the punishment whereas Estha and Rahel, the children, had to bear separation from their mother as well as from each other. Velutha was wrongly charged, implicated and beaten to death in custody by the police while Ammu was forced to leave Ayemenem, alone, to struggle for survival. Ammu finds a job but due to her deteriorating health, is unable to keep it and dies alone in a quiet chamber, paying heed to the call of the man in her heart. The underlying moral fabricated in this story is the sudden death of the girl Sophie Mol who is as pure and saintly as saint Joans. This death of innocence, before the ghastly episode ahead, signifies the death of humanity. The home coming of Sophie Mol and the entire sequence melts into each other so smoothly that one finds it difficult to separate them. It seems as if the platform of seduction was laid by God, the almighty—the return of Margaret to her first husband, the meeting of Velutha and Ammu on their way to airport, the regermination of the forgotten love in their hearts, the nocturnal meetings, the stormy night, the death of Sophie Mol, the revelation of their sexual relation and the punishment. The serpent society had dug its fangs at the right place and its venom had had its right affect. The moral vision that Roy intends to portray from this semi-autobiographical story is quite dispersed in approach. The idea that she wishes to convey is simply that no offence goes unnoticed. It is the God who is the originator and director of the entire episode. He scripts certain plots to forward a moral to the society. The first moral that surfaces out of the whole process is that love knows no bounds of caste, creed, religion, colour or any other distinction. It is free from all the norms and laws laid by the society. The second moral is that its killing is as murderous and ugly as the slaughter of an innocent lamb at the altar, in the name of divine sacrifice, and is despised even by God. The third logical moral that the novel puts forth is that one should abide by the laws of the society in order to maintain a balance of peace and tranquil in the environs in which one survives: "Laws are made to breach" is not always the right concept of the theory. Practical implication of theory churns out an entirely opposite solution.

Thus, *The God of Small Things* is not just a simple love-affair story to read and enjoy but a story based on complex phenomena of the complicated theological society that is to be chewed and comprehended and digested. So deeply engraved are the imprints of the events in the novel that it would forever remain etched in one's memory. Through a delicately woven, sensitive story, Roy has easily raised a cumbersome topic to the fore and made unthinkable; thinkable. The moral angle that she provides to her maiden novel is highly commendable. The concluding dialogue 'Nalye' spoken by Ammu resounds long after one has finished reading the novel, connecting its reader emotionally with the character. Here, in fact, lies the beauty of the novel.

The non-fictional scripts of Arundhati Roy are equally touchstone in them with milestone achievements. She began her journey in this secluded land with her essay "The End of Imagination", stunting the imagination of every reader. Though the essay focuses Roy as an important literary and media figure; it also examines the powerful literary voice that resounded around the world. The article is indeed an important artefact of peace activist in a national and regional climate where most were liable to rejoice nuclear testing by India, rather than to detract. It marks the start of Roy's post-Booker Prize career as an activist with a moral vision. She gains recognition as transnational feminist and continues to write and deliver speeches at significant global forums; therefore, her anti-nuclear essay is noteworthy and historic.

India carried out its first test for a nuclear device in 1974. Since then, it has maintained moral ground as a peace-loving nation for it has not used its nuclear know-how to devise a bomb. The question that Roy has raised in her essay is that why did then India choose to perform a series of nuclear tests between May 11 and 13, 1998 in Pokhran, Rajasthan. Almost predictably Pakistan tested its own nuclear arsenal within 11 days, on May 28, 1998. This bold step had an immediate News coverage of the issue in the *New York Times* during May and June 1998 and told an interesting story. The United States was struck more by the inability of its intelligence agencies to foretell this act than the occurrence of the testing event itself. The *New York Times* Columnist, Tom Weiner, while ironically implying that US would never take this step, simultaneously berated the CIA of mirror-imaging or believing another nation to have priorities similar to the US. In hindsight, the reaction of other nuclear arms bearing nations to the act of nuclear testing by India can be described knee-jerk and undeniably hasty at best—a rap on the knuckles for refusing to ratify the CTBT. Policy analyst Bhaskar Roy (2008, July 18) reported that the Indian scientists and engineers working in the USA under bilateral agreements were bundled out of the country over night. Indian scientists were also blacklisted from visiting the US even for international conferences. Economic and trade sanctions were imposed by Japan, US, Denmark, Sweden, and other western nations, amidst apocalyptic accounts of a possible nuclear war in the region.

Using the nuclear bomb as political currency to assert global and regional supremacy reveals itself as having been a conscious strategy of the Indian Government. The logics and narratives of nationhood need to be continually built so as to maintain the nation's saliency. In the wake of mass scale celebration, it seemed that Mahatma Gandhi's philosophy of non-violence and secularism for post-colonial India may have failed to give citizens the sense of nationality and cohesively that the possession of the bomb apparently has. Even the strongest critics of nuclear weaponry nodded in agreement that nuclear arms are important global currency to maintain self-respect. Indian peace activists denounced state-centred justifications of testing for the sake of countering border aggression from Pakistan and China, and for exposing the hypocrisy of nuclear arms bearing western nations. They urged politicians to keep their thoughts and their national budgets focused on issues concerning nation's upliftment. Yes, Roy's writings do carry vital importance in the contemporary era of confusion and Chaos. She says, quite blatantly, in her defence that she's not an activist, nor the leader of any mass movement, and she's certainly not the voice of the voiceless.

At the Sydney Peace Prize the Lecture delivered by Arundhati Roy clearly speaks about her moral approach towards the world as a society. When the Sydney Peace Prize was bestowed on Roy she was taken by a surprise because she knew well that the people called her *'the biggest trouble maker'* and that she didn't have a single peaceful bone in her body. But the fact remains that she was chosen and invited and she was readily there to accept it and refute certain charges piled on to her, quite humbly and gracefully. When at the gathering she spoke, it was as usual mesmerising and charismatic with her blunt and bold and brave approach to the topic. Arundhati Roy's chief characteristic feature is that she is honest and genuine in her speech. She dare's to call a spade a spade and a thorn a thorn. She finds it ironic that she, who is considered to be the person who spends most of her time thinking of strategies of resistance and plotting to disrupt the putative peace, is given a peace prize.

Arundhati Roy, it should always be kept in the mind, comes from an essentially feudal country and there are few things more disquieting than feudal peace. "Sometimes there is truth in old clichés". There can be no peace without justice. And without resistance there can be no justice. Roy feels that today it is the idea of justice that is under attack. The assault on vulnerable, fragile sections of society is at once so complete, so cruel and so clever, all encompassing and yet specifically targeted, blatantly brutal and yet unbelievably insidious, that its sheer audacity has eroded our definition of justice. It has forced us to lower our sights, and curtail our expectations. She calls it 'an alarming shift of paradigm'. Dwelling upon the most ironical fact of our lives she writes: "Almost unconsciously we begin to think of justice for the rich and human rights for the poor. Justice for the corporate world, human rights for its victims. Justice for Americans, human rights for Afghans and Iraqis. Justice for the Indian upper castes, human rights for Dalits and Adivasis".[1]

Arundhati Roy firmly holds the opinion that violating human rights is an inherent and necessary part of the process of implementing a coercive and unjust political and economic structure on the world. Without the violation of human rights on an enormous scale, the neo-liberal project would remain in the dreamy realm of policy. But increasingly, Human Rights violations are being portrayed as the unfortunate, almost accidental fallout of an otherwise acceptable political and economic system. As if they're a small problem that can be mopped up with a little extra attention from some NGOs. That is why in areas of heightened conflict in Kashmir and in Iraq—Human Rights Professionals are regarded with a degree of suspicion. Many resistance movements in poor countries which are fighting huge injustice and questioning the underlying principles of what constitutes 'liberation' and 'development', consider: "Human Right NGOs as modern day missionaries that've come up to take the ugly edge off imperialism—to defuse political anger and to maintain the status quo."[2]

Focusing on the America's invasion of Iraq, Roy says: "The invasion of Iraq will surely go down in history as one of the most cowardly wars ever fought."[3] It was a war in which a band of rich nations, armed with enough nuclear weapons to destroy the world several times over, rounded on a poor nation, falsely accused it of having nuclear weapons, used the United Nations to force it to disarm, then invaded it, occupied it and are now in the process of selling it. Roy admits that she speaks of Iraq not because everyone is speaking of it but because it is a sign of things to come. Iraq marks the beginning of a new cycle. It offers us an opportunity to watch the corporate—military cabal that has come to be known as '*Empire*' at work. She urges us to peep behind the curtain of blood and says if we can find ourselves doing that then we would glimpse the pitiless transactions taking place backstage. In 1991, US President George Bush senior mounted Operation Desert Storm (the Stage). Tens of thousands of Iraqis were killed in the war. Iraq's fields were bombed with more than 300 tonnes of depleted Uranium, causing a fourfold increase in cancer among children. The truth is that for more than 13 years, twenty-four million Iraqi people have lived in a war zone and have been denied food and medicine and clean water. Roy's morale invokes the people to awaken to the facts and remember it always that: "The level of cruelty did not fluctuate whether the Democrats or the Republicans were in the White House. Most pathetically, half a million Iraqi children died because of the regime of economic sanctions in the run up to 'Operation Shock and Awe,"[4] Until recently, while there was a careful record of how many US soldiers had lost their lives, we had no idea of how many Iraqis had been killed. US General Tommy Franks had proudly said, "We don't do body counts."

The UN's Chief Weapons Inspector Hons Blix said he found no evidence of nuclear weapons in Iraq and ironically now it has been proved correct. Every scrap of evidence produced by the US and British governments was found to be false-whether it was reports of Saddam Hussain buying Uranium, or produced by British intelligence which was discovered to have been plagiarized from an old student's dissertation. And, a country, for no good proof, was bombed into oblivion. Roy, a human being with a heart for humanity is deeply wounded and cries back to ease off her pain. She is always misunderstood to be supporting the wrongdoers, but unperturbed by the allegations piled against her, she yearns to talk and talks at a length on the illegal invasion of a country and the mass murder of its people. However, to imagine that the world would change was naive. The tragedy with the entire episode was that their political rivals had no real dispute with their policies. The fire and brimstone of the US election campaign was about who would make a better "*commander-in-chief*" and a more effective manager of the American Empire. The bottom line of the entire story is that "democracy no longer offers voters real choice. Only spacious choice."[5]

Bechtel has footprints around the world. That's what being a multinational means. In India, Bechtel along with General Electric sported the trick. The Enron contract, which legally binds the government of the state of Maharashtra to pay Enron a sum of 30 billion dollar, was the largest contract ever signed in India. The Enron contract, which was India's first '*fast track*' private power project, has come to be known as the "most massive fraud in the country's history". The electricity that Enron produced was so exorbitant that the government decided it was cheaper not to buy electricity and pay Enron the mandatory fixed charges specified in the contract. "This means that the government of one of the poorest countries in the world was paying Enron 220 million US dollars a year not to produce electricity!"[6] Now that Enron has ceased to exist Bechtel and General Electric are suing the Indian Government for 5.6 billion US dollars. This is not even a minute fraction of the sum of money that they actually invested in the project. Arundhati Roy sketches the true picture of the entire scene naked before us. She not only herself plunges deep but also provides a swimming ground to its readers and listeners to submerge; float and probe into the vast sea of problems to dig out a solution.

To a visionary like Roy, what does moral mean in this unpeaceful, savage, corporatized, militarized world? What does it mean in a world where an entrenched system of appropriation has created a situation in which poor countries which have been plundered by colonizing regions for centuries are stooped in debt to the very same countries that plundered them, and have to repay that debt at the rate of 382 billion dollar a year? What does peace mean to people in occupied Iraq, Palestine, Tibet and Chechnya or the Dalits and Adivasis and Muslims of India? What does it mean to the millions who are being uprooted from their homes by dams and development projects? What does peace mean to the poor who are being actively robbed off their resources and for whom everyday life is a grim battle for water, shelter, survival and above all, some semblance of dignity? For them, peace is war. Utterly concerned about the world peace, she argues: "We know very well who benefits from war in the age of Empire. But we must also ask ourselves honestly—who benefits from peace in the age of Empire? War mongering is criminal. But talking of peace without talking of justice could easily become advocacy for a kind of capitulation. It's easy to blame the poor for being poor. It's easy to believe that the world is being caught up in an escalating spiral of terrorism and war. That's what allows the American President to say, 'You're either with us or with the terrorists'. But that's a spurious choice. 'Terrorism is only the privatisation of war'. Terrorists are the free marketers of war. They believe that the legitimate use of violence is not the sole prerogative of the state."[7]

Roy firmly affirms that it's mendacious to make moral distinction between the unspeakable brutality of terrorism and the indiscriminate damage of war and occupation. Both kinds of violence are unacceptable. We cannot support one and condemn the other. The real tragedy is that most people in the world are trapped between the horror of a putative peace and the terror of war. These are the two sheer cliffs we're hemmed in by. The question is: How do we climb out of this crevasse? But for that who is morally uncomfortable, the first question we must ask is do you really want to climb out of it. She herself produces an answer to the question put forth and suggests that if one really wants to climb out, there's good news and a bad news too. The good news is that the advance party began the climb some time ago. They're already half way up. The bad news is that the colourful demonstrations, weekend marches and annual trips to the World Social Forum are not enough. There have to be targeted acts of real civil disobedience with real consequences. She concludes her lecture at Sydney Peace Prize 2004, by saying: "May be we can't flip a switch and conjure up a revolution. But there are several things we could do. For example, you could make a list of those corporations who have profited from the invasion of Iraq and have offices here in Australia. You could name them, boycott them, occupy their offices and force them out of business. If it can happen in Bolivia, it can happen in India. Why not? That's only a small suggestion. But remember that if the struggle were to resort to violence, it will lose vision, beauty and imagination. Most dangerous of all, it will marginalise and eventually victimize women. The point is that the battle must be joined. As the wonderful American historian Howard Zinn puts it, 'You can't be neutral on a Moving Train.'"

Speaking of the vision of Roy, one can't ignore the Gandhian philosophy that seeps through her speeches and writings, so evidently. Roy quotes about Gandhi's salt march: "Gandhi's salt march was not just political theatre. When, in a simple act of defiance, thousands of Indians marched to the sea and made their own salt, they broke the salt tax laws. It was a direct strike at the economic underpinning of the British Empire. It was real."[8] Gandhiji's non-violence was real. The implication appears to be that there is some other kind of activism that is either not real or has some lesser degree of reality. In several texts Roy gives two examples to show the reality of Gandhi's non-violence. The one to which the quote above alludes was the Dandi Salt March. The British had declared a monopoly for themselves and their permit holders on the manufacture and sale of salt. Through the monopoly, they burdened salt production with a tax which resulted in higher salt prices for the customer. The actual fact is that everybody uses salt. In India's hot climate, where masses of people sweat gallons of salty water day after day, many tons of salt are needed regularly to maintain body fluids at normal levels. Salt is easy to manufacture and its raw material are plentiful. But by decreeing itself to be the only legal maker and seller of salt, the British Empire cordoned off for itself a rich source of easy money.

It is not necessarily wrong for a government to cordon off a source of easy money for itself. One good reason why the Indian salt tax was wrong was that it was imposed on the people by an illegitimate government—'Taxation without representation.' Similarly, quoting the past happening, Arundhati Roy wants to say that Gandhi argued fervently that it was a moral duty to give up one's freedom in order to help out the impoverished villagers. Gandhi was a self-described protectionist. What actually happened was that a populace deliberately kept uneducated and disempowered was compelled to pay a salt tax by the superior force of British arms. The British did not actually devote the money to building schools and hospitals. Most of it went to fund their own military and police. Unfortunately, Roy observes, today's flawed Indian democracy is still close to being a Hegelian state overfeeding the military at the public trough while starving health and education.

These considerations provide some context for Roy's declaration that Gandhi was a political genius who practised real non-violence, not just political theatre. Gandhi knew how to bring non-violence to bear where it would do the most good, where it would transform the fundamental causes of violence, where it would break the links of the chains that held India in bondage. If the Indians would make their own salt then the British scam would not work. Roy has unkind words for people who treat non-violence as political theatre. They may indeed appeal to the conscience of the oppressors and seek to win hearts by self-suffering; they may get attention and dramatize their views; they may go to jail or on hunger strikes. The second example Roy gives to show Gandhi's realism is the Khadi based alternative economy to which Gandhi gave most of twenty-five years of his life. The main motive that brought the British to India was to make money and the day they found that they can no longer make money, they would leave.

There is a passage in *The God of Small Things* where a character who appears to speak with the voice of the author speculates that when all is said and done, it is not economics, and it is not any of several other plausible candidate for being first in the order of causes, which, at bottom, determines what happens. "It is the laws of love, the ones that say who should love whom, and how much."[9] This suggestion about which cause is the most potent one in human life fits in with the main theme of the novel, which is that all hell breaks loose when a touchable loves an untouchable. In acknowledging all the important questions that might be discussed, I do not mean to say that Roy has become obligated to produce a comprehensive and consistent theory just because she used the word "*real*" to praise Gandhi. But what I really intend to do is to shift to a slightly different sort of question, "What is going on when Roy, or anyone, talks of economic causes?" I think this slight shift will make it possible to articulate more clearly some relationships between the way she thinks and the way saints think.

Roy says in one of her interviews with David Barsamian that militarism has become an economic necessity for the Empire. I take this statement to be equivalent to saying that economic causes explain militarism, i.e. for economic reason there has to be militarism. The author suggests two economic causes of militarism. In addition to these she mentions several aspects of the psychology of daily life that are conducive to paranoia and to nationalist frenzy. Her vision when she says that a new possible world is fast approaching and she can already hear her breathing; indeed startles and surprises us.

She is among the many people of goodwill who are not easily persuaded to such dangerous elements of typically non-modern traditions as religion and communal bonding that could be put to good use for filling up the holes in modernity. She is not sure which is worse, traditional society or modern society. She grew up in a small town as the independent daughter of an independent mother. She grew up fearing the traditional norms that would have compelled her to marry. Rahel's marriage in *The God of Small Things*, no doubt drawn from life, illustrates the disasters she feared. But later in life she found that the promises of modernity were also hollow. She found herself among many people who pick and choose, trying to select the best of tradition and the best of modernity. She calls it a high wire act. Meanwhile, the enemies destroy her country with a pincer movement that combines the worst of tradition with the worst of modernity, global capitalism.

Recently, Amy Goodman interviewed Arundhati Roy to capture her views on 'war, poverty and India's Maoist Rebels'. Roy quite confidently, convincingly and comfortably answered to all his queries unfolding her heart that yearns for solidarity and brotherhood. The '*media hungry*'; '*camera crazy*' Roy was transformed into a '*human loving goddess*'. Roy thinks that the big lesson today is that America, having attacked and made war on the poorest countries; could not win a single war. It lost Vietnam, Afghanistan, and Iraq and surely would lose Kashmir. She hold's America soaked in all these war crimes. She says it has expanded the war in Afghanistan and moved it articulately into Pakistan. It was America which had forced the Taliban to raise heads and now America wants them to garret the pit that they grew in their own backyard. She writes in her article "An Ordinary Person's Guide to Empire" that America has interfered with Pakistan from the beginning, and Pakistan is now paying a terrible price for that mean, I don't know if it had a choice...when America wants to interfere, it doesn't give anyone a choice. So, it's destroyed Iraq. And it will destroy India. The author's obvious fear, I suppose. Indian Government need to awaken to this reality that war cannot be won. So it's about time somebody realised that and decided to change the way the world thinks about war and weapons and putting soldiers on the ground. There are several wars going on in India—a fully fledged war. Kashmir is up in flames and the northeast, how can one ignore it?

Roy presently has been framed up with certain anti-patriotic charges and her loyalty is under the scanner for her anti-national speeches. She has written and spoken vastly on Naxalites' and Maoists' role in creating violence and the government's efforts in trying to curb and control the situation. Her open sympathy and empathy has created a great degree of debate and controversy. Her article "Walking with the Comrades," before Dantewada seem to instigate Dantewada episode. Questioned about her sympathy towards the Maoist Roy says: "I think that you got to look at the very depth as a terrible tragedy. In a system, in a war that's been pushed on the people and that unfortunately is becoming a war of the rich against the poor...." Who will then break the cycle of violence? The state argues that the state has to cleanse or sanitise the area because whenever it initiates development works on bridges or starts school; those are blown up by the Maoists. Arundhati Roy here gives the example of Vinayak Sen's description of nutritional aids. She draws aside the curtain to reveal the true scenario. She describes that when you go into the schools you see that they are used as barracks. So, the very idea that Maoists blow up schools and that they are against development, sounds a bit ridiculous.

Arundhati Roy's plain motive behind such talks is nothing but non-violence which she has been preaching through her own style since she stepped into writing. Her 'Narmada Bachao Andolan' experience has taught her a lot about patience and non-violence. Called as the 'apologist for Maoists' and the 'sophisticated face of Naxalism', Roy says that the terrible structural violence is actually creating a 'genocidal situation' in those tribal areas. If anyone bothers to look at the malnutrition and the levels of absolute desperation, any responsible person will surely say that the violence will stop when the state stops pushing those people. Speaking on Indian judicial system and democracy she has written in her essay "Democracy's Failing Light" that India is a fake democracy because it doesn't work for the mass of the people. She quotes: "...You have institution which has been hollowed out, you have institution to which poor have no access and when you look at the institution of the democracy, look at the elections, at the court, at the media and you look at the judiciary. You have a very dangerous system building.... It works for some and it doesn't work for others depending on where you want to place your feet."[10]

On a very serious note, Roy has set her foot in the danger zone. Her morality is highly condemned by the people and she is called a controversial writer. People love to hate her, love to direct her hate mails and accuse her of saying unacceptable things. But what they forget is that one has to do the impossible to perform the possible—the harsh truth of today's world. When questioned about a 16-year old with a gun, that seemed so beautiful with a lovely smile Roy says countering her statements in one of her interviews that when she sees a victim of rape, at the hands of CRPF men, standing up and saying I'm going to fight this. She would feel terrible.... But it's far better than having the girl accept her inhalation.

For 'Narmada Bachao Andolan' Arundhati Roy was chiefly targeted and put behind bars convicted to have raised anti-judiciary slogans which she declined. Arundhati Roy, since that particular day, has continued her battle with India's judiciary and has travelled a long way in the course. The time and event has passed but the whole episode did put another dent in democratic Indian's battered international image. Just days earlier, vengeful mobs had run amok, murdering hundreds of Muslim families in their homes in Gujarat as police stood by. To the outside world, looks like an episode from the middle Ages. The country's finest legal minds put India in the same league as the tawdry Third World dictatorships that jail intellectual opponents, drawing peasants battling the impending flooding of their homes. Probably no contempt could have caused greater damage to the reputation of the court, but the judges may have thought that at least they had defended their dignity from their high-profile tormentor. Roy's sole motive was to defend freedom of speech in India for which she decided to lodge an appeal in the court. She also made it quite clear and loud that she was not just angry but more than that. Angry was too mild a word to describe how she felt about it. It was not about her and the court but an issue of freedom of speech of any citizen of a democratic nation.

Many of the worst affected are tribal people and poor, low-caste farmers called Dalits, many of whom have already been forced out of ancestral lands into regular refugee camps with little or no compensation. Roy condemns the current '*fascistic atmosphere*' in India after the slaughter of hundreds of Muslims in Gujarat by angered mobs. She is immensely touched and pained at the wounds on the nation's body. She can literally see them gaped and profusely bleeding. She writes in the preface of her book *The Shape of the Beast:* "To the Muslims of Gujarat they brought genocide. To more than a hundred thousand farmers they brought suicide.... To the adivasis of Dantewada they brought enforced displacement and a brutal, government sponsored civil war. To people in Kashmir, Manipur, Nagaland, they brought continued military occupation elaborately dressed up as 'normality.'"[11] In the book, while speaking to David Barsamian about her popularity and her success, she spoke in order to make it clear to the people that it's not fame she is looking for but the attention towards what she writes. She is against the democratic fashion that India enjoys. She calls it '*Demon-crazy*'. The kinds of upheavals that are going around in the nation make her keep her fingers crossed, for nothing worse than the present should take place. Can we add another question to the cart? Is there life after democracy? I wonder.

Moral culture is infested deep in Arundhati Roy's character. She is a woman with a sensitive heart; a heart that melts easily and a heart that mourns profoundly. But the sensitivity of her heart doesn't make her weak and timid. She's as bold and fearless as a tigress which pounces, if attacked, and never spares the culprit. Here, she is attacked by the frail and moth eaten system that dishes out its own profit. Roy, dwelling on the nations' present state of violence says: "Right now we're sipping from a poisoned chalice—a flawed democracy laced with religious fascism pure arsenic."[12] The choice of topics, her harsh comments and the outrageous style have not only dragged her into isolation but also imposed threats on to her precious life. She inhales it, its toxic smell is pungent and awful but she's not a bit scared about the situation. Rather she enjoys the flavour and in a conversation with N. Ram, when asked about the difficulties faced in performing such daring act Roy puts forth: "It's true that I write about contentious things. Closer to home, there's some hostility. Each time I step out I hear the snicker-snack of knives being sharpened. I catch the glint of scimitars in the sun. But that's good. It keeps me sharp—fit, alert, it focuses my thought, hones my arguments, makes me very careful about what I say and how I say it."[13]

Her courage is impeccable. Even Ram Chandra Guha, her staunch critic, applauds her for her bravery and endurance. I salute her for her loyalty towards nation and its people. In a conversation with David Barsamian, when questioned about the experience of '*writers block*' and whether she did face any difficulty in writing and if yes, what was the technique that she applied in order to get out of it, Roy instantly replied that she hadn't gone through such a situation yet and revealed that she never took writing as a profession or a career because she doesn't want to enter an arena that she knows will consume her soul. But it's very hard to keep quiet. Arundhati Roy's fiction and non-fiction are our world laid bare, with great courage, passion and eloquence, by mind that has engaged unhesitatingly with its changing realities, often anticipating the way things have moved in the last decade. In her non-fiction, she examines the nature of state and corporate power as it has emerged during this period, and the shape that resistance movements are taking. As she speaks, among other things, about people displaced by dams and industry, the genocide in Gujarat, Maoist rebels, the war in Kashmir and the global war on Terror, she raises fundamental questions about democracy, justice and non-violent protest.

Unabashedly political, through the talks and comments, she speaks about the necessity of taking a stand, as also dilemma of guarding the private space necessary for writing in a world that demands urgent, unequivocal intervention. She also discusses with rare candour her ambiguous feelings about success and the pressures and the freedom that come with it. As it tracks the fault lines that threaten to destroy India's precarious future, it asks basic questions about democracy itself, a political system that has, by virtue of being considered 'the best available option', been put beyond doubt and correction. The hundred million dollar moral question that it puts on the platter is—'What happens once democracy has been used up? When it has been hollowed out and emptied of meaning?' She says in one of her interviews: "Deep at the heart of the horror of what's going on lies the caste system: this layered, horizontally divided society with no vertical bolts, no glue, no intermarriage, no social mingling; no human—humane—interaction that holds the layers together. So when the bottom half of society simply shear off and falls away, it happens silently. It doesn't create the torsion, the upheaval, the blowout, the sheer structural damage that it might, had there been the equivalent of vertical bolts."[14]

NOTES

1. Arundhati Roy. *An Ordinary Person's Guide to Empire*. Viking, Penguin Books India, 2005. Article—"Peace and the New Corporation Theology" (01). Print.
2. *Ibid*., 02.
3. Arundhati Roy. *An Ordinary Person's Guide to Empire*. Viking, Penguin Books India, 2005. Article—"Instant-mix Imperial Democracy" (144). Print.
4. *Ibid*., 154.
5. *Ibid*., 155.
6. Arundhati Roy. *An Ordinary Person's Guide to Empire*. Viking, Penguin Books India, 2005. Article—"Peace and the New Corporation Theology" (04). Print.

7. Arundhati Roy. *An Ordinary Person's Guide to Empire*. Viking, Penguin Books India, 2005. Article—"Confronting Empire" (85). Print.
8. Arundhati Roy. *An Ordinary Person's Guide to Empire*. Viking, Penguin Books India, 2005. Article—"Peace and the New Theology" (03). Print
9. Arundhati Roy. *The God of Small Things*. IndiaInk, 1997 (33). Print.
10. Arundhati Roy. *Listening to Grasshoppers*. Hamish Hamilton, Penguin Books, India. 2009. Article—"Introduction: Democracy's Failing Light" (p. xxxi). Print.
11. *Ibid*., p. vii.
12. Arundhati Roy. *Listening to Grasshoppers*. Hamish Hamilton, Penguin Books India, 2009. Article—"Democracy Who's She When She's at Home" (04). Print.
13. *Ibid*., 25-26.
14. Arundhati Roy. *The Shape of the Beast*. Viking, Penguin Books. India, 2008. Article—"Scimitars in the Sun" (06). Print.

WORKS CITED

"Acclaimed Indian Author Arundhati Roy on Obama's Wars, Poverty and India's Maoist Rebels". Interview by Amy Goodman. N.P. 8 Nov., 2010. Web. Downloaded 15 Feb., 2011. <http://www.democracynow.org/>.

Ghose, Sagarika. "Interview of Arundhati Roy". N.P. India. 15 Apr., 2010. Web. Downloaded 17 Feb., 2011. Google search.

Kapoor, Priya. "Of Moral Positions and Nuclear War: Novelist Arundhati Roy as Peace Activist". Global media, Fall 2009. Web. Downloaded 15 Feb., 2011. Google search.

"Kashmir: Moral and Political Dilemmas of the Right of Nations to Self-Determination". *Gabbar News*. 12 Nov., 2010. Web. Downloaded 15 Feb., 2011. <http://www.thegabbar.org/>.

Roy, Arundhati. The Gandhi Series. "Gandhi"—Chapter VII. Web. <http://howardrichards.org/>. Downloaded 16 Feb., 2011.

Roy, Arundhati. "Walking with the Comrades". N.P. 8 Apr., 2010. Web. Downloaded 17 Feb., 2011. Google search.

Sharma, Jyotirmaya. "Reality, One Bite at a Time". India, Asia and the World. 01 May 2010. Web. Downloaded 25 Feb., 2011. Google search.

11

Aravind Adiga's *The White Tiger*

Neha Vatsal

There is a galaxy of writers who have established themselves as significant Indian English writers such as Anita Desai, Arundhati Roy, Salman Rushdie, Bharti Mukherjee, Kiran Desai, Manju Kapur, Jhumpa Lahiri, Shashi Despande, Vikram Seth, Vikram Chandra and Amitav Ghosh. The latest to arrive on this horizon is Aravind Adiga. He started his career as financial journalist in *Financial Times*. He was subsequently hired by *Time* where he remained a South Asia correspondent for three years before going freelance. During this freelance period, he wrote *The White Tiger*. Aravind Adiga now lives in Mumbai, Maharashtra, India. He won *Booker Prize* in 2008 for *The White Tiger*, after Salman Rushdie, Arundhati Roy and Kiran Desai. His award winning book, *The White Tiger,* was a critical view on an India of light and an India of darkness, *The White Tiger* is the ninth winning novel to take its inspiration from India or Indian identity. His book, *The White Tiger*, has been published by Atlantic Publishers. Michael Portillo, Chairman of the judges of the Man Booker Prize in 2008, said that in many ways it was "the perfect novel." He went on to say:

> "The judges found the decision difficult because the shortlist contained strong candidates. In the end, *The White Tiger* prevailed because the judges felt that it shocked and entertained in equal measure.

> The novel undertakes the extraordinary difficult task of gaining and holding the reader's sympathy for a thorough-going villain. The book gains from dealing with pressing social issues and significant global developments with astonishing humour."

Portillo went on to explain that the novel had won overall because of its originality. He said that *The White Tiger* presented "a different aspect of India and was a novel with 'enormous literary merit'".

Most of the European critics echoed this view and praised Adiga's courageous attempt to reveal the dark picture. It is totally different from the picture of shining India. Reviews of the book in mainstream publications including *The Economist* present it as "glimpse into real India".

Poverty is one of the main issues which attracts the attention of writers. When we talk about poverty, we suddenly recalls the names of Charles Dickenson, George Orwell, Munshi Prem Chand, Sarat Chandra Chatterjee. Dickens portrayed the slum children of Victorian society who faced urban poverty, deprivation and the misery. Prem Chand wrote about rural field. These writers presented the real face of poverty. In Aravind Adiga's novel *The White Tiger*, we meet the narrator and protagonist Balram Halwai, an intelligent man who was born into poverty. The novel is told in the form of letters from Balram written to the premier of China who is to visit India. When Balram was a young child, he was identified as the White Tiger, the rarest creature in jungle. Due to hard circumstances he left his studies and worked as a cleaner to help his family. Balram eventually rises from poverty and he becomes a driver of a wealthy businessman in Delhi. Aravind Adiga has concentrated on Balram Halwai and the poverty all around him in *The White Tiger*. He depicts the real picture of India in front of us. The government hospitals, the liquor shops and the brothels that turn up in the novel are all based on real places in India that he had seen in his travels. He admitted:

> Balram Halwai is a composite of various men I've met when traveling through India. I spend a lot of my time loitering about train stations, on bus stands or servants'

> quarters and slums, and I listen and talk to the people around me. There's a kind of continuous murmur or growl beneath middle class life in India, and this noise never and faucets in your house stared talking.[1]

There is another shocking portrait of Indian corruption and social injustice at a time when the media has tended to focus on sunnier tales of nation's economic transformation:

> Unpretentious and compulsively readable.... Arvind Adiga's auspicious debut novel is at once a fascinating glimpse beneath the surface of an Indian economic "miracle," a aftermath, and a meticulously conceived allegory of the creative destruction that's driving globalization.[2]

Adiga presented a very pathetic picture of poverty before us. Some people cannot vote because they are poor, some cannot follow their religion because they are poor and they want job in a house where a child cannot call himself captain of Indian Cricket team, Azharuddin because the captain is a Muslim. Aravind Adiga depicted a miserable condition of driver no. 1 (one)—Ram Parsad who is actually a namazi Muslim, forced to become Ram Parsad just to earn his livelihood. Adiga says in an interview:

> The only alternative to Indian democracy, which has failed over 500 million people by leaving them in abject poverty, is an improved vision of Indian democracy. My point in *The White Tiger* is to puncture the sense of complacency that too many Indians have—this feeling that, oh, we're a democracy. All our problems are fixed.—*The White Tiger* is an edgy book—and I did want it to start a debate within India about where the country is headed.[3]

The scene of accident brings forth another real picture of poverty that the children of poor loiter here and there "with no one to look after them" (165). They are homeless and live under the flyovers and bridges. Poor people are poor as they have no control over population. In this regard, Chairman of the judges, Michael Portillo said,

> It changed my view of certain things like what is real India and what is the nature of poverty...what is this

> one apart was its originality. For many of us this was entirely new territory, the impossibility of the poor escaping from their lot in India.[4]

Adiga presented before us that in the Darkness, poor are filthy and dusty, but most of the times honest too. He gives the example of poor rickshaw-puller who delivers the furniture, takes the money worth his one year's salary everyday and he 'never takes a rupee of it' and gives it to his owner. A chauffeur also transfers big amount of money in the black suitcase where his master wants. Adiga lays bare their mindset ironically that they never take a single penny not because they are honest but because they are in the trap in the rooster coop. Indian man is the family man. He will live in the poverty. Adiga depicted two words together. He says, "The dreams of the rich, and the dreams of the poor they never overlap, do them? See the poor dream all their lives of getting enough to eat and looking like the rich. And what do the rich dream? Losing weight and looking like the poor."[5]

The poor parts of India are referred to as the Darkness which is a world filled with hunger, servitude and life-long debt. Modern Delhi is referred to as the light. This is a world where men and women have air conditioned cars, mobile phones and guarded apartments with large TVs and computer games. But light has some very murky aspects to it—bribery, corruption and murder. Balram Halwai, the white tiger of the book's title, presents the narrator's sharp and satirical eye for the realities of life, for India's poor. Halwai's lesson is that poverty creates monsters and he himself is just a monster. *The White Tiger* offers a story of coruscating wit, suspense and questionable morality. Balram Halwai is a complicated man: Servant, Philosopher, Entrepreneur: Murderer. Over the course of seven nights, by the scattered light of a preposterous chandelier, Balram tells us the terrible and transfixing story of how he came to be a success in life—having nothing but his own wits to help him along.

Born in dark hart of India, Balram gets a break when he is hired as a driver for his village's wealthiest man, two house Pomeranians (puddle and cuddle), and the rich man's (very unlucky) son. Balram's new world is a revelation from behind the wheels of their Honda City car. While his peers flip through the pages of *Murder Weekly* ("Love–Rape–Revenge!"), barter for girls, drink liquor (thunderbolt), and persecute the great Rooster Coop of Indian society, Balram wades his employers bribe foreign ministers for tax breaks, barter for girls, drink liquors (single-mates Whiskey), and play their own role in the Rooster coop.

Balram learns how to siphon gas, deal with corrupt mechanics, and refill and resell Johnnie Walker Black Label bottles (all but one). He also finds a way out of the coop that no one else inside it can perceive. Balram's eyes penetrate India as few outsiders can the cockroaches and the call centers; the prostitutes and the worshippers; the ancient and Internet cultures. And with a charisma as undeniable as it is unexpected, Balram teaches us that religion doesn't create virtue, and money doesn't solve every problem—but decency can still be found in a corrupt world, and you can get what you want of life if you eaves-drop on the right conversations. From the rich new perspective offered to him in this more interesting job, Balram discovers New Delhi, and the vision of the city changes his life forever. The real achievement of his book is, in its picture of two Indias: the bleak, soul—destroying poverty of village life and the glittering prizes to be in the big city.

The White Tiger reminds us *The Death of Vishnu* and *Bangkok 8* in ambition, scope and narrative genius, with mischief and personality of its own. Amoral, irreverent, deeply endearing, and utterly contemporary, this novel is an international publishing sensation—and a startling, provocative debut. *The White Tiger* is an unexpected journey into the minds of poverty-stricken Indians. Arvind Adiga in an interview with Elaine McCartly said:

> I am an optimist on the future of India, I think young Indians want real change and are determined to reduce the corruption and mis-governance that are the root cause of poverty in parts of India that have good governance—in the southern state of Kerala for instance and I think that if young Indians step up the pressure on the political

> system, poverty can slashed in the coming decade—and action has to start now.[6]

Aravind Adiga's *The White Tiger* also faces adverse criticism: the author is accused of accused of selling an inauthentic picture of Indian poverty to the Western market for coming into the limelight. The corrupt politicians, executives and the business community are ruthlessly exposed, making a poor show of the much advertised 'shining India'. The satire is direct everywhere. The protagonist writers to the Chinese Premier who is reported to have made a plan to come to India to witness the progress in technology:

> Apparently, sir, you Chinese is far off in every respect, except that you don't have entrepreneurs. And our nation, though it has no drinking water, electricity, sewage system, public transportation, sense of hygiene, discipline, courtesy, or punctuality, especially in the field of technology. And these entrepreneurs—we entrepreneurs—have set up all these outsourcing companies that virtually run America now. (4)

Comparing the Indian mass to the roosters. He writes,

> When you get here, you'll be told we Indians invented everything from the internet to hard-boiled eggs to space-ships before the British stole it all for us. Nonsense. The greatest thing to come out of this country in the ten thousand years of its history is the Rooster Coop. Go to Old Delhi, behind the Jama Masjid, and look at the way they keep chickens there in the market. Hundreds of pale hens and brightly colored roosters, stuffed tightly into wire mesh cages, packed as tightly as worms in a belly, pecking each other and shitting on each other, jostling just for breathing space; ...they see the organs of their brother lying around them. They know they're the next. Yet they do not rebel. They do not try to get out the coop. The very same thing is with human beings in this country. (173-74)

Breaking the myth of poor but honest Indian people he writes that the poor people in India appear honest, because they do not have the courage to steal: "It's because 99.9 percent of us are caught in the Rooster Coop just those poor guys in the poultry market" (175). In page after page, Adiga teases his Indian readers with facts disturb the state of euphoria they are in. Some facts, however, particularly the fact of corruption in administration, are publicly discussed, thanks to the democratic rules in India that tolerates the freedom of speech. The driver also has the freedom to discuss the corruption in high places:

> You see, a total of ninety-three criminal cases—for murder, rape, grand larceny, gun-smuggling, pimping, and many other such minor offences—are pending against the Great Socialist and his ministers are the present moment. Not easy to get convictions when the judges are judging in Darkness, yet three convictions have been delivered, and three of the ministers are currently in jail, but continue to be ministers. The Socialist himself is said to have embezzled one billion rupees from the Darkness, and transferred that money into a bank account in a small, beautiful country in Europe full of white people and black money. (97-98)

The protagonist, rickshaw-puller's son turned to a driver who gains, turn out to be an entrepreneur after murdering his master, is in no way a reader-friendly narrator. Rather, he shocks the readers who almost belong to the murdered master; if not to the class of feudal landlords the master's family belongs to. Adiga knows that his readers will take the side of the target of attack—and will also identify them with him. Like any aspiring middle-class Indian, Ashok studied in America and came back with a Christian wife, one who continues behaving as feudal lords, Ashok treated the servant class with sympathy and some times he also appeared reluctant to bribe the ministers for a smooth running of their family business.

Adiga brings out the duplicity in Mr. Ashok only to give his readers a rude shock in a cleaver way, holding the mirror to their faces. Ashok liked to express his concern for the country whenever he had any opportunity. To his American wife he said, "The thing is, he (the driver) probably has...two, three years of schooling in him? He can read and write, but he doesn't get what he's read. He's half-baked. The country's full of people like him, I'll tell you that and we entrust our glorious parliamentary democracy...to characters like these" (7). This is how the educated and well-established Indians usually criticize the function of democracy in India, without any attempt at self-analysis. Adiga mercilessly exposes the façade of such people.

Though Ashok repeatedly told his brother Mukesh and his wife Pinky that their driver Balram must be treated as a human being—he even raised his salary without being asked for it—and that he must not be humiliated for his bad English or any other thing, he remained silent when the crime of Pinky was bestowed on Balram. It was Pinky who took the driver's wheel from Balram was made to take the blame—he had to sign a paper prepared by Mukesh that contained his confession of the crime—luckily though, the police did not bother to investigate the death of an urchin and he was saved. This incident of car accidentally is introduced in the novel as a method of shock-therapy for the readers who easily identify themselves with Ashok and get terrified to find the protagonist's grudge against the master class people.

Again it was Ashok who bribed the minister regularly in Delhi so that his family would be exempted of income tax. He knew it very well that this illegal way of getting exempted of income tax is meant for depriving the country old development the expenses of which are met through the taxes collected from the citizens. There seems to be much difference between the theory he uttered and the practice. He rudely caught Balram by the collar calling him names and almost pushed him against the balcony after he learnt that Balram had taken Pinky to airport. He was not ready to hear anything from Balram and charged him of ruining his family's reputation. "The landlord inside him was not dead and chest was over the edge now, and if he pushed me even a bit more I was in real danger of flying over" (182). Any well-to-do man in India is expected to behave in this way in such circumstances.

Beside corruption, the middle-class people's narrow mindedness and petty regional prejudices (as in the remark), "I don't believe a word. The south is full of Tamils. You know who the Tamils are? Negroes. We're the sons of the Aryans who came to India. We made them our slaves. And now they give us lectures" (233) are also exposed in the novel. And thus the book is not an easy reading any way. The readers of English novels in India largely come from families that are habituated to take service from servants and who usually have their own vehicles. They don't feel comfortable when they read that the driver Balram has no grudge against the rich Americans who are compelled to do all the odd jobs at home themselves, there being no facility of appointing servants at low price as it is found in India. Vijay Nair says: "*The White Tiger* traverses the familiar territory of class and caste divide, poverty and exploitation and the triumph of the human spirit that one expects in a book that unfolds from a place called 'darkness' in Bihar and draws its protagonist from an impoverished family of rickshaw-pullers who were in the business of making sweets before fate intervened."[7]

Adiga presents India as vast and dark jungle where hierarchy, sycophancy, corruption, ruthlessness are the rules of the day. He feels that after independence jungle law replaces zoo law where the most furious, the hungriest are the rules of the day. He feels that after independence jungle where the most furious, the hungriest are eating the weaker and making their bellies big, where the youths are out of job and have become helpless. Instead of struggling and facing the challenges of life, they are busy in nonsense gossiping and watching photographs of film actresses. Adiga remarks:

Things are different in the darkness. There, every morning, thousands of young men sit in the tea shops, reading the newspapers, or lie on a charpoy humming a tune, or sit in their rooms talking to a photo of a film actress. They have no job to do today. They know won't get any job today. They've given up the flight.

Adiga challenges secular fabric of India where a Muslim has to change his name as Ram Parsad and remain Hindu as Hindu because being a Muslim he cannot get a job in the Hindu family. "What a miserable life he's had, having to hide his religion, his name, just to get a job as a driver" (110).

Balram becomes a witness to the dark India of social, political and religious unjust systems where fatal accident caused by the drunken owners are not reported, the police is greased to keep silent, drivers are compelled to sign confessionals, servants are treated worse than animals corruption, elections are meant to disturb nation's economy and to make fun of democracy, the Ganga has become a black river, people change religion to get petty jobs, "where girls going into buildings late at night and coming out with so much cash in the morning," (128) where the father of the nation also seems to be in darkness coming to the light where prostitution, debauchery, deceit and falsehood are the accepted norms of social life.

This monster of evil transforms Balram into an evil monster and he becomes so passionate that he doesn't hesitate to murder his master Mr. Ashok. It is his way of getting social justice and in somewhat predictable manner Balram moves very fast to reach Bangalore through a criss-cross journey, along with his nephew. He establishes himself as a successful entrepreneur, with the seven lakh rupee that he has stolen from his master. He never seems to repent for what he has done but justifies his act of murder as an act of class warfare. With the murder of Mr. Ashok, he also kills the character of Balram and appears as Ashok Sharma and is the proud owner of sixteen SUVs which he uses as taxis and has drivers working for him. He treats his driver in entirely different way. He establishes a dignified employer-employee relationship. He admits: "I was a driver to a master, but now I am a master of driver. I don't treat them like servants—I don't slap, or bully, or mock anyone. I don't insult anyone of them by calling them my 'family', either. They are my employees; I'm their boss, that's all. I make them sign a contract and I sign it too, and both of us must honor that contract" (302). His transformation from Delhi to Bangalore makes a sharp comment on Indian legal system where after committing murder a man can easily protect himself by changing name, profession and city. But like a real hero of black comedy, he is also not free from the corruption of dark India. When his driver hits a boy on a bicycle, he also shows the same loss of moral and humanitarian values that he inherited from his master. He deals the case in his favor. Here Adiga's intentions to show the role of money in Indian legal system and how legal system has become the handmaid of corrupt businessmen and politicians. Money can change the number plates of the car and make another car a substitute. By the end of the novel Adiga puts a big question mark on India's sixty-two years old Independence. He compares working men and women of Bangalore with animals who sleep in the day and work all night because they have to work according to the time of their master's country: "See, men and women in Bangalore live like animals in forest do. Sleep in the day and then work all the night until two, three, four, five o'clock, depending, because their masters are on the other side of the world, in America" (298). No doubt Adiga presents a dark jungle where all social, political, legal and religious systems as a White Tiger who survives beyond the bondages of the cage. The image of the White Tiger is evoked for the final time by Balram to take money, and start a school—an English language school—for poor children in Bangalore, a school where the kids are taught the facts of life in place of hollow idealism. By the end of the novel, the murderous protagonist becomes very optimistic regarding the bright future of India and makes a golden prediction: My humble prediction: in twenty years' time, it will be just us yellow men and brown men at the top of the pyramid, and we'll rule the whole world. No doubt, *The White Tiger* is a shocking tale that throws light on every dark of modern Indian but even amid this darkness the writer seems to be very optimistic for a 'New and Shining India.'

In his debut novel, *The White Tiger*, Adiga exposes the real but ugly face of India's heart of darkness, particularly the rural India, Indian Political system and government machinery. Rural India is represented by the village Laxmangarh, District Gaya, Bihar. The protagonist Balram Halwai alias Munna, son of Vikram Halwai, the rickshaw-puller, belongs to this heart of darkness. In his childhood, he is forcibly taken by the family for the marriage of his sister. The real picture of the village is contrary to what is shown by the government to the outside world, to the organizations like UNO. The village lacks the basic amenities like electricity, drinking water, sanitation and even food. "Children—too lean and short for their age, with oversized heads from which vivid eyes shine, like the guilty conscience of the Government of India". Laxmangarh is accessible by boat. It receives supplies every Monday. Poor sanitary conditions and substandard food items are the fate of its residents.

> There is one street in the village; a bright strip of sewage splits it into two. On either side of the ooze, a market: three more or less identical shops selling more or less identical adulterated and stale items of rice, cooking oil, kerosene, biscuits, cigarettes, and jiggery". (19)

The image of villages conveyed to the outside world is that of a village paradise. The tone here is marked by irony:

> Your Excellency, I am proud to inform you that Laxmangarh is your typical Indian village paradise, adequately supplied with electricity, running water, and working telephones; and that the little children of my village, raised on a nutritious diet of meat, eggs vegetables, and lentils, will be found, when examined with tape measures and scales, to match up to the minimum height and weight standards set up by the United Nations and other organizations whose treaties our prime minister has signed and whose forums he so regularly and pompously attends. (19)

The village is inhabited by two classes, i.e. the landlords and the laborers or to be more specific the dominated the rich and the poor. The wealth and resources are owned by the landlords in every possible way. They take the major share of their earnings and sexually exploit their women and even men. They are given animal names according to their greed and appetite. The Buffalo is the greediest of all the landlords. Others are the Stork, the wild Boar and the Raven. They feed on the village and everything that grows in it. The laborers have very few employment opportunities. They are equated with human spiders. Rickshaw-pullers are human beasts of burden and are treated like donkeys. Their condition remains the same for generations. Balram's brother Kishan has the same fate as that of his father:

> They would do the same thing to him that they did to Father—scoop him out from the inside and leave him

> weak and helpless, until he got tuberculosis and died on the floor of a government hospital, waiting for some doctor to see him, spitting blood on this wall and that! (86)

Those who cannot find work in the village move to bigger cities like Calcutta, Delhi and Dhanbad to find work. Their number is so large that they pack the inside of mass unemployment. Government is taking no steps to control this heart of darkness.

Balram also gives a picture of Delhi, India's political capital as seen by him while serving as a chauffeur to rich landlord's son Ashok. We also learn how Delhi works: "Delhi is the capital of not one but two countries—two Indias. The Light and the Darkness both flow in to Delhi. Gurgaon...is the bright modern end of the city and...old Delhi is the other end" (251). "We need a fixer. He'll get us the interview with a minister that we need" (121).

Corruption and bribery are the trademarks of this political system. The poor who have come from the Darkness to work in Delhi live under the huge bridges and overpasses. The condition of the poor, the working of masses remains the same whether they are in rural India or Delhi. The urban poor work for the rich, for the development of fast forwarding India but their existences are poles apart: "These people were building homes for the rich, but they lived in tents covered with blue tarpaulin sheets, and partitioned into lanes by lines of sewage" (260).

The novel exposes the class-based Indian society divided into the rich and the poor, the belly and small belly people. Big belly people eat up the share of the poor yet the poor raise no voice against them. They have compromised with this slave-master position, believing it to be natural and God-given. Age-old slave like mentality of underprivileged and poor people is the cause of their poverty and oppression. Indians have allowed themselves to be ruled and dominated since long. They are not free even in free India Indians were first ruled by muslims and then the British and now the powerful few. Adiga beautifully describes it as a rooster coop situation:

> Go to Old Delhi, behind the Jama Masjid, and look at the way they keep chicken there in the market. Hundreds of pale hens and packed as tightly as worms in a belly, pecking each other and shitting on each other, jostling just for breathing space; the whole cage giving off a horrible stench—the stench of terrified, feathered flesh. On the wooden desk above this coop sits a grinning young butcher, showing off the flesh and organs of dark blood. The roosters in the coop smell the blood from them. They know they're next they do not rebel. They do not try to get out the coop. (173)

The very same thing is done with human beings in this country.

Human beings are treated like caged animals, boned labor and slaves. Unless they dream for betterment and freedom, no change or improvement is possible. Even renowned Urdu poet Iqbal gives similar view about the mental make up of slaves: "They remain slaves because they can't see what is beautiful in this world" (40).

Balram Halwai alias Munna, the underdog protagonist of *The White Tiger,* has been able to break this coop because he decided not to remain a slave. As he got the opportunity to better his life, to be a master and not a slave, he slit the throat of his master, decamped with cash and only then has got the position of a master, an entrepreneur. He has no regrets. This novel conveys a very clear message to the poor and the underprivileged that are having a slave-like existence to join successful revolutions from the World History; to free the slaves and kill their masters. Alexander, the Great, Abraham Lincoln and Mao Zedong have led successful revolutions to overthrow the ruling masters. Now is the time for 'An Indian Revolution' and they have to wage this war. They have to take the initiative. "People in this country are still waiting for the war of their freedom to come from somewhere else—from the jungles, from the mountains, from China, from Pakistan—that will never happen.... The book of your revolution sits in the pit of your belly, young Indian. Crap it out, and read" (304).

This is a wake up call to the poor with slave-like existence to get out their age-old slumber of oppression and slavery, to snatch their due from their masters. This can be done only if they dream of a beautiful life which is their right. Since it is denied to them, they have to take it by force as is done by Balram alias Ashok Sharma, the entrepreneur. From a slave, he has risen to be a master—a self-taught entrepreneur. All this has been achieved because of his desire to get rid of slavery. "Even as boy I could see what was beautiful in the world: I was destined not to stay a slave" (41).

He could see the beautiful in the world, did not believe that his condition is God-given and beyond change. They have to rise up against the ruling masters to change the system. Adiga's outlook is very much the Marxist one—a way to change the world/system through action. Change will not come on its own; it has to be brought by creating awareness and realization. Situation can improve with the empowerment of the working masses. The coming of Chinese Premier to India can be read as the arrival of communism in India, i.e. throwing out the rich as a done by Naxals through shooting and by "this man called Castro who threw the rich out of his country and freed his people". It will lead to equal distribution of wealth and resources in the country. It is possible by overthrowing the rich and while doing it one may have to spill a little blood. Revolution is the need of the hour. It is a wake up call to Indians of the heart of India's Darkness to take the initiative, shed their weakness and grab their share. Only then can there be a healthy society and progressive India. Revolution alone can change the Dark Indian of today into a bright tomorrow.

The book *The White Tiger* presents a class struggle in India with Halwai juxtaposing the rural, downtrodden sections of the Indian society as against the rich elite. Author's existential and crude prose animates the battle between India's wealthy and the poor. The novel portrays a satirical picture of class struggle in India. It is a brilliant and unflinching vision of modern India. But Adiga said that although India has "an extreme division between the rich and the poor". His book wasn't a social commentary.

The novel undertakes the extraordinarily difficult task of gaining and holding the reader's sympathy for a thorough-going villain. The book gains from dealing with pressing social issues and significant global developments with astonishing humor Adiga dedicated the prize to New Delhi, where he has lived for many years. "It's a city that I love and a city that's going to determine India's future and the future of a large part of the world. It's a book about Delhi, so I dedicate it to the people that made it happen,"[8] he said. It's a thrilling ride through a rising global power; a place where, we learn, the brutality of the modern city is compounded by that of age-old tradition.

Through Balram's personal story of murder and uncertain success, we are drawn into the vortex of India's underbelly where, as the narrator says, "The story of a poor man's life is written on his body, in a sharp pen" (7). It is precisely this perspective, "the dark side of India," (interview 2008) which according to Michael Portillo, chairman of the five-member panel of judges, was entirely new territory. "Clearly, the book's 'originality' set it apart from the others on the shortlist. Mr. Portillo revealed further that Mr. Adiga's book was chosen because it "shocked and entertained in equal measure," successfully engaging the reader with a "thorough-going villain" and dealing with social issues with "astonishing humor". "It is a fact that for most of the poor people or through politics, which can be a variant of crime," Adiga, the fifth Indian-origin writer to win the prize, told the BBC.

These people at the bottom have the same aspirations as the middle class—to make it in life, to become businessmen, to create business empires. They need to be given their legitimate needs—the schooling, the education, the health care—to achieve those dreams. If not, as I said there are only two ways up: crime or politics.

The White Tiger by Aravind Adiga is a study of metamorphosis of an uneducated chauffer Balram who influenced by urban and cosmopolitan ways of life murders his master Ashok and becomes an entrepreneur. The novel is a monologue in epistolary from addressed to Chinese Premier Jiabao, a visitor to India to entrepreneurship. Balram's tale deals with "How he was corrupted a sweet, innocent village fools into a citified fellow full of debauchery, depravity, and wickedness" (197).

In a confessional mood, Balram narrates his success story to his Excellency Wen Jiabao and calls himself a "real entrepreneur". He communicates to the Communist leader the rags-to-riches story if his own life as a microcosm of the "new India". Balram has changed his identity and location to fulfill his selfish interests. In the beginning he was "Munna", a name without any identity and it is his teacher who gives him the name Balram. The seven night actions cover the whole life span of Balram which has brought a significant change in his life. His multiple identities are created according to history and in relations of power, they can also be remade. Identities can be' seen as sites of contention: "Each of us lives with a variety of contradictory identities.... Behind the quest for identity are different and often conflicting values. By saying who we are, we are also trying to express what we are, what we believe and what we desire. The problem is that these desires are often patently in conflict, not only between communities but with individuals themselves" (98-99).

Through a close reading of Aravind Adiga's *The White Tiger*, it is a novel written in the realistic mode that holds a mirror to the Indian reality, especially its ugly side. While the paper has no intention to summarily reject the above claim, it tries to point out the importance of the target readership for the author and how that has influenced his writing, both in terms of content and language. It is my contention that Adiga mostly writes for a Western audience and that has informed his writing to such an extent that instead of depicting reality of any kind, mainstream or alternate, it actually reinforces many of the Western stereotypes about India. It is pertinent to place *The White Tiger* in the ream of Indian Writing in English. While giving an overview of the major concerns of Indian Writing in English, R.K. Dhawan points out, "Raja Rao deals with Indian metaphysics, Anand is concerned with the underdog, Markandaya presents rural India, Malgonkar recreates history, Nayantara Sahgal draws upon the Indian political situation" (7). Adiga's *The White Tiger* can be seen as a portrayal of the life of an underdog through a rags-to-riches story and holds forth the dirty underbelly of the 'shining India' that he terms as Darkness. Keeping in mind the above dominant themes of

Indian Writing in English, it can be safely surmised that Adiga is not breaking any new ground, expanding on the theme earlier explored by writers such as Anand and Malgonkar.

The setting of the novel, for a major part is Delhi and Bangalore. While the former is the capital of India, hence, the most representative of Indian cities, the latter, as is often referred to in the novel, is the I.T. capital of India. Thus, Adiga chooses to select two cities as the setting for his book that is the two most recognizable cities from India, for a western reader. Just like his urban setting, his rural setting is very typical as he chooses the Gangetic belt (or, Darkness as he keeps mentioning throughout), as his rural setting. By selecting Delhi, Bangalore, and the river Ganga, arguably the three most recognizable entities from India, for a western reader, Adiga makes it crystal clear at the very outset as to who his target readers are. Adiga also seems to be suffering from "anxiety of Indianness,"[9] to quote a phrase from Meenakshi Mukherjee, when he desperately tries to not only keep his settings typically representative of "Indianness" as pointed out above, but also in his overt unlike a seasoned craftsman who would do so through careful characterization, Adiga tries to thrust his protagonist's Indianness on his reader.

It is brilliance of the vision of Adiga that he successfully shows the conversion of the psyche of Balram. The innocent rustic becomes a monster to devour the fifth represented in the high-tech society of Delhi of which Ashok is a representative. He learns the aesthetics of violence to keep body and soul together and to save his mind and spirit from the loss of oblivion. One day, he punches Ashok with the vigorous comments, "What blindness you people are capable of. Here you are, sitting in glass buildings and talking on the phone night after to Americans who are thousand of miles away, but you don't have the faintest idea what's happening to the man who's driving your car!" (257). He becomes impatient to articulate the voice of the poor of India. He is disgusted either all-pervasive uncertainty or flux of the conditions of life. Regarding the impact of civilization and the impact of city, he declares, "But Delhi is a city where civilization can appear and disappear within five minutes" (281). He finally kills

Ashok and uses his money to begin his life a new in the city of Bangalore. Adiga leave many things unsaid, but implication gives a waking call to the entrepreneurial and ambitious youth today to see through the subtleties and dreadful complexities of the materialistic challenges. The ever-widening gulf between the haves and have-nots, master and servant, employer and employee is treated dexterously, focusing on the deep-rooted corruption, exploitation and atrocities. The novel on the whole, as described by the Booker judges, is an extraordinary work that paints a portrait of Indian Poverty, and brutal injustice prevailing in the society, where the protagonist's incessant quest for status culminates in heinous crime.

BOOKS CITED

Arvind Adiga. *The White Tiger*, New Delhi: Harper Collins, 2008.

Jefferies Stuart, Interview with Adiga, 16 October 2008 with India today Group.

Note: All the quotations has been quoted with page numbers.

NOTES

1. Book review in *The New York (www.nytimes.com)*
2. Aravind Adiga in an interview with Colm. (Tibin.adiga interview. htm.) 15 Oct. 2008.
3. Michael Portillo, 15/10/2008 web http//www.themanbookerprize. com/news/stories/146, 14 Sept. 2013.
4. Arvind Adiga, *The White Tiger*, New Delhi: Harper Collins 2008, 225.
5. *Arvind Adiga in an interview with Colm Toibin.adiga interview. htm*
6. Kamala Markandaya, *Bombay Tiger* (cover page), Penguin/ Viking, India, 2008.
7. Vijay Nair, *The Hindu Literary Review*. 132: 1. January 4, 2009, 2.
8. "Indian Novelist Aravind Adiga wins Booker Prize". Agencies. Express India. 15 October 2008. Archived from the original on 17 January 2010. Retrieved 2008-10-16, p. 275.
9. M. Mukherjee (1993). The anxiety of Indianness: Our novels in English. *Economic and Political Weekly*. 28(48), 2607-2611.

12

Vijay Tendulkar: An Explorer of Contemporary Social Phenomenon

Deepa Singh

Drama in India has a long history. Dating back to the days of Bhasa, Bhavabhuti and Kalidasa, drama can boast of a rich and chequered history. The earliest plays were written in Sanskrit, based on the *Vedas* and the *Upanishads*. Down the centuries, Indian drama has undergone various metamorphoses and it still continues to flourish in all regional languages. It enjoys almost an equal status along with two other major literary genres, namely fiction and poetry, though, by and large, fiction has overshadowed drama and poetry.

By and large, the plays written in regional languages dominate the Indian theatre, as they are easily intelligible to the audiences. Actors too can easily improvise in them, thereby giving vent to their histrionic talents in a natural and uninhibited way. Early Indian English playwrights could not enjoy the patronage of an English-knowing elite audience and, hence, the growth of Indian English drama could not flourish. English, being a foreign language, was not intelligible to the masses, and playwrights, too, found it difficult to write crisp, natural and graceful dialogue in English. Since they did not grow up in an English environment, and they had acquired their knowledge of English only at a fairly advanced age, the dialogue they wrote proved to be somewhat artificial. At this juncture it would be in the fitness of things to hatch a graph of Indian drama which started as a result of the impact of English studies.

R.N. Tagore (1861-1941) wrote his plays at a time when the impact of civilization of the west had resulted in the disintegration of old values. No wonder Tagore felt the compulsive urge for a search of new values and his plays are a result of this search. He tried to adopt the old myths and legends so as to make them acquire a new symbolism and magnificence in his plays like *Chitra* (1892), *Post Office* (1912), *The King of the Dark Chamber* (1910).

Sir Aurobindo (1872-1950) wrote his plays in regular poetic dramas. He has written five full length plays in blank verse. His plays are *Rodogune* (1958). *Perseus, The Deliverer* (1942), *Vasavadutta* (1957), *Viziers of Bassora* (1959), and *Eric* (1960). In these plays, he closely follows Shakespeare and Elizabethan's both in the verse and dramatic form. *Perseus, The Deliverer* (1942) has a very strong resemblance to *The Tempest* of Shakespeare. His verse is closely modelled on Elizabethan blank verse with more than a touch of high Miltonic manner, Aurobindo does not deviate from the beaten tracks of those who have written poetic dramas in pale imitation of Elizabethan blank verse and consequently in an artificial language.

Harindranath Chattopadhya's *Five Plays* (1937) are based on the tradition of socialist realism and show his social consciousness. His plays are *The Window* (1937), *The Parrot* (1937), *The Sentry's Lantern* (1937), *The Coffin* (1937), and *The Evening Lamp* (1937). The play *The Window* provides a lacerating account of the slum life of the workers. And the play *The Parrot* is dedicated to all whose morality is not a parrot's café and concerns only three characters: Man, Woman and Tramp.

Fyzee Rahman's *Daughter of India* (1940) is a story of an untouchable girl in love with her idealistic master, as Englishman. The main weakness of the play is the employment of a strange technique that vitiates the realistic atmosphere, which is necessary for the success of a play. The playwright makes flower speak and a narrator comments on action and thus the story does not develop through effective dialogues.

In *Slaves of Ideas* and other plays (1941) A.S.P. Ayyar is seen to be a vigorous critic of contemporary life. In these plays the dramatist tries to portray modern Indian life when old ideas are being gradually displaced by the new ones. In A.S.P. Ayyar's play and Fyzee Rahman's play *Daughter of India* the dialogue does not rise above ordinary conversation and is dull and drab, flat and artificial.

Asif Currimbhoy however, has achieved a certain degree of success in his plays. His famous plays are *The Tourist Mecca* (1961), *The Clock* (1962), *The Dolddummers* (1962), *The Dumb Dancer* (1962), *Om* (1962), *Thorns on a Canvas* (1968), *The Restaurant* (1968), *The Captives* (1968), *Darjeeling Tea* (1968), *The Dissident MLA* (1968). After reading his plays one gets the impression that they are products more of craft than art. The dramatist has no individual vision of life or at least he fails to communicate it through his works.

Gieve Patel's *Princess* (1970) is a play about two families in a Parsi village in Gujarat. The conflict and tension in the play arise from the struggle of two families for the possession of a child who in the play becomes an invalid and dies. In the play, Gieve Patel succeeds in giving his language a touch of the local idiom, which, therefore, is more refreshing and natural. It is a landmark in the history of Indian English drama for in it the dramatist has successfully tackled the problem of dialogue.

The problem of adapting language is not a difficult one for the Indian dramatist in English if his characters are drawn from the cross-section of society. This cross-section includes not only the Anglo Indians but also those who have had their education in English and to whom English is a natural medium of conversation. This limits the scope of the dramatist but it makes for greater realism and authenticity. This is the advantage that Nissim Ezekiel has in *Nalini* (1969) and *Marriage Poem* (1969) included in his *Three Plays* (1969). Both plays have naturalistic dialogues. Both plays are naturalistic and probe the psychological tension experienced by individuals in certain moments of life.

Modern Indian drama highlights the two major characteristics. One is, Indian playwrights have gone back to tradition for their themes and techniques and the other is, they are making use of what are considered modern trends in the theatre. These two characteristics are specially seen in theatrical events in the 1960s and 1970s which led to an unconscious awareness of the oneness or "Indianness" of Indian theatre.

The regional drama in India is slowly paving a way for a "national theatre" into which all streams of theatrical art seem to coverage. The major language theatres are active all through the turbulent years of rejuvenation and consolidations. These are Hindi, Bengali, Marathi and Kannada. Plays written in various Indian languages are being translated into English and other languages. They are being produced and appreciated in the various parts of the country. A closer contact is being established between the theatre workers from different regions and languages through these translations.

According to Indranath Choudhary, "When the Sahitya Akademi was set up in 1954, Dr. S. Radhakrishnan spelt out its objective as the promotion of the unity of Indian literature, despite India's geographical, political, social, and linguistic diversities" (Choudhary 28).[1] Dr. Radhakrishnan gave a slogan to the Akademi that Indian literature is one, though written in many languages. It now seems certain that we can talk of the entire Indian literature as a single entity. It is in this context that the plays of Girish Karnad, Mohan Rakesh in Hindi, Badal Sircar in Bengali and Vijay Tendulkar in Marathi assume significance. According to Arundhati Banerjee:

> In the 1960s four dramatists from different regions of India, writing in their own regional languages, were said to have ushered modernity into the sphere of Indian drama and theatre. They were Mohan Rakesh in Hindi, Badal Sircar in Bengali, Vijay Tendulkar in Marathi and Girish Karnad in Kannada, Rakesh's untimely death left his life's work incomplete, and Karnad has written only intermittently. Sircar, of course, has been almost as active as Tendulkar, though his plays can be divided into three distinct periods. Tendulkar, however, has not only been

the most production but has also introduced the greatest variations in his dramatic creations (Banerjee 7).[2]

Mohan Rakesh (1925-1972) is one of those rare literary personalities who never accept the traditional set up but always aspire to find and project something which is challenging and new. Rakesh's language separates him from other Hindi playwrights and puts him on a higher level of competence. His plays *Ashadh Ka Ek Din* (1958), *Lehroon Ke Rajhans* (1963), *Adhe-Adhure* (1969) express the character's mental conflict, frustration, dissatisfaction and the resulting anger in a unique manner. According to N. Choudhary, "With Mohan Rakesh Hindi drama makes a departure from pseudo-modernism and traditional symbolism to the drama of non-communication. The modern man's failure to understand himself or to understand the other person and their mutual failure to understand each other, which is the real tragedy of modern life" (Choudhary 512-13).[3] Mohan Rakesh has paid much attention to the internal conflict in the minds of his characters. He has made efforts to grapple with the problem of man-woman relationship on different levels in this place. The depiction of the complexity of human heart, man's helplessness and the chains of relationship attract audience and readers.

Badal Sircar (1925-), the great Bengali playwright uses contemporary situations and social problems to show life-in-death attitude of modern life. The main theme of his plays is a sense of utter meaninglessness of our existence which leads to a state of metaphysical anguish. Sircar's plays *Evam Indrajit, Baki Ithihas* and *Seish Nai* are based on political, social and psychological problems. In fact, Badal Sircar stands in the fore-front of a new theatre movement in India. His focus shifts from the individual to the society. Sircar writes "A character may be too limiting in its individuality, a story may be too specific to the subject" (Gowri 75).[4] Badal Sircar has sympathy for communists but he differs from them. According to a famous critic, "He does not wish to create new myths in the place of the old. He prefers to raise consciousness and create awareness of the issues" (Dutta 8).[5] Sircar aims at effecting awareness in such manners that it make people feel guilty of their indifference. He does not provide solution to the problems but only hints at them.

Girish Karnad (1938-) was a senior bureaucrat, a famous T.V. and film artist and director and successful playwright. He wanted to become an English poet but he wrote plays in Kannada. His plays *Yayati* (1961) emerged from his resentment at being suffocated by the responsibilities thrust on him by his parents. His other plays show the strong impact of his rebellion against cultural hegemony. He borrows his themes from Indian history, myth and legend and employs in his plays techniques of classical and folk theatre of India. He does not want to waste his time in inventing stories and he wants to make use of culture to destroy its own false values. He argues: "The energy of folk theatre comes from the fact that although it seems to uphold traditional values, it also has the means of questioning these values of making them literally stand on their head" (Karnad 14).[6] He shares the disillusionment of modern Indian intelligentsia. He borrows his themes from history in *Tughlaq* and *Tale Danda* from myth in *Hayavadana* and from folklore in *Naga-Mandala*. He has shown to the Indian theatre and the world theatre community how our past and present can coalesce to give our present day existence meaning and to theatre activity a direction.

According to Arundhati Banerjee, "Vijay Tendulkar has been in the vanguard of not just Marathi but Indian theatre for almost forty years" (Banerjee 7).[7] He started his career as a dramatist with his play, *Shreemant* (The Rich Man) in 1955. He has not pioneered only the experimental theatre movement in Marathi but also guided it. Chandrasekhar Barve expresses his opinion about Tendulkar's contribution to Marathi theatre:

> We can say with certainly that Tendulkar has guided Marathi drama that seemed to have lost its proper track, and has kept leading it for over two decades. His place and importance in this respect shall remain unique in the history of Marathi drama. There may be controversies regarding his greatness but his achievements are beyond question. (Barve 25)[8]

Vijay Tendulkar (1928-2008) was a leading contemporary Indian playwright, screen and television writer, literary essayist, political journalist and social commentator. A lifelong resident of the city of Mumbai Tendulkar was the author of twenty-eight full length plays and twenty-four one act plays, several middles, articles, editorials and eleven plays for children since then. New York's Indo-American cultural council dedicated October 2004 as a tribute to Tendulkar's prodigious literary contribution, presenting in English a wide range of his plays and films. He began his career as a journalist in 'Marathi Weekly'. He remains in this job a number of years. In 1948, he became the assistant editor of the *Navbharat Times,* all this while he had been writing starting with short story writing. First that it included more dialogue than narrative, he switched to writing one act plays, writing full length plays was natural progression, from his very first play, *Grihastha* (1957) to *Safar* (1992). Tendulkar has written basically all his plays in his native language 'Marathi'. It is contribution or co-operation of many translators who has translated his plays in English and in many other languages. But English version is more popular than that of other language versions. And if we talk about the theme and the source of his plays it would not be wrong to say that all of his plays are based on his experiences and his direct observation of society. Tendulkar is basically a social reformer and through his plays he wants to reform the society, picking up some burning problem of society.

In this regard, Tendulkar selected the fields of his observation, 'in Middle Classmen' their social condition, and their behaviour and attitude toward society. In this respect, he selected especially women problem and in most of his plays he has tried to light upon the women problem in society. In his observation whatever he found, illegal, not proper, imbalanced and deformed he has tried his best to expose those problems through his plays using satirical method to make cure society from such types of burning problems. His plays are useful for reading as well as stage performance. There is discussion on some of his plays which gives the proof of his dramatic shaping and achievements.

Tendulkar became one of the leading Indian playwrights with his play, *Silence! The Court is in Session* in the late sixties. And his *Ghashiram Kotwal* won the Kamala Devi Chattopadhyay Award in 1970. He won various awards and fellowships which include the Nehru Fellowship in 1973-74, Sangeet Natak Akademi's Award for playwriting in 1971, National Award in 1977, Film Fare Award in 1980, and the Padma Bhushan Award the highest in literature in 1984.

He was bitterly criticized and was even attacked by people for his plays. His *Ghashiram Kotwal* was branded as an anti-Brahmin play and his *Kanyadaan* as an anti-Dalit play. Talking about the reaction to his *Kanyadaan*, Tendulkar says: "You are honouring me with the Saraswati Samman today for a play for which I once had a slipper hurled at me. Perhaps it is the fate of the play to have earned this honour and that insult—As a creator, I respect both verdicts" (Tendulkar, *Kanyadaan* 71).[9]

Tendulkar watched several plays and some Hollywood films in his childhood. The visuals had a good impact on him. This exposure to the theatre at an early age has had its strong influence on him as a successful dramatist. He is the author of original stories and screen plays for eight films. His films are: *Akrosh, Gahrayi, Manthan, Nishant, Kamala, Musafir, Ardhasatya* and *Umbartha* (*The Threshold* 1981), a ground-breaking features film on woman's activism in India.

Tendulkar's urge to write has not been simply an urge to wield the pen and see it make attractive squiggles on blank paper. He has been propelled by an urgent need to discover, to express, to assert, to reveal and occasionally, to explode. It is his compulsion to lock with life on paper that has brought forth this stupendous output. But, having so engaged himself, his artistic consciousness has shown him the way to disengage himself too, allowing his characters and their lives to grow on paper, so to say, giving his plays the ring of socio-psychological truth.

Tendulkar has been charged that his dispassionate approach to his characters gives the impression of non-involvement and that his writing in general, suggests a pessimistic view of life. Negating this charge he says his urge to create is born out of involvement with life. He holds that creation is the result of grief over something, anger at something, joy about something in life. These in no way are signs of neutrality. But he believes that the characters and situations he creates have their own independent existence and logic. Accordingly he allows them to live by them. It does not mean that their sorrows do not sadden him, their joys do not make him happy as they do any other member of the audience, but he does not intervene.

As for pessimism his experience of his times, his life have shown him that the individual is largely disempowered, made abject, reduced to the role of spectator by the logic of certain events and social grouping. He says that the history of human culture has taken very complex twists and turns. Yet, even today, his inspirational strength lies in the hope with which he looks forward to tomorrow. He says, "I have consistently depicted the indomitability and grit of the human spirit in my writings. But I have never allowed that to lead me into drawing unreal, comforting conclusions" (Tendulkar, *Natak Ani Mee* 1997).[10]

This account gives us some idea of the social and aesthetic ideas that inform Tendulkar's playwright. They explain his themes and forms which he has used to explore. They also explain why, even at the height of the "back to roots" movement of the seventies, he felt neither the urge nor the temptation to write a play in a folk form until the theme of *Ghashiram Kotwal* took hold of his mind and literally drove him to make that choice. It is important to note in this context, that he has not used a similar form again since then, despite the phenomenal success of the play.

The work of writers and artists often falls into clear phase generally chronological in nature. Writers tend to move from one phase of the themes and forms to the next in a linear fashion. For some, the act of writing itself is an inquiry into the means, the limitations, and the possibilities of their medium. It is an aesthetic search. For Tendulkar, the primary compulsion is and has always been humanistic. Man's fight for survival, the varied moralities by which people live, the social position of women, the covert or overt violence in human beings, these are his abiding concerns. They appear in his play in different forms:

> By his own admission, characters are the most vital trigger to his playwriting. "I was never able to begin writing my play only with an idea or a theme in mind. I had to have my characters first with me...living persons leading me into the thick of their lives where they would give me the theme." (Tendulkar 15)[11]

It makes sense then, to approach Tendulkar's work through his characters, and to examine the language, structures and forms he uses through them. Tendulkar has created memorable male and female characters, but it is his women, on account of their unique position in society, who help to reveal his social conscience, and it is they who emerge as the columns and beams on which he builds his structures.

Many of his plays like *Ghashiram Kotwal, Kamala* and *Silence! The Court is in Session* etc. document the degeneration of the socio-political fabric in past as well as contemporary society. They are concerned with cyclical structure of power. They explore dynamics of power in personal, social and political space and portray violence as means of exercising power. While the play *Kamala* unfolds domination of woman in both personal and public spaces, *Silence! The Court is in Session* is about suffocating and hypocritical social standards and portrays the subordination of women in Indian society through the medium of a 'mock-trial', which turns all in real. Similarly, *Sakharam Binder* is a play about sexual power whereas *The Vultures* is about domestic violence and moral collapse of a family. As a whole, his plays are potent comment on concentric circles of power which control and direct individual and social action. The lack of moralizing gives his plays a very open-ended feel and leaves room for individual interpretation and response.

Tendulkar has always maintained the form which always follows character, situation and theme. A quick look at some of his plays bears out what he says. *Shrimant* and *Manus Navacha Bait* are about the urban middle class. They are written in the conventional drawing room in naturalistic or melodramatic mode complete with exposition, complication and denouement. *Sari Ga Sari* (Necklace Oh Necklace! 1964) is cast as a tamasha because it tells a farcical tale which finds its natural expression in that form. *Pahije Jatiche* is like prose keertan, with the main protagonist addressing the audience directly with the akhyan which, in this case, is the story of his life, interspersing it with events that are enacted as illustrations. *Shantata! Court Chalu Ahe* has a naturalistic appearance, but, being the presentation of a game, it becomes an allegory where make-believe can easily blend with reality. *Gidhade* is an expressionistic play while *Sakharam Binder* is consummately naturalistic. *Kamala* and *Kanyadaan* aim to be naturalistic but are flawed in execution. In the midst of all this is *Ghashiram Kotwal* (1972), the only major play Tendulkar wrote in a blend of folk forms. It is a fine example of how this may be done to further a modern purpose.

The theme of his plays ranges from the alienation of the modern individual to contemporary politics, from exploration of man-woman relationship to historical episodes, from socio-individual tensions to complexities of human character. He takes the stories for his plays from real life incidents. He deals with the upper as well as lower middle class milieu in his plays. He deals with physical as well as psychological violence.

In his plays, Tendulkar has a deep-rooted commitment to the society and the concept of social justice, which form the bedrock of a morally coherent political system. Many of his plays like *Ghashiram Kotwal, Kamala* and *Silence! The Court is in Session* etc. document the degeneration of the socio-political fabric in past as well as contemporary society. He displays rare sensitivity and accuracy dealing with social issues. The lack of moralizing gives his plays a very open-ended feel and leaves room for individual interpretation and response.

Tendulkar's plays are concerned with cyclical structures of power as is evident in *Ghashiram Kotwal, Kamala, Silence! The Court is in Session, Sakharam Binder, The Vultures* and *Kanyadaan*. They explore dynamics of power in personal, social and political space and portray violence as means of exercising power. While the play *Kamala* unfolds domination of woman in both personal and public spaces, *Silence* is about suffocating and hypocritical social standards and portrays the subordination of women in Indian society through the medium of a 'mock-trial', which turns all too real. Similarly, *Sakharam Binder* is a play about sexual power whereas *The Vultures* is about domestic violence and moral collapse of a family. As a whole, his plays are potent comment on concentric circles of power which control and direct individual and social action.

As Tendulkar's plays are studies in corruption as a means and function of power, they show that corruption in moral fabric leads to corruption in social and political structures and the social situation is defined by money, power and their subsequent misuse. They explore the phenomenon of deep-rooted corruption that creates morally twisted structures of dominance and power and points to 'the growing nightmare outside his creation.'

Another important feature of his plays ranges from the alienation of the modern individual to the social-individual tensions and the complexities of human character. His *Kamala* raises cardinal questions regarding value system of modern success oriented generation which is ready to sacrifice human values even in the name of humanity itself. In fact, each character in Tendulkar's plays, steps on to stage straight from life and it is this immediately identifiable quality of his characters, which erases the dividing line between truth and fiction. His *Vultures, Silence* and *Sakharam* present a raw chunk of life in all its ugliness and crudity, which performs necessary function of jolting the public conscience and start the necessary process of introspection.

As a whole Tendulkar's plays are concerned with an individual set against the backdrop of a hostile society. They portray the loss of values in an individual as he comes in contact with structure of power. His plays neither moralize nor engage value judgments. What becomes apparent in his plays is the abiding concern with the plight of the individual, his solitude and alienation in an urban and industrialized society.

Most of the plays of Tendulkar are stories of violence, power and repression in different forms in the contemporary

Indian society. His preoccupation with violence manifests itself in the male-manipulated cruel game garbed as 'mock-trial' in *Silence! The Court is in Session,* in an ambitious young journalist's craze for investigative journalism in *Kamala,* in the creative Dalit young man's sadistic treatment of his Brahmin wife in *Kanyadaan.* Further *Sakharam Binder* claims the boastful proclamations of insatiable 'itch' in the eponymous, the cruelty that the two brothers and sisters practice in *The Vultures.* For the ruthless human punishment Ghashiram Kotwal meets both the innocent and the guilty in *Ghashiram Kotwal.* All these plays are, in fact, spectacles of violence, overt or covert.

Tendulkar's plays focus on the basic hypocrisy and double standards on which our society is founded. Revealing the essential nature of the game of politics and the basic craving for power, here he portrays the whole gamut of situations and context which characterize our private and public lives. His plays signify departure from the mainstream Marathi drama of the 60s that mostly dealt with the more privileged sections of society. His plays explore the texture of modernity and social change in post-independence, industrialized Indian society. His tense and gripping plays are charged with undercurrents of violence, uncertainties and anger, and concern themselves with questions that are crucial to all societies grappling with change and social barriers. The studies, which have been undertaken in the past, focus on either a particular time-span, or on the thematic concerns in Vijay Tendulkar's plays. The scholars treat Tendulkar's plays as political, social and feminist his plays, which jolts audiences out of their complacency each time that accounts, more than any other element, for their immortality.

NOTES

1. Indranath Choudhary, "Indian Literature after Modernism". *The Commonwealth Review* 5.1 (1993-94), pp. 17-26.
2. Arundhati Banerjee, "Introduction: *Five Plays* of Vijay Tendulkar." Bombay: Oxford University Press, 1992.
3. N. Choudhary, "Hindi Drama: *Comparative Indian Literature.* Ed. K.M. George. Madras: Macmillan India, 1984.
4. Ramnarayan Gowri. Quoted. "The Endless Road of Badal Sircar's 'Free Theatre'." *Frontline* (August 28, 1992), p. 75.

5. Ella Dutta, "Introduction: *Three Plays* of Badal Sircar". Calcutta: Seagull Books, 1985.
6. Girish Karnad, "Three Plays." Delhi: Oxford University Press, 1994.
7. Arundhati Banerjee, "Introduction: *Five Plays* of Vijay Tendulkar". Bombay: Oxford University Press, 1992.
8. Barve Chandrashekhar. *Vijay Tendulkar*. New Delhi: Prestige Books, 1990.
9. Vijay Tendulkar, *Kanyadaan*. Delhi: Oxford University Press, 1996.
10. "*Natak Ani Mee*." Interview with Shirish Pai, Priya Tendulkar. Dimple Publication: Thane, 1997.
11. *The Play is the Thing*. Sri Ram Memorial Lecture X, Sri Ram Centre for Performing Arts. New Delhi, 1997, Part 1, p. 2.

13

Sharankumar Limbale's 'The Outcaste *Akkarmashi*': A Dalit's Assertion for Caste Identity

Ghanshyam Kumar

"India is generally known as the classic land of castes and creeds. Caste is said to be in the air, and even Muslims and Christians have not escaped infection."[1] The phrase 'even Muslims and Christians' shows that the followers of Sanatan Dharma have been strictly maintaining and retaining the rigid caste system since time immemorial. We can easily experience that a man having no caste identity is good for nothing with a socio-political point of view. And if a person has no intervention in social as well as political affairs, then he or she can't be treated as a socially human being in the real sense of the term. Thus we find that caste plays a vital role in the formation of the personality of an individual. Caste factor ensures an individual identity especially in the Indian perspective. Our economic status, political grip and social identity depend on our caste acquaintance. Caste here in India is more than a human being and more than a social being. A man feels dehumanized in case of his not belonging to any specific caste. Being an outcaste he suffers from indignity, humiliation, exploitation, suppression, oppression, atrocity and what not from the cruel hands of the well organized upper-class people who represent the centuries' old Brahmanic hegemony.

The word 'outcaste', as per *The Concise Oxford Dictionary's* definition, means "a person who has no caste, esp. in Hindu society or a person who has lost his or her caste". In case of Sharankumar Limbale's 'The Outcaste *Akkarmashi*', the unification of these two definitions—a person who has lost his or her caste esp. in Hindu society—is more befitting and appropriate. An outstanding autobiographical endeavour, The Outcaste *Akkarmashi* tells of an untold plight of one of the worst Dalit sufferers who is none other than the protagonist himself. Limbale acknowledges very bitterly, "My mother is an untouchable while my father is a high caste from one of the privileged classes of India. Mother lives in a hut, father in a mansion. Father is a landlord; mother, landless. I am akkarmashi (half-caste). I am condemned, branded illegitimate. What is more, he poignantly postulates further deepening his own agony, High-caste people look upon my community as untouchable, while my own community humiliated me, calling me akkarmashi.... It is the pain of millions in India."

True, that this personal pain is not personal in itself, but of the millions of his likes who remain unnoticed and unacquainted. It is because unseeability and untouchability are the hallmarks of the identification of the mute sufferers who drag their lives out of the mainstream society. M.K. Naik writes, "Almost every fourth Indian is a Dalit and is easily identified. He may be a beggar near a temple or a church, a permanent squatter, a prematurely old person in his forties, a child laborer in a factory, a pauper in a village, child domestic help, a porter a rickshaw-puller in a city, a bonded laborer, and a migrant slum dweller. And a Dalit woman is always ill clad, a bag of bones, often with a malnourished child in her arms, a temple Devdasi. Although they constitute a significant number of the country's population, they remain unseen and unnoticed...."[2] Sad to say that as many as more than thirty crore Dalits, if estimation is true, are accursed to live a marginalized life. They are required to be brought back to the centre from the periphery for the harmonious social structure. Isn't it improper that on the one hand, the technological innovations have brought about tremendous worldwide changes and a sizeable majority of Dalit population in India is naturally forced to live cats and dogs life on the other? Pejorative and derogative connotations labelled against Dalits, such as Chandal, Rakshas, Malechchh, Antyaj, Panchama, Harijan, Scheduled Caste and Scheduled Tribe and so on, aggravate their woes and agony to a great extent. Dr. Ambedkar in his book *Ostracized Bharat* writes, "Dalithood is a kind of life condition that characterized the exploitation, suppression and marginalization of Dalit people by the social, economic, cultural and political domination of the upper castes Brahmanical ideology" (97). De facto, it is the Brahmanical ideology that Kancha Ilaiah, a Dalit activist and writer of a wide repute, terms as 'intellectual goondaism'. In his recent book *Post-Hindu India* Kancha Ilaiah explicitly views, "Though the concept of 'goondaism' appears to be modern, it existed all through even since the Indian society began to operate as a civil society."[3] He holds Lalit class people (upper castes people) responsible for keeping their hegemonic attitude that causes damaging effects to the very interests of productive Dalit masses. Kancha Ilaiah continues, "In India, the modern democratic state has been seized by the intellectual goondas"... who "have done more damages to the socio-economic, political and civil societal life processes in India than the street goondas could do".[4] However, economic crisis is supposed to be the root cause of social evils to a great extent. It breeds many a problem.

The dearth of money forces a man to drudge and to clean shit for satiating his hunger. Hunger drives one to do some immoral and unethical deeds as well. Most of the time it is felt that economic crisis is shrewdly created by the Lalit class people in the various forms of exploitation, by flexing their muscles and displaying the power of wealth. Dr. Amartya Sen rediscovers that the reason behind starvation is nothing but the unequal distribution system. It is not that equal distribution of the needful is not possible. Status quoism is deliberately kept up by the Brahmanical mind setup.

Again, it is hunger that drives Masamai to satisfy the physical desire and sexual deliberation of the Patil of Baslegaon, Hanumanta Limbale, whose son the protagonist himself is,

Sarankumar Limbale avers, "My mother was once the keep of Hanumanta, whose son I am and at present she is Kaka's kept woman" (31/TO). An already married Masamai divorced her own husband Ithal Kamble because her alluring beauty caused a lust Hanumanta to get attracted towards her, and she was infatuated by him. Limbale very rightly remarks, "To be born beautiful among Dalits is a curse" (37/TO). The Outcaste *Akkarmashi* depicts the awfulness of hunger with intense feelings, creating pathos and sympathy among readers. Such depiction of hunger is really rare in other literary work. Originally written in Marathi by Sarankumar Limbale and later translated into English by Santosh Bhoomkar, the narrative leaves an indelible impression on the mind of readers for its exemplary portrayal of the protagonist's plight. 'Murdahiya', a Dalit Hindi autobiography recently launched by well-known Dalit writer Tulsi Ram, also deals threadbare with the harsh realities of the life Chamar Community he also belongs to. But the intense depiction of hunger shown in The Outcaste *Akkarmashi* has outclassed the same in 'Murdahiya'.

However, it is due to his being an illegitimate child that Limbale felt humiliation and denial of self-dignity right since his early boyhood. He had to suffer a lot and felt dehumanized almost every time, everywhere. It is the identity crisis that compels him to be assertive for caste identity. Frankly speaking, his mother's sleeping with the high caste Patil of Baslegaon happens to sow the seeds of indignation in the young mind of the protagonist at the prevalent social behaviour of Indian society. And like fish out of water he feels about himself among the people of his own community as well as others. The binding nature of the bitterness of casteism makes him realize that man without social identity is just like a rudderless boat. Expressing his extreme hatred towards the very idea of untouchability, he poignantly remarks, "We hated the very idea of untouchability. With our education there grew in us a sense of pride. Casteism made us bitter" (76/TO). Education is a liberating force while illiteracy is a binding stigma. Real self-esteem is enjoyed by the qualified. Realization of unusual inner strengths depends on self-dignity and self-esteem. Only the spread of education among the uneducated or illiterate Dalit people can make them free from the bondage of life. Good education also brings an independent social recognition to an individual. Limbale has "realized that self-esteem had unusual strengths..." (76/TO). He asked a number of pointed questions throughout his narrative that remain unanswered and unresponded till date. He recalled his schooling days and felt alienated as he had been unlike other children. Not to speak of the social environment even the school environment was poisoned with discrimination between child and child belonging to different socio-economic background with various caste identities. He found himself in the school just like the garbage thrown outside. "There is saying, 'Children are the flowers of God's abode' but not us. We are the garbage the village throws out. There were so many caste factions in our school.... We had grown up like aliens since our infancy" (5/TO). Limbale is absolutely right when he remarks that "It is man who is hindrance to religion" or caste. From birth to death in the caste ridden Hindu society there is no escape from rites and rituals on various occasions such as after-birth celebration, marriage ceremony, after-death ceremonial rites and rituals and so on. Religious dogmas and spiritual fascist forces cause disintegration in the Indian social setup.

In lack of caste identity even the village barber Ishunath refused to have his hair cut or shave his head. Even Shivram, owner of tea stall, displayed social discrimination in his small shop, "There was a small tea shop in our village owned by Shivram where separate cup and saucer were kept for Mahars and Mangs.... Everywhere we were condemned...our caste had been thrust upon us even before we were born" (76/TO). To his utter dismay, he failed to enjoy the social harmonious life in lack of caste identity and socially valued hierarchy. It seems that he was not even a human being, not to speak of his being a social being at all. Limbale expressed his agony very indignantly, "But a man is recognized in this world by his religion, caste or his father. I had neither religion nor a caste. I had no inherited identity at all" (59/TO).

> Hutton is of opinion that caste is a good institution which has proved its worth and should be reformed not rooted out...the broken poisoned finger should be amputated, not that whole hand.

Limbale could not get certain papers signed for school because he (sarpanch) could not properly identify his caste by his mother or father and they could not accept his grandmother as his guardian she lived with a Muslim.

In the long established social pyramid, there is no room of those living on the periphery. In the social pyramidal structure Brahmins who form the least number of the total population sit on the top. Just below them come Kshtriyas, further followed by Vaishyas. Shudras stand on the lowest stratum. Among the conventionally recognized four Varnas outcastes have no place at all. The pain of being out of the caste system is very deeply felt in the following lines, "The life of man who suffered not only through this caste system but also the pain of not even being allowed into the caste system. He was an outcaste, below everyone else" (96/TO). In India, caste plays a key role from electing a village Sarpanch to forming the government, state and central. For strong social bastion one must be the essential part of a particular caste or class, lower or middle or higher so that he/she might not only exercise his/her franchise with pride but also live a societal life properly. It is not hidden from us that the political game in India is played following the caste and class equation. The significant role of caste identity can be understood even from this fact that one's self-respect always remains on the wane in case one fails to be worthy to assert oneself with no identity crisis. Limbale found himself between what-to-do and what-not-to-do situation in absence of his social and caste status. He wanted to know asking a volley of questions, "She (Masamai) will die blemished, an object of someone's lust, but what about us? Will anyone marry my sisters? Will society accept us? When we die, will people from the Maharwara undertake our funerals?" (64/TO). It is a matter of fact that if the question of caste identity gets its proper solution only once, many social diseases are supposed to be easily cured. But it seems to be a pipe dream in the existing socio-political circumstances of India. Limbale, knowing the cruel rigidity of caste system in the Hindu society and the riotous attitude between Hindus and Muslims, took a peaceful refused under the calm and serene shadow of Buddhism. Having taken inspiration from the revolutionary move of Dr. Ambedkar, who, along with thousands and thousands of Dalits (who failed to share the social interests of the mainstream society), adopted Buddhism at Nagpur in 1956, Limbale not only embraced Buddhism but also took active participation in the Dalit Panthers movement to awake the people of his likes. He explicitly revealed, "I was afraid of my caste because I could not claim my father's caste and religion. In a sense I was not a Mahar, because high caste blood ran in my body. The agony I lived through is my own as much as that of my village" (82/TO).

When there came time for marriage, he could not even married to an outcaste girl because his blood is not pure; he was not wanted anywhere. Eventually a drunkard who had offered Limbale his daughter would allow her to leave after the wedding because of Limbale's background. He expressed a dig at Hindus' social modes and behavior. Limbale was dead against solemnization of his own marriage, following Hindu rituals and customs. As did he opine, "I don't believe in Hindu rituals. We are going to be wedded according to Buddhist rituals" (99/TO).

After having got a job as a telephone operator, Limbale faced a lot of problems in finding a house on rent in a new town for his accommodation. Casteism chased him there as well like his foe. In his own words, "I faced the problem of finding a house in a new town and my caste followed me like an enemy.... Every town and person was caste conscious. This casteism has dehumanized me everywhere" (106/TO).

When Kusum, his wife informed him that she had given birth to a male baby, Limbale, as if predetermined, christened his child with Annarya. This is really a culmination of his anger and indignation at the hegemony of the elite of the Indian society. He avowed, "I got news that my wife Kusum had had a baby boy. I have already thought of a name for him. It was Annarya" (112/TO).

Limbale wants the coming generation not to suffer the brunt of caste discrimination and oppression because caste is a prominent status marker in the Hindu society. However, The Outcaste *Akkarmashi* tells an untold tale of a Dalit who rose from penury to privilege. The struggle of the protagonist instills in other Dalits radical thoughts to wage a silent war against the rotten stinking caste system that has maimed and paralysed the cordiality and harmony and the sense of togetherness among the people in general.

To conclude, such a noteworthy autobiography has not only helped enriched and strengthened the sensibility and consciousness of Dalit literature but it has also created a new trend in post-Independence India. Now Dalit literature is not confined to the Indian subcontinent alone but it has attracted the global attention towards it by setting up its analogy with the Afro-American Black Literature in many respects as well as forming the essential part of the world literature.

It is true that the Dalit literature created or being created with the sympathetic point of view can't exactly express the same intensity of atrocity mated out to the worst sufferers. This can be easily analyzed after going through the two different views being expressed below by the two stalwarts of modern Hindi literature belonging to Dalit and Dalit class respectively: Omprakash Valmiki remark "How will you understand the pain of the horse, his emotion towards his master once he is tied to the Khunta after a whole day long labour, hungry and thirsty?"[7] is a straightforward reply to Kashinath Singh's view "It is not necessary to be a horse, to be able to write on horses."[8]

NOTES

1. D.N. Majumdar and T.N. Madan, *An Introduction to Social Anthropology* (1986), Mayoor Paperbacks.
2. Authorsden.com

3. Kancha Ilaiah. *Post-Hindu India* (2006), Sage Publication, 23.
4. *Ibid.*, 37.
5. Gyanoday (Hindi Monthly Magazine), November 2011. Editor: Ravindra Kalia. Pub. Bharitya Gyan Peeth, New Delhi.
6. The Outcaste *Akkarmashi*: Sharankumar Limbale, translated by Santosh Bhoomkar, Oxford University Press.
7. Om Prakash Valmiki, Joothan, *An Untouchable's Life*, 1997, Translated from Hindi by Arun Prabha Mukharjee: Columbia University (97).
8. Kashinath Singh (2011), Rehan Par Regghu. Raj Kamal Prakashan (47).

NB: "TO" used in the paper in the bracket refers to Sharankumar Limbale's. The Outcaste (*Akkarmashi*) and the digit before it is the page nos.

14

My Feudal Lord: A Saga of Feminist Politics

Faraha Naqvi

My Feudal Lord is a literary sensation of Tehmina Durrani which takes up the issue of female emancipation. Tehmina Durrani, a woman of high rank, belongs to an affluent family and brought up in a fairly comfortable background. Her father S.U. Durrani was in Pakistan International Airlines. Though she belong to one of the most influential and reputed families of Pakistan, she never enjoys the exalted position of her life under the querulous atmosphere of her home. She suffered alienation, estrangement in relationships, suppressions and humiliations from the hands of her own people. She first time married to the Personal Security Officer at the governor of Punjab, Anees Khan, at the age of seventeen and later on she divorced him as the feeling of love vanishes soon from their married life. She second time got attracted and married to Mustafa Khar, one of the founders of Pakistan People Party (PPP) and close ally of Zulfiqar Ali Bhutto and his chief minister in Punjab, Pakistan. It was his sixth marriage with Tehmina which hailed a storm in her life as he was true 'Feudal Lord' and the couple soon realized the bathos.

After suffering for thirteen long years she decided to break the tradition of silence and take a strong step to unveil the cruel reality of Janus-faced sophisticated people who were responsible for her constant plight through her autobiographical novel *My Feudal Lord*. This autobiographical novel won Bellasario prize and give world-wide recognition to Tehmina Durrani. It got translated into several other languages and became a sensational bestseller. She has also written the novel, *Blasphemy* which was another success for her as a writer. She has also worked on Abdus Sattar Edhi's narrated autobiography, *A Mirror to the Blind*. She is currently married to Mian Muhammad Shahbaz Sharif, a former well-known political figure and it is the third marriage for both Tehmina and Sharif.

My Feudal Lord, a brilliant novel which articulate the pain and suffering of the mute and the suppressed Tehmina who suffered disabling oppressions throughout her life. It is stalwart protest and a frank portrayal of all that events which has remained silent for the sake of woman's modesty. The rebellious note in the novel is very much reflecting through its title which is suggestive and has symbolic significance. The novel made a clarion call and presents before us the constant struggle of the woman against their incessant exploitation, torture and suppression which they undergo because to the feudal conservative framework who considered marriage as not a pious relationship but a point of domination of a man over woman. She has emerged as a bold and courageous writer who gave strength to other women who suffered quietly in the four walls of the households, to fight for their rights and raised their voice against any injustice towards them.

The feminist politics galore the whole novel and secured a distinctive place in the twentieth century. It is a common belief that man is not always a proper judge to evaluate women's writing and therefore feminist critic fight against the one-side evaluation of literary output. In the realm of literature, it is male who dominates and considered females as a subservient, unimportant, marginal and ordinary things. In this context, Simon de Beauvoir writes in her *The Second Sex*, 'one is not born as a woman, one becomes so'. She cites a clear distinctive between masculine and feminine with their respective values and says that the distinction is a cultural production. The female writing is based on a universal concept...a universal woman nature and culture. Femininity is actually and essentially a cultural product. The feminists have challenged the concept of patriarchy, gender and evaluation of literary output by which women constitute various common ideologies regarding their subaltern position in the male-dominated society. Literature now come to be studied both as an expression of feminism and as an expression of masculinity.

It was feminist criticism which made possible to the world that is a tradition of female creative writing which has its own rights for existence. Feminism is an expression of resentment at the unjust treatment meted out to women. Patriarchal powers tyrannize the female which creates an unequal relationship among human being. Literature is filled up with the expression that provide secondary place to woman in the binary opposition of man-woman. But women have always raised their voice for liberation. One of the earliest examples in English literature can be seen in the following lines of Anne Bradstreet,

> I am obnoxious to each carping tongue, who says, my hand a needle better first a poet's pen, all scorn, I shall thus wrong, For such despite they cast on female wits; if what I do prove well, it won't advance they all say its stolen or else, it way by chance.... (29-30)

Lets Greeks be Greeks, and let women be what they are, men have however precedence, and still excel. It is but vain unjustly to wage a war, men can do best, and woman knows it well. Feminist movement is based on the realization of a female that she is a 'female' in the beginning of it, Gayle Graham Yates writes in *What Woman Want*, "Many people date beginning of the international feminist movement—and at each of its stages it was an international phenomenon." From the publication in 1792, in England of Mary Wollstonecraft's book, *A Vindication of the Rights of Woman*; It was a mind-blowing thesis on the inception of feminist thought, Andrew Sinclair writes on her thesis—*The Better Half*:

> The first object of laudable ambition is to obtain a character as a human being; regardless of the distinctive of sex...trifling employment has rendered woman a trifler...

> for man and woman, truth if I understand the meaning of the word, must be the same. (49-50)

From this moderate attempt to define feminine self of feminist movement which has seen several strides in the form of different 'feminisms'. The development of feminine sensibility can be traced in:

1. Articulation
2. Intervention
3. Discovery of selfhood.

It is also termed as the politics of gaining hegemony. Whatsoever is the connotation and metaphor with the feminist discourse, *My Feudal Lord* has emerged as a significant forum for realizing and empowering the feminine self. Tehmina Durrani, Maxine Hong Kingston, etc. belongs to the ideology of oriental feminism which talks about female enunciation and maintained by the writers of the Third World. In the Third World, fiction is the struggle of human beings for betterment of communal life either by preservation of traditional order or by progress towards a new order. The human efforts ultimately lead to failure and frustration or at times to fulfillment and satisfaction. The best of the Third World fiction has thus communal or collective tone which the literatures of advanced countries do not have. It is because of the fact that in the Third World divergent elements is inherent in the very scheme and fabrics of life. The confrontation of opposite forces portrayed in the fiction leads to a conflict between two different orders embodying different scales. *My Feudal Lord* is a seminal text of feminism that is a saga of devastating indictment of women's role in Muslim society. Tehmina Durrani's marriage to a prominent Muslim statesman in Pakistan turned out to be nightmare and the couple soon realized the bathos. Unlike the baby-doll image of a Muslim bride, Tehmina waged a war of liberation and made a clarion call of feminist ethos. The auto-novel explores and manifests the emotional trauma of the typical Muslim protagonist turning into an Amazon.

The novel is almost a culture-clash and more than that is the clash of two selves with each other and life struggling to reconcile the opposite tendencies. A writer herself is governed by the dual pattern of value and modern forces subverting her. The author writes in her notes, preceding the novel,

> When I decided to write the book, I was aware of the perils of exposing the details of my private life to a male-dominated Muslim society. But I had to cast aside my personal considerations in favour of the greater good. There is a deep-rooted deficiency in the feudal value system; it must be diagnosed before it is treated. (9)

My Feudal Lord is a novel of social change where Tehmina Durrani, in a very firm and vocal tone explains the saga of a Muslim lady who adopts total frankness and ultimately emerges as a woman to be admired. This autobiographical novel was later translated into several languages. This fictional autobiography *My Feudal Lord* describes her traumatic mar. Mustafa Khar who was an important politician in the Zulfiqar Ali Bhutto Government and he later became the chief minister of Punjab. He was a charismatic champion of democracy but on the personal front he was however an inveterate wife abuser. Mustafa Khar represents the value and norms established by a patriarchal society. *My Feudal Lord* is divided into three parts respectively.

1. Lion of the Punjab
2. Law of the Jungle
3. Lioness.

Throughout these sections one can trace the progress of Tehmina Durrani from an ordinary elite emancipated human being contesting for equal rights and women's empowerment. The novel is a feminist affirmation of woman's strength and it is also suggestive nature of woman. Tehmina Durrani, born into well-educated and elite class of Lahore in Pakistan. She had a political background and she married one of the most eminent political figures, Mustafa Khar. For thirteen long years, she lived under constant fear, as the battered sixth wife of a landlord-politician, silently enduring her husband's beating, his philandering and his abuse of their children. Gradually, Mustafa Khar succeeded in cutting her off from the outside world. For fourteen years, she suffered alone, in silence. She decided to break the silence and found the courage by leaving her husband Mustafa Khar and writing her autobiography which gave the real picture of her marriage, and exposing feudalism or male domination in its true light.

Tehmina Durrani, speaks to Sehar Ali in Lahore, about the personal tragedy that sparked off an inspired fight against injustice. Once this desire to expose the reality kindled in her, a broken lady performs an unachievable task. Raising voice against the predicament and breaking the silence all alone after suffering for thirteen years she displays exemplary courage and bravery schooling.

She became rebellious to marry because he was the first man who falls in love with her and she felt that he was her only chance for happiness. But Anees in the shape of husband could not realize her feeling to him. Life does give her in some measure what she might have. She was attracted to Mustafa Khar. He had charismatic and powerful personality. She called him as "an exotic, tall, dark and handsome man, with flashing eyes and a rake". She was weakened by her attachment to Anees because he had carried no weight to strengthen her. Anees was a dull man, Mustafa Khar had a series of wives but not as him. She was attracted to him looking for a pillar which she might not had in her life. At the same time she felt an underlying guilt because it was not easy for her to cheat and deceive a man who had trusted her so much. Mustafa Khar was a professional seducer. He was a master in the art to seduce women. The seduction is a fine art of sexual and psychological persuasion used by men to gain the desired effect. He trapped her in his art and she became the victim of him. She became irrevocable in her decision to remarry to Mustafa Khar. She did not pay any heed when her family threatened her to boycott. Once again she probes happiness in new relationship with Mustafa. The marriage soon turned into a nightmare. Her love for the man had now turned into a fear. She got broken when she faced the cruel reality of a man whom she loved truly. He was a feudal lord who had been exposed to the modern world, and his philosophies were eclectic. His class believed that a woman was as instrument of a man's carnal pleasure. She could not tolerate her marriage because it did not fit into the fictionalized accounts that she had craved for. She missed the bliss, ecstasy, and passion that she hoped she would find in this marriage. But then again he treated her as a companion. A Pakistani woman holding the values of oriental culture to her heart will endure almost anything in order to hold a marriage together. Tehmina's conventional upbringing conditioned by her patriarchal social environment, in which she lived, made Mustafa's physical assaults that were the social ethos into which Tehmina's mother always pressurizes her to live life quietly. Her mother's comment aptly illustrates this: "if a husband behaves in a strange or unreasonable manner, you should treat him like a sick human being, like someone who needs medical care and treatment. Deal with him like a psychiatrist" (*MFL* 130).

The novel very much attack against the traditional concept that women should always endowed by men and endeavored to understand him in any good or bad situation just as a psychiatrist. Yet Mustafa is neither sick nor reasonable. He is simply insanely and irrationally possessive. He beats the pregnant Tehmina brutally.

When Mustafa Khar reveals his relationship with Tehmina to Sherry that time she was expecting the baby and the shock of Sherry later on suffered by Tehmina are tremendous. When she became subjected at the same situation then she realized that how Sherry got hurt. This is into him a feudal master who treats his wife as a possession. She had a passionate desire to share her predicament with her mother but she could not do so as she never tried to understand her plight since her childhood. Her mother's inability to understand her own daughter's sufferings and restlessness leads her goes through various degrees of neglect, humiliation, withdrawal and alienation. She had none with her to share her plight and she bears all alone that cruel reality. Anybody else in her place may have given up long back but for Tehmina Durrani that wasn't ever an option. Though she slipped into morass of despair and depression when she tried to commit suicide but she picks herself up for children.

For the first time in her life she considers divorce but realizes that she might not be right over her daughter. So she once again reconciles with her destiny. There was a tremendous desire in Tehmina for maintaining her dignity and self-respect before society. These unfulfilled desires lead Tehmina to keep quite. In the course of time, when Mustafa develops an illicit relationship with her younger sister Adila, she could not tolerate this particular aspect of Mustafa. She tells in the presence of all; "your marriage according to Koran, was over years ago when you slept with my sisters. I have been living with you in sin. The contract stood null and void long ago" (*MFL* 362).

It was the time when she completed the divorce proceedings and also began to write an autobiography. Her courage had established her as a woman who was willing to take on the powerful feudalism. Patriarchal discourse limits and transcribes the image and identity of Tehmina but she inverts the social and familial contrast of woman. She pretended to her mother and to society that she has a good relationship with her husband Mustafa Khar but in reality she suffered with a hand of shattered relationship. The kind of physical trauma she suffered anyone can run from that situation.

Yet Tehmina Durrani appears in the long run a loser, because she lost her husband and custody of her children. Although she has deprived everything and strives against all odds but she not lose her hope and courage to fight against her husband's brutality. She becomes a woman who wants her individual worth realized and attempt to break through the suffering that traditional society offers her. She decided to break the tradition of silence. The auto-novel focuses on woman's awareness of her predicament, her wanting to be recognized as a person than as woman and her wanting to have an independent social image. Tehmina is urging her readers and others repressed sisters to rediscover their marginal self and thereby gain emancipation and empowerment.

We meet the inferences that *My Feudal Lord* is ultimately a treasury of female experiences in the form of an enthralling account which confirms the conviction that a woman is all powerful to eradicate the evils and oppressions if she realizes her existence and gives her' self a voice in the form of a Shero.

Tehmina Durrani's *My Feudal Lord* emerges as a beacon light to those oppressed and perturbed woman in the usual chores of life.

WORK CITED/CONSULTED

Beauvoir, Simon de. *The Second Sex*. 1949. English translation & Ed. By H.H. Parshley. London: Jonathan Cape, 1983.

Bradstreet, Anne. "*The Prologue*", published in Exilent Kraditor, Ed. UP From Pedestal, (Chicago: Quadrangle Book, 1968).

Durrani, Tehmina. *My Feudal Lord*, London: Corgi Books, 1995.

Sinclair, Andrew. *The Better Half*, New York: Harper and Row, 1965.

Yates, Graham Gayle. *What Woman Want*, Cambridge; Harvard University Press.

Note: Page numbers are given after every quotation taken from the text.

15

A Peep into the Life of Jhumpa Lahiri through Her Female Characters

Gunjan Saxena

The emergence of modern Indian feminist ideology in literature seems to cover the victimization of the educated and middle-class urban women and conspicuously highlights such exploitations in the cultural background that marginalizes the existence of Indian women and places male authority in superior position. Jhumpa Lahiri who is an Indian by ancestry, British by birth and American by immigration, deserve the dignity as one of the eminent writers in Indian English Literature. De facto, the personal life of Jhumpa Lahiri is the very prototype of diasporic culture. Having spent more thirty years in the United States, she still feels a 'bit of an outsider' because of the roots of Indianism in her existence. Her "Interpreter of Maladies" (which won her the Pulitzer Prize for fiction in 2000), "Unaccustomed Earth" and her first novel *The Namesake* (which spent several weeks on *New York Times* bestseller list) thrive on nuance and subtlety to address the baffling issue of female identity. Lahiri has acknowledged her personal experience with a hyphenated, split cultural background in interviews—"As a young child, and therefore somehow negated, by my American Environment and vice versa, I felt that I led two very separate lives."[1]

Lahiri uses her acute powers of observation together with her personal experience to create stories that transport readers to an imaginary landscape exploring and exposing the frailties common to all of humanity. She always tried to show that motherhood is a glorious stage for a woman but for a migrant in a foreign alien land, loneliness and strange surroundings nearly kill such feelings. Similarly woman in Indian English Fiction is depicted as the silent sufferer and upholder of the tradition and traditional values of family and society. If we analyze psychologically almost all the female characters of Jhumpa Lahiri seem the victims of conflicts in cultural beliefs and dysfunctional relationship created by the influence of cross-cultural interactions.

Most of the women in "Interpreter of Maladies" and "Unaccustomed Earth" suffer a kind of typical psychological trauma, living as a 'tree without roots'. They are presented as a citizen of two countries so their national and cultural identities remain uncertain and confused. They feel alienated in their own host country. In fact, Lahiri has poured out the essence of her own experience in the depiction of her female characters. In the portrayal of these characters, Lahiri appears to be blessed with a bia-cultural perception and wider analytical dexterity.

The title story of "Unaccustomed Earth" reveals the painful consequences of diasporic isolation. It is woven around 38 years old Ruma whose conflicted position lie within the sense of exile and loss from her parents. This story clarifies that children of immigrants are not born as blank slates. Rather, they are 'contaminated' by their parents' migrant experience. Ruma is very intimate to her mother who is a traditional Bengali woman. She seems to be a representative of Indian culture and traditions even after living in the United States. Her sudden death creates the distances between Ruma and her father. Ruma is shattered and deeply shocked by this incident while her father remains quite neutral towards it. After selling the family house, a cruel act of "wiping out her mother's presence in Ruma's eyes, he started travelling all around Europe enjoying the freedom of a widower". His irrelevant and limited visits to his daughter reveal the shattered father-daughter relationship. Ruma remains seeking the roots of her existence and adopts the social isolation due to the frustration and discontentment. This appears quite contrary to her father's socializing and travelling adventures. It is the father who comes across as less burdened by circumstances or 'traditions' while the daughter discovers an unsettling truth about her father, and via him, about herself. But to her father, his freedom and enjoyment provide the opportunity to avoid from everyday obligations. Ruma discovers ultimately that her father is not unaware of her worries and tensions. His weekly visit in Seattle finally succeeds in rejuvenating the long lost closeness without verbal acknowledgement. Some issues remain unsolved but the initial barrier seems to be overcome in the final act of reconciliation. Talking about the predicament of immigrants, Jhumpa Lahiri says—

> I think that for immigrants the challenges of exile, the loneliness, the constant sense of alienation, the knowledge of and longing for a lost world, are more explicit and distressing than for their children.[2]

In another story 'Hell-Heaven'—an 'upside-down' version of the Bengali expression 'akaash-pathal' that signifies vast difference—Lahiri does her take on the chestnut an immigrant man befriending a married immigrant woman and her husband, and entering the closed, precious world of an immigrant couple to upset its equanimity. The story is told by the daughter of the couple, who remembers the delightful 'Pranab kaku' and his special place in the household. Like 'Bhupati' in Tagore's novella *Nashtamir* (The Broken Nest), the husband in this story is blind to the loneliness of his wife and Pranab becomes more than a friend to this diasporic version of Charulata. "It is clear to me now that my mother was in love with him," the narrator tells us, "he wooed her like no other man had, with the innocent affection of a brother-in-law."[3]

In the stories of *Interpreter of Maladies*, Lahiri has dexterously poured out the dilemma of baffling questions regarding the sandwiched existence of women between "the strict tradition they've inherited and New world they must encounter every day."[4] Almost all the stories are centered on the woman protagonists and we are forced to peep into their inner strife and mental agony. In the title story "Interpreter of Maladies", the whole theme is woven around a female protagonist, Mrs. Das, who with her family of five, comes to Orissa from America. She is represented as a sober lady who controls her painful passions and achy feelings in a sensible manner. But her cold behaviour towards her husband and neutrality for her children seem bizarre to their guide Mr. Kapasi who is continuously capturing the trials and tribulations of this family. He observes that her dressing sense is completely western "a red-and-white-checkered skirt that stopped her knees, close fitting blouse styled like man's undershirt."[5]

Yet in the context of western feminism, her nature seems quite contradictory. When Mr. Das relishes the natural scenes through his camera, she "gazes out another window, at the sky where nearly transparent clouds passed quickly in front of one another."[6] In fact, she endeavours to seek the lost affection and warmth of marital life in the emptiness of firmament. The pain of not very happy marriages is dealt in a very sensitive manner. "After marrying so young, she was overwhelmed by it all, having a child so quickly, and nursing and warming up bottles of milk and testing their temperature against her wrist while Raj was at work, dressed in sweaters and corduroy pants, teaching his students about rocks and dinosaurs. Raj never looked cross or harried, or plumps as she had become after the first baby."[7] The marriage of Mr. Kapasi is also no better. He compares his lifeless marriage with that of theirs. "The signs he recognized from his own marriage were there—the bickering, the indifference, and the protracted silences."[8]

Mrs. Das takes keen interest in Mr. Kapasi when she comes to know about his profession as an interpreter for Gujrati patients who can't speak the local language. It seems to her something 'romantic' and she decides to spit out her darkest of secrets into his ears that one of her sons is not conceived by her husband. She tells him she has been striving with this secret for the past eight years and has confided to none. She wants to be relieved from the nameless pain and mental agony:

> I feel terrible looking at my children, and at Raj, always terrible. I have terrible urges, Mr. Kapasi, to throw things

> away. One day I had the urge to throw everything I own out the window, the television, the children everything.[9]

She desires to unburden her eight year torture to someone sympathetic. She finds Mr. Kapasi appropriate to share her secret because of his bizarre profession of interpreting illness of patients. She urges for an interpretation of her own malady by Mr. Kapasi.

> It means that I am tired of feeling so terrible all the time. Eight years, Mr. Kapasi, I've been in pain eight years, I was hoping you could help me feel better, say the right thing. Suggest some kind of remedy.[10]

Thus the inner struggle of Mrs. Das is the focal point of the story. What is worth noticing is the portrayal of Mrs. Das and like her other women characters without any emotional melodrama, declaring the verdict of their critical dilemma themselves. Mrs. Sen in Lahiri's another story 'Mrs. Sen's' suffers a kind of typical psychological trauma living as a 'tree without roots'. She remains unable to detach herself from Indian memories and simultaneously finds it obscure to adopt to American ways like driving the car, which she hates utterly. Thus her cultural and national identities remain uncertain and confused. In fact, Lahiri's depiction of women characters with diasporic feelings justifies her bicultural perception and wider analytical dexterity. Every time Mrs. Sen reminds of her home India:

> At home that is all you have to do. Not everybody has a telephone. But just raise your voice a bit, or express grief or joy of any kind, and one whole neighbourhood and half of another has come to share the news, to help with arrangements.[11]

She has a penchant to return to her roots and Lahiri needs not fumble the words to emphasize such emotions. They emerge spontaneously having the real sense in them. In order to pacify her sense of isolation, Mrs. Sen starts a day care centre. A typical American Kid Eliot observes the action and reactions of Mrs. Sen and contrasts them with those of his mother. Her obsession with fine Indian sarees, letters from India and buying fish, all makes her feel better. One thing more is to be noted here that Mr. Sen is quite neutral and impersonal towards his wife. His non-co-operative behaviour enhances the deep-rooted pain of loneliness in the heart of his wife and it becomes more difficult for her to cope with the new culture. Her smiling face and jovial gestures hide a bitter fact that she misses India badly "Here, in this place where Mr. Sen has brought me, I cannot sometimes sleep in so much silence."[12]

The same experience is reflected in the character of Twinkle in "The Blessed House" who insists on installing a sculpture depicting crucification of Christ on the mantle of their new house in spite of her husband's objection. The inner struggle of Miranda, who is not an Indian, is highlighted by the author in 'Sexy' with the notion that she is in love with a married Indian man. These characters are depicted waging a battle within themselves. Shoba in "A Temporary Matter" is a sentimental protagonist striving to find the solidity of her marital life. She tries her best to avoid the aching void left by the neutral behaviour of her husband, Shukumar but fails. In the beginning she seems to be the replica of modern woman who is independent and confident of herself. But adverse circumstances compel her to lose the control over herself. In fact, she has gone through the saddest tragedy of her life and that is to give birth to a dead child. Instead of consoling her, her husband tries to overcome his grief by shutting himself off from the rest of the world. The schism between them becomes wide; Shukumar makes no move to cover up the signs of negligence throughout the house that he holds Shoba responsible for when his own apathy and grief are to blame as well. One day they receive notice that their electricity will be out for one hour every night for five days. They spend each of these nights in dark sharing secrets with each other, things they had never shared before. Each confession becomes more bold and reveals a larger flaw in their marriage, until their imminent separation becomes clear:

> These were the things he had told her. He had held his son, who had known life only within her, against his chest in a darkened room in an unknown wing of the

> hospital. He had held him until a nurse knocked and took him away and he promised himself that day that he would never tell Shoba, because he still loved her then, and it was the one thing in her life that she had wanted to be a surprise.... Shoba had turned the lights off. She came back to the table and sat down, and after a moment Shukumar joined her. They wept together, for the things they now knew.[13]

Lahiri has the credit to portray the everyday middle-class women with dexterity particularly in 'A Real Durwan' and 'the treatment of Bibi Haldar'. The plight of these poor women is treated with special sensitivity and delicacy. "The treatment of Bibi Haldar; is about Bibi who suffers from a bizarre incurable illness. She lives with a distant cousin who barely feeds her and in return makes her work in wretched conditions. Bibi in spite of these miseries has dreams and aspirations as any young woman would have. The story ends with Bibi becoming pregnant which cures her of her illness. Thus the story reveals the triumph of the spirit of motherhood. Boori Ma in 'A Real Durwan' is not very fortunate enough to have a caring family. She is a resident sweeper of a Calcutta chawl. She is a refugee from Bangladesh. According to herself, she belongs to an affluent family but fate has not been in favour of her and she ends up sweeping the stairs of the chawl. The situation which she has relished before and the circumstances which she is facing now are quite contradictory. As the story progresses, one of the tenants in that chawl gets a couple of ceramic sinks and installs one of them in the common areas. That sink becomes the cynosure of all eyes. Everyone wants a sink in his home. One fine day, the sink is stolen and all the tenants blame Boori Ma for this and throw her out on to the road and declare that they need a real durwan.

> Then they tossed out Boori Ma. All were eager to begin their search for a real Durwan. From the pile of belongings Boori Ma kept only her broom. "Believe me, believe me", she said once more as her figure began to recede, she shook the free end of her sari, but nothing rattled.[14]

The thematic treatment of another story "Sexy" appears quite different yet significant and relevant to the current notion. Unlike other stories its protagonist is an American rather than an Indian female. The treatment of the female psyche clarifies here that in the diasporic identity-crisis which occurs as a direct result of the clash of two very difficult cultures, it is not always the immigrant Other who is victimized but also the native Self can fall prey to the process of othering. In this story the young woman Miranda gets involved in an affair with a married Indian man named Dev. As portrayed in Miranda's fascination with Indian culture upon meeting Dev, native Self covertly takes an interest in knowing and locating the immigrant Other. Miranda is intrigued by the thrill of exploring the other—a sense of thrill which causes her to visit an Indian grocery or go to an Indian restaurant as to try to learn more about India and Indian culture. This Self/Other confrontation then posits Miranda's identity on the verge of openness to the other. But other is not as open as Native Self. According to Spivak, the ideal relationship is the one which "engages the other in non-essential, non-crisis terms" but is also reciprocal and so requires the same very act of opening up from the other.[15] Dev in 'Sexy' has a misplaced stereotypical view of Miranda as an exotic woman of high sexual appeal all through the story. Thus, he cannot take part in creating "the ethical stance of making discursive room for the Others to exist".[16] In this way, the one single attempt on the part of female subject is unanswered, silenced and doomed to fail.

Lahiri's novel *The Namesake* is also not untouched with her minute observation and imaginative potency in the realm of feminism and that potency emerges out of the essence of her own analytical observation of the life. In this novel, the main female protagonist Gauri falls in love with and marries Udayan Mitra. Udayan Mitra and his elder brother Subhash are inseparable in childhood and generally regarded as 'mirror images' of each other. When Udayan meets Gauri, Subhash is in America, pursuing higher studies. Udayan is caught up in the banned Naxalite Movement and eventually is killed by the police in stark view of his parents and wife. This earth-shattering event permanently scars each one of them, especially the two women, one the mother whose favourite son has been taken away from her and the other, his young pregnant wife. Subhash, the elder brother returns to mourn the younger brother's death. On seeing the discrimination meted out to Gauri and the police and the investigation agencies still harassing her with questions concerning her dead husband and her comrades in crime, he decides to give her a means to escape. Against his parent's wishes he marries her and takes her to America. "To take his brother's place, to raise his child to come to love Gauri as Udayan had. To follow him in a way that felt perverse, that felt ordained. That felt both right and wrong."[17]

Gauri gives birth to a daughter Bela, but soon begins to feel suffocated in both the marriage as well as in her role as a mother. She continues to be haunted by the memories of her first husband.

> Even now, part of Gauri continued to expect some news from Udayan. For him to acknowledge that their lives, aware of him, unaware of him, had gone on.[18]

In "Towards a New Psychology of Women", Jean Baker Miller recognizes that "women are seen as nurtures and caregivers and that their selves were almost totally determined by what the dominant culture believed it needed from women".[19] Thus, the so-called feminine virtues are cherished in women and like, Gauri, if they want to break free, they are branded as failed mothers and wives. So Gauri continues to feel alienated in her own home. She is acutely aware of her shortcomings as both a wife and a mother, but chooses to continue on this path. Women have also "traditionally built a sense of self-worth on activities that they can manage to define as taking care of and giving to others".[20] By negating her feminine self, she does not find peace or self-fulfillment. She is definitely a successful professional but ends up as a lonely individual.

As a crux of matter Lahiri's anthology of short stories and other works reveal her genius approach to female psychology. Her female characters engage in creating identities thereby emphasizing on individualism. They noisily assert that meaning of life and suffering both depends on individual and agencies that engage in constructing identity. Lahiri explains that creation of identity has to endure resistance. It must also be reiterated that Lahiri does not differ between female and women as existentialists. She emphasizes that inability to adapt and adopt creates marginalization and sub-alternate. She proves herself dexterous in the portrayal of something different women characters whose image imprint in our mind forever. Amy Tan in one of her reviews captures the styles of Ms. Lahiri very succinctly when she says, "...(Ms. Lahiri has) an eye for nuance and ear for irony....."[21] De facto, her collection of short stories as well as novels depicts and celebrates the womanhood and the femininity of everyday woman in its entirety.

NOTES

1. Leyda Julia, "An Interview with Jhumpa Lahiri", *Contemporary Women's Writing*, Vol. 5, Issue 1: 66-83, Oxford University Press, 2011.
2. ———, Jhumpa Lahiri Author Interview—Book Browse. (www.bookbrowse.com)
3. J. Lahiri, (2008), "Unaccustomed Earth". New York/Toronto: Alfred. A. Knopf. 57.
4. C.V.B.T. Sundari, "Women in Interpreter of Maladies by Jhumpa Lahiri." 84.
5. J. Lahiri, (1999), "Interpreter of Maladies". Boston: Mariner Books. 46.
6. *Ibid.,* 50.
7. *Ibid.*, 63.
8. *Ibid.*, 53.
9. *Ibid.*, 76.
10. *Ibid.*, 65.
11. *Ibid.*, 116.
12. *Ibid.*, 115.
13. *Ibid.*, 22.
14. *Ibid.*, 82.
15. M. Kilburn, Glossary of key terms in the work of Gayatri Chakravorty Spivak. Post-colonial studies at Emory: Retrieved

20 July 2010, From www.englishemory.edu/lahiri/glossary.html. (3)

16. D. Landry and MacLean, G., The Spivak Reader. New York and London: Routledge 1996, (6).
17. Lahiri, Jhumpa, *The Namesake*. Houghton Mifflin, 2003: 115.
18. *Ibid*., 154.
19. Jean Baker Miller, "Towards a New Psychology of Women." Boston: Beacon (17).
20. *Ibid*., 153.
21. J. Lahiri, *Interpreter of Maladies*, Flamingo, 2000-05-15, p. 20.

16

Gender Issues in Mahesh Dattani's *Where There's a Will* and *Tara*: A Study

Jyoti Vishnoi

Mahesh Dattani is one of the most powerful and potent dramatic voice in the Indian English dramatic world. His plays reflect comprehensive dramatic soul as he has a strong passion for the theatrical art as a writer. He is one of India's most daring, innovative and important dramatists as he deals with many burning issues that afflict societies the entire world over. He writes originally in English and deals with the radical themes such as the unexplored soil of homosexuals, HIV positives, eunuchs, physically challenged people, gender discrimination, communalism, etc. His famous plays are *Where There's a Will*, *Dance Like a Man*, *Tara*, *Final Solutions*, *Seven Steps Around the Fire*, etc. Rozario Ignatius remarks:

> Mahesh Dattani is one of the few leading Indian dramatists. Other popular names in this genre are Gurcharan Das, Gieve Patel, Shashi Tharoor, Uma Parameswaran and Manjula Padamanabhan. The greatness of Dattani lies in the fact that he expresses himself easily and naturally in a voice loud and clear.... A reading of Mahesh Dattani's plays brings to the fore many burning issues that beset the post Independence Indian Society. (*Contemporary Social Issues* 106)

As a renowned playwright, he has considerably enriched and enlightened the tradition of Indian English Drama. In his plays, he deals with various problems and pent up feelings of the subalterns in a very realistic and authentic way. He is one of the exponents of modern Indian Drama as he has a modern approach to theatre and deals conventional themes with modern outlook. As the multi-faced literary and dramatic figure, he deals with various themes, techniques and devices. As a dramatist he has given a new height and dimension to Indian English Drama.

Gender discrimination is one of the most recurring themes in his plays. He is considered as the spokesman of the marginalized people and his plays reflect his deep concern for gender subalterns, the marginalization of women. Many writers deal with gender issues and raise voice against the miserable plight of women. Feminism has given birth to two opposite attitudes namely pro-feministic and anti-feministic attitude. The writers who have favorable attitudes towards feminism are called pro-feministic and those are against or oppose this attitude are designated as anti-feministic. Mahesh Dattani belongs to the pro-feministic group. Though he has no specific agenda of feminism, he tries to present various aspects of gender discrimination. As a realist, he presents the constant battle between the feminine psyche and patriarchal order and raises questions regarding gender inequality as in an interview with Anjum Katyal, he says: "Gender is a major part of it... it has to do with my own comfort with both the feminine and the masculine self in me...the masculine self is very content; it doesn't need to express itself. But the feminine self seems to seek expression..." (Of Page and Stage, An interview).

In his very first play *Where There's a Will* he satirizes patriarchy and gender discrimination and explores the dichotomy between the male and the female roles in a patriarchal society. Even in modern times women are being treated as sex objects and exploited physically and mentally. Feminism self has not being restored yet. In his interview with Laxmi Subramanyam, Dattani says:

> They are humans. They want something. They face obstacles. They will do anything in their power to get it. All eyes focus on in the powerlessness of sensibility for political correctness either. My only defense is to say that I am not biased against women. (*M.V.* 134)

However, it is a fact that the women are not treated at par with man in all areas of human activities. They are confined to their homes, marginalized, suppressed and oppressed. In a patriarchal society a woman is never treated on equal terms and is given the secondary role. She has no individual existence and treated as an object. In the play *Where There's a Will,* Dattani presents how women in their own homes are marginalized. Though the kitchen or home is described as the kingdom of women, they are no longer ruling over them as they are pushed on the margin of invisibility. There are two kinds of images of the women in the play. First, there is a woman who suffers throughout her life. Sonal Mehta, the wife of Hasmukh Mehta has been victimized and exploited by the patriarchal social system. She is the silent sufferer. Secondly, there are women who opposed the patriarchal unjust authority as they were aware of their rights and duties. They are capable to observe their deeds, decision and position in society. Kiran Jhaveri and Preeti are assertive, confident and bold as they can at times, defy. They are able to contend with patriarchal authority. Both are shrewd, cunning and money-minded. They are scheming and have guts to oppose what they consider wrong.

Dattani satirizes the patriarchal domination with the help of some comic situation. The story revolves around the life of a man, Hasmukh Mehta, a rich and successful businessman and his family. He is the boss of his familial as well as business world. He is the embodiment of patriarchal norms and tries to control family even after his death through his will. The family in the Indian society is dominated by male and it is he who is considered as the head of the family. The power that he enjoys over his family members is unquestionable. Since he is the head of the family, the freedom is hardly given to the other members of the family especially for women. The male has the right to take the important decisions such as education, marriage etc. Hasmukh is the autocratic head and demands unquestionable obedience from his family members while his wife Sonal has no choice of her own. She has learnt how to obey her husband.

Hasmukh is anti-thesis to her. He rules his family when he was alive. After his death he tried to control his family from his grave through his will. Kiran remarks: Hasmukh was intoxicated with his power. He thought he was invincible. That he could rules from his grave by making this will (*C.P.* 508).

Kiran is a new woman who has guts to fulfill her needs. She has both brain and body and knows how to use any of them to satisfy herself. She is sharp, open-minded and confident. On the other hand, Sonal is ignorant, innocent and devoted wife to her husband Hasmukh who is a rude and perverted creature. Sonal is ignorant of her husband's Sexual lust and his enjoyment with night women. While Kiran is intelligent enough to read Hasmukh's mind, she maintains her relation with Hasmukh only to satisfy her needs as she has no emotional attachment with him. Through her experience with him, she tells Sonal:

> He depended on me for everything. He thought he was decision-maker. But I was. He wanted me to run his life...he saw in me a woman who could father him! Men really never grow up. (*C.P.* 510)

Kiran is a modern woman who is the symbol of gendered strength. She behaves with all the family members very nicely and thwarts the ambitions of the patriarch and undermines his domination. Asha Kuthari Chaudhary remarks:

> Dattani's perception of gendered strength is invariably that of a woman like Kiran Jhaveri, marginalized, almost invisible, suddenly thrust into the action and pluckily accepting the challenge for what it is worth. She is nobody's fool and wields authority with the sensitivity that is perhaps peculiar to women. (Mahesh Dattani 59)

Dattani is of the opinion that women suffer while they have no faults of their own as they are victims of men's vain pride and false ego. Male ego or pride is the main cause of the present plight of the women in our society. It is a fact that education and economical empowerment make women strong but education and economic independence would not help them gain their proper place unless the male ego undergoes a complete change. Through the conversation between Kiran and Sonal, Dattani expresses his views regarding education and women empowerment. Kiran, a well-educated, a hard-headed woman is the marketing executive in the company of Hasmukh Mehta. Sonal is uneducated and considers Kiran as a fortunate lady as she says:

> Sonal: You are so lucky, you are educated, so you know all this.
>
> Kiran: Wrong, I learnt my lessons from being so close to life. I learnt my lessons from watching my mother tolerating my father when he came home every day with bottles of Rum wrapped up in the newspapers. As I watched him beating her up and calling her name, I learnt what life was when my mother pretended she was happy in front of me and my brother so that we wouldn't hate my father and I learnt when I kept my mother away from my father so that in return he would remain silent for these three hours when he came home and before he fell asleep at the dining table too drunk to harm us anymore. I served him those drinks waiting for that moment when he would become unconscious and I would say a prayer. (*C.P.* 508)

Kiran who has unhappy childhood falsifies Sonal's notion by narrating her unhappy past. But the fact cannot be neglected that modern education has helped women to be aware of their rights and duties. Education makes them capable to observe their deeds, decisions and position to oppose patriarchal unjust authority.

Through Kiran, Mahesh Dattani expresses his wrath and anguish at the continuation of sorry state of women from one generation to another:

> Kiran: Isn't it strange how repetitive life is? My brothers! They have turned out to be like their father going home with bottles of rum wrapped up in newspapers. Beating

> up their wives and I too am like my mother I married a drunkard and I listen to his swearing. And I too have learnt to suffer silently. Oh! Where all this end? Will the scars of our parents remain forever? (*C.P.* 508)

At the end, Kiran and Sonal join hands to eradicate the evil of sexual colonialism. They are endowed with the ability to assess and subsequently shaking of the unjust shackle of patriarchy. Thus Dattani presents the theme of women empowerment and development besides the theme of patriarchal domination, subordination of women in the play.

In his famous play *Tara,* Dattani presents the bizarre reality of the women playing second role in society. It presents injustice done to women. As an assertive playwright he represents the reality that there is always a difference between a male and female child and importance is given to the male. The play is a story about how Indian society deals with girl child and the situation gets worse if the girl is physically or mentally handicapped. Sangeeta Das remarks:

> Tara is neither Chandan's tragedy nor is it really Tara's. Tara is sacrificed because she was a girl and had no right to have a better life than her brother. The idea of a complete girl child and an incomplete male child is so shocking that sacrifice of the girl child is acceptable than a handicapped male child. The tragic events depicted in the play are tragic actions belonging to everyday life. (*I.C.W.T.* 115)

Dattani reveals how the power of wealth and patriarchy deprives the girl child of what is hers. Tara and Chandan are twins and are separated after the three months of the year of birth. They were conjoined from the chest and had three legs. The chances of survival of the third leg were more with Tara but it was given to Chandan. Dattani reveals the bitter fact that woman's life is always structured and governed by patriarchal force. Tara's grandfather uses his money and political power and the third leg was given to Chandan instead of Tara. The cruel decision of grandfather and his mother takes the life of sister and ruins the life of brother in one of his interviews with Laxmi Subramanyam he says:

> I see Tara as a play about the male self and female self. The male self is being preferred in all cultures. The play is about the separation of self and the resultant angst. (*M.V.* 134)

Though both Tara and Chandan are separated physically, they are emotionally united and share similar mental agony which is quite obvious in the play. Mr. Patel, their father tries to separate the twins emotionally as he has a little hope of Tara's life expectancy. Chandan belongs to new generation and believes in equality of womanhood. He represents radical values and respects Tara's talent and identity. When Mr. Patel wants Chandan to attend the office with him, he does not wish to do so without Tara:

> Patel: I was just thinking...it may be a good idea for you to come to the office with me.
>
> Chandan: You can take Tara. She'll make a great business woman.

Actually He's not ready to go anywhere without Tara as he says:

> I will not go to college without Tara.

Chandan believes in Tara and her strength and opposes his father, a firm believer in old values. He asks his father to value Tara's talent and intelligence. Chandan is against gender discrimination and he belongs to the new generation regarding this gender discrimination. Swami Vivekananda said:

> It is very difficult to understand why in this country so much difference is made between men and women, whereas the Vedanta declares that the one and the same conscious self is present in all beings. Liberty is the first condition of growth. (S.V. 76)

Bharati's decision of giving her kidney to Tara maybe seen as an act of expiation as she feels herself guilty for Tara. Her love for Tara is pure but her maternal love is marginalized as a woman and her old values compel her to take decision in favor of Chandan.

It is remarked:

> Dattani establishes that mother and daughter relationship is ultimately subordinated to the directives of patriarchy. It makes obvious that women's lives are organized and manipulated by the patriarchy in all ages, roles, gender perception and prescribe unequal means to achieve the wholeness for women. (Agarwal 80-81)

Dattani presents that Chandan suffers emotionally as he feels that he is responsible for Tara's suffering. Bharati, the mother of the twins develops a guilt complex and is also very close to a mental breakdown. She belongs to the old generation of Indian women who preserve the family tradition and old values and so she takes decisions in favor of male child as she wants a healthy son but Bharati also suffers as she loves her daughter very much and is concerned for Tara's career and future:

> Bharati: It's time Tara decided what she wants to be. Women have to do that as well these days. She must have a career.
>
> Chandan: She can do whatever she wants. Grandfather's trust will leave us both money, isn't it?
>
> Bharati: Yes! But she must have something to do. She can't be aimless all her life. (Dattani 348)

Though Tara is the victim of gender discrimination in patriarchal society, she is confident, intelligent and courageous girl she is much attached to her mother as she says: I am strong. My mother has made me strong (Dattani 330).

As a modern woman, Tara is assertive and expresses her resentment when Roopa insults her.

> Roopa: How dare you! You one-legged thing!
>
> Tara: I would sooner be one-eyed, one-armed and one-legged than be an imbecile like you. (Dattani 369)

Tara asserts her identity and does not consider herself different from Chandan. She is not ready to accept the tradition of treating male child and female child differently. When Roopa tells her about the tradition of killing girl child by drowning into milk in the houses of Patel, she says:

> How absurd!... Absolutely hilarious.... Is that what Mummy was trying to stop you from telling me? (Dattani 349)

As a modern woman, she is frank and does not hesitate to express her hatred for her father and accepts that she does not care for anybody except her mother, "I don't care! I don't care for anyone except Mummy!" (Dattani 370).

As a new woman she opposes gender discrimination and thinks of her self-identity. Thus, Dattani presents the gender politics in Indian society. Though gender difference is not new in Indian society as women are deprived of liberties and rights in our society, the woman of today is confident, assertive and courageous. She is capable to prove herself. His plays *Where There's a Will* and *Tara* reveal his concern for women's plight. Tara is an emerging new woman who fights for her identity. Kiran Jhaveri is also a new woman who is independent, confident and hard-headed.

WORKS CITED

Agrawal, Beena. *Mahesh Dattani's Plays A New Horizon in Indian Theatre*. Jaipur: Book Enclave, 2008.

Chaudhary, Asha Kuthari. *Mahesh Dattani*. New Delhi: Foundation Books Pvt. Ltd., 2005. Print.

Das, Sangeeta. *Identity Crisis of Women in Tara. The Plays of Mahesh Dattani: A Critical Response*. Ed. R.K. Dhawan, Tanu Pant, New Delhi, Prestige Books, 2005.

Dattani, Mahesh. *Collected Plays*. New Delhi: Penguin Books, 2000. Print.

Ignatius, Rozario. *Contemporary Social Issues in the Plays of Mahesh Dattani*. The plays of Mahesh Dattani: *A Critical Response*. ed. R.K. Dhawan and Tanu Pant. New Delhi: Prestige Books, 2005. Print.

———. Of Page and Stage. An interview with Mahesh Dattani by Anjum Katyal. *Seagull Theatre Quarterly*, 24 January, 2000.

Subramanyam, Laxmi (ed.). *Muffled Voices: Women in Modern Indian Theatre*. New Delhi: Shakti, 2002.

Vivekanand Swami. *My India the Indian Eternal*. Kolkata: The R.K. Mission Institute of Culture, 1998.

17

Study of Diasporic Vision in Naipaul's *Half a Life*

Seema Srivastava

The term 'diasporic', originally used for the Jewish externment from its homeland, is now applied as a "metaphoric designation" for expatriates, refugees, immigrants, exiles, homeless individual, rootless persona etc. 'Diaspora' refers to the work of exiles and expatriates and all those who have experienced unsettlement and dislocation at the political, existential or metaphorical levels. Today the exiles have taken over the stage and crossed national boundaries and exchanged cultural codes. Surprisingly, it is significant that diasporic writers are different from the western writers in the sense that the western writers have not lost their 'real' countries and seem stuck with alienation which is a kind of Psychological exile. On the other hand, for the immigrant writers, it is a matter of maintaining a delicate balance between culture of origin and culture of adoption. They can go back to the culture of origin only in imagination.

The Indian diaspora is a generic term to describe the people who migrated from territories that are currently within the border of the republic of India. It also refers to their group composed of "NRIs" (Non-Resident Indians, in other words Indian citizens not residing in India). The Diaspora covers practically every part of the world. It is an interesting paradox that a great deal of Indian writing in English is produced not only in India but in widespread geographical areas of indenture, Indian diaspora in the South Africa, the Caribbean, the South

Pacific, Mauritius, and the contemporary Indian Diaspora in U.S.A., the U.K., Canada, Australia and New Zealand.

With the settlement of more and more writers of Indian origin into Foreign countries and their involvement in creating Literature of their domicile, the theoretical problem of the critical parameters defining and assessing their work arises. Writers like Nirad Chaudhary, Rushdie, V.S. Naipaul, Nissim Ezekiel and Ramanujan and other significantly differ from one another. The diasporic experience includes the quest for identity which has a broad spectrum meaning and it has been manifested in various ways in the will to exist despite all odds and to survive all odds.

V.S. Naipaul, the Nobel laureate, has been considered the leading novelist of the English speaking caribbean. His writings—Fiction as well as non-Fiction deal with the cultural confusion of the third world and the problem of an outsider, a characteristic of his own experience as an Indian in the West Indies, a west Indian in England and a nomadic intellectual in a post-colonial world. Actually the unique combination of circumstances which related Naipaul to three societies which formed his sense and sensibility has played a prominent role in shaping the thematic matrix of his creative works.

Naipaul is a writer belonging to the Indian diaspora. As Naipaul is a world champion writer of the theme of dislocation, disintegration and consequent loss of identity. In his novel *Half a Life* (2001), Naipaul goes back to his favourite theme: the dilemma of an immigrant.

Interweaving the tales of three generations of an Indian Brahmin family "*Half a Life* is the story of a race in search of a familiar face in the mirror of time. The irony, however, lies in the fact that the mirror reflects the images which are weird and not even recognizable." Just as in *The Mystic Masseur* Ganesh Ramasumair's search for roots takes him to various stages of transformation and finally the face that he could discover is that of G. Ramsay Muir and Mohun Biswas's search for a house is a metaphor for his search for selfhood in the mirror of time, *Half a Life* is apparently an extension of this incessant quest recorded through the search of Willie Somerest Chandran for his face and identity in limbo. This novel presents two sets of father-son stories each of whom has his own fears, his own solitariness and his own loss but sadly there is no channel of communication between them and their disintegration is inevitable destiny. Out of these three, however, it is only the youngest one—the Protagonist who is given a name even. His father and grandfather, despite having strongly influenced his story, are left anonymous—again a symbolic presentation of loss of identity.

The novel opens with the beginning of Willie Somerest Chandran's search for his roots as he awakes one day to the realization that his middle name sounds alien. He asks his father; "Why is my middle name Somerset?"[1] This question regarding the very essence of a person's existence brings into light the irony of Willie's background of his half-life in half-made societies with the people who are themselves leading a life which is half discovered, half-realised and half-lived. Willie's quarry unleashes a torrent of memories unfolding before him a complicated picture which relates to his roots. A probing look reveals that this man is as much an amalgam of drastically different traits as is his name an admixture of different and even antagonistic streams. It is his destiny that half of his name does not belong to him, it is borrowed from the famous writer Somerset Maugham; his first name proclaims him as a Christian whereas his surname signifies his mixed ancestry. It is this revelation that breeds contempt in the mind of this twenty-year-old son of a half-rebel Brahmin father and a low caste mother. His incompleteness becomes the cause of his self-hatred and thus begins Willie's attempt to run away from the shadow of his past. His low parental status instills in him a sense of shame and he resolves to live in a world of falsehood and he make believe identity. But past is a shadow one can never betray and in the vain attempt to wash one's hands of the past, one always stakes one's present and future. Willie's search for his roots takes him backward because his roots are entwined with those of his father and grandfather. Willie's socio-cultural disintegration begins in his childhood and leads to his Persistent attempts to negate his weird self and to find some other concrete image even if it is made of falsehood. His whole life is doomed by the scar of his father's misplaced ideal in marrying a low caste woman and initiating the alienation which brings punishment to descending generation. Cultural alienation is in Willie's blood because his father had revolted against the tradition and negated the history by marrying a low caste woman. Those were the times of the national movement and the impact of Gandhi was in air. Gandhi's call for the upliftment of the neglected segment of society—the untouchables who were discriminated against, and Willie's father—the son of priest decided to marry a low caste woman simply to show acquiescence to the ideal of sacrifice. There was no question of love; instead the very sight of the girl bred repulsion. The austerity and discipline imposed on senior Chandran by his father had bred immense dissatisfaction in him and his restless soul was yearning for an anchor. Years later, he tells his son Willie; "I was in a great mess feeling that we were all living in a false security, feeling idle, hating my studies and knowing that great things were happening outside."[2]

It was a maddening impulse which sought satisfaction only in destroying itself. Negating history is a sin and Willie's father had to bear the punishment for his foolish decision to become a scapegoat for his people with vested interests and illusionary ideals. This disgusting story, told, by his father in reply to Willie's question, creates contempt in the heart of son who is destined to bear the burden of this cursed ancestry on him. Being a half Brahmin he cannot relate fully to the low caste and being a low caste mother's son he is not complete and whole-heartedly acceptable in Brahmin community. This halfness of Willie's identity leads him to reject his roots and to make desperate attempts to create a new image of selfhood for which he travels all around. Willie hopes to reverse the tradition when he decides to go outside the periphery of his ancestral establishment for searching a meaningful identity away from conservative mould of his parental existence. Willie's hatred for his parents goes deep in his psyche and is apparent in his reluctance to show this composition to his father. The realization comes to the father thus; "But I have him nothing. He is not me. He is his mother's son."[3] Willie's story is set up in post-independent India, then in London and then he travels to a pre-independence African country which is closely modeled on Mozambique and then for a brief period appears in Berlin.

In London for a while Willie is lost, the education that he was getting was absolutely devoid of perspectives. He pursues everything half-heartedly:

> The learning he was being given was like the food he was eating, without savor. The two were inseparable in his mind. And just as he ate without pleasure, so with a kind of blindness, he did what the lecturers and tutors asked of him, real the books and articles and did the essay. He was unanchored, with no idea of what lay ahead.[4]

In the process of settling down in the London life, Willie comes close to a few people, each of whom is leading a half life in their own way. There is Percy Cato who was "a Jamaican of mixed Parentage and was more brown than black."[5] Percy Cato is in many ways like Willie. He is ashamed of his background and instead of presenting facts about life, like Willie, he believes in presenting fiction. He tells Willie that his father went to Panama as clerk when Willie understands he is lying: "That's a foolish story. His father went there as a labourer. He would have been in one of the gangs, holding his pickaxe before him on the ground, like the other, and looking obediently at the photographer."[6]

The bohemian culture of Notting Hill is alien for Willie but not being able to define his own culture. Just a week or so later, he was glad he hadn't said anything. Percy took Willie to a party in Notting Hill. There he recognized that the girl, Willie sleeps with is not his friend and lover but the lover of his friend because June shows no objection in having sex with Percy. By this Willie also was learning the English life. In the fluidity of existence in London, Willie is drawn to the 'bohemian' immigrant community of the post-war city, its dingy West-End clubs, lonely Pavements and odd sexual escapades. Floating in the bottomless sea of Multiculturalism, Willie comes to realise the gruesome consequences of his distance and freedom from his tradition. For the purpose of gaining a new image he has lost his old face and now floats in uncertainty with no hope at revival. It is not only Willie, almost all the expatriates are in the miserable predicament of no entity, uncertainly and alienation. In London, Willie seems to have found his ground for a while when, all of a sudden, he comes to a reconciliation and realization that he did not need to rebel for the simple reason that distance from his root socio-cultural background has left him unanchored and in a state of unbridles freedom. In search of his identity in this strange world Willie adopts the defence mechanism of projecting a borrowed, make-believe identity and ventures to live with this superficial image once again:

> .... He adopted certain things he had read and spoke of his mother as belonging to an ancient Christian Community of the subcontinent, a Community almost as old as Christianity itself. He kept his father as a Brahmin. He made his father's father a 'courtier': So playing with words, he began to remake himself. It excited him and began to give him a feeling of power.[7]

While making his efforts to settle in London, Willie realizes that there are numerous immigrants there leading a bohemian life in the limbo in their own eccentric ways. When Willie takes these immigrants close to his heart and hopes for some emotional support, they shrink away giving only a few words of formality. The Plight of helplessness and lack of belongingness causes more pain and fear Psychosis to Willie than his real half-life identity. Willie, who had not forgiven his father even in stories, now, realizes that life after all, was not easy for his father also. On being disillusioned with a bohemian life in limbo, Willie earns wisdom as he speaks: "I misjudged my father. I used think that he world was easy for him as a Brahmin and that he became a fraud out of idleness. Now, I began to understand how hard the world must have been for him."[8] This rediscovered shadow of his father figure, now keeps haunting Willie, in all the weak as well as strong moments of his life hereafter. He is split within himself and is in a dilemma of internal conflict in his bid to achieve assimilation or acculturation which is the only option left to the alienated immigrants in the alien society where he or she is merely a marginalized vagrant. Sexual Promiscuity is witnessed in the Third world immigrants living in the liberal Western world as an existential activity with no sense of permanence and the inhibitions and taboos of the Parochial society have no reason to survive at all. His repeated sexual failures make him realize that his mind can't get pleasure until and unless he re-establishes his affinity with his father whom he misses every minute now. He realizes: "Where my father told me his life story and talked about his sexual impotence. I mocked him. I was a child then. I discover I am like my poor father."[9]

Another important factor in the diasporic existence is that the language is the power of expression and life is meaningful unless it is experienced and comprehended appropriately. Naipaul seems to convey that displacement brings the dispossession of the language power and thus aggravates the sense of alienation. The immigrant is always at a disadvantage in the foreign land and his escape depends on the degree of his adoptability to those aspects which are essentially alien to him. None but Naipaul could understand the agony of losing one's culture and language and in case of Willie the loss of proper language is ironically painful since he is emerging as a writer. On the publication of his first book Willie is introduced as "a subversive new voice from the subcontinent."[10] With his remigration to African country Willie's voice itself becomes a victim to the despotic forces. While travelling to Ana's African country from Southampton Willie's mind is occupied by the confusion that are caused by such frequent changes in the setting. The Novelist writes: "Willie was trying to deal with the knowledge that had come to him on the ship that his home language had almost gone, that English was going, that he had no proper language, no gift of expression."[11]

Even his relationship with Ana is based on the similarity of their predicament in alien surrounding. While hunting desperately for wholeness authenticity in life, Willie discover a kind of reciprocity in Ana and the halfness in both the expatriates strikes a bond and mutual attraction with a hope of finding completeness through entering into a merger on physical level. Strangely enough, the halfness of Ana makes him forget his own lacking and though temporarily, her company strengthens and allows him to push back the shadow of inadequacy which otherwise looms large in his life. The third person narrator remarks thus: "As and what was most intoxicating for while was that for the first time in his life he felt himself in the presence of someone who accepted him completely. At home his life had been ruled by his mixed inheritance. It spoilt everything. Even the love he felt for his mother, which should have been pure, was full of the pain he felt for their circumstances."[12]

Willie goes with Ana to the African country with all expectations to belong there but it is ironical that his fate becomes more than worst, in it floats his existence. Though the description of the land is modeled on Mozambique, Naipaul maintains the anonymity to intensify the sense of limbo in the existential predicament of the Protagonist. Walking in the streets of the town he feels that he is "Walking as if in Wilderness" [*HAL* 134]. Willie becomes a 'Nowhere man' and reflects on his loss of belongingness: "I don't know where I am. I don't think I can pick up my way back. I don't ever want this view to become familiar. I must not unpack. I must never behave as though I am staying."[13]

The novel ends at the moment of Willie's decision to leave Mozambique. He is in his early forties: thus 'half-a-life'? But Naipaul means his title more blackly too, Willie has lived only half-a-life because, of mixed Parentage himself, he is only "*half-and-half*".[14] Willie chooses to spend most of his life in colonial Mozambique, a half-and-half society. More deeply, Willie is half a man because his father's baleful shadow has cut across his life, scything it in two. Nationally free to make himself a new, Willie finds that in truth he is doomed to repeat the sacrificial frigidity of his father's life. Nationally free of the artifice of coast and race, he is in fact as imprisoned by it as his father, with the difference that at least his father chose to imprison himself when he married his 'backward' wife, where Willie never asked for his imprisonment.

In his efforts to wipe away the stigma of his historical past inferiority, Willie goes in the wilderness of double exile and procures nothing except a more painful status of being in the fluidity of existence and lack of recognition as an individual. He has faced an agonizing trauma of deracination and marginalization just like so many other uprooted people of mixed race and un-pedigreed class. The loss of identity, sense of alienation and exile is the lot of mixed crossbreed, un-pedigreed class. Another stigma of being a second rate citizen keeps Willie prepossessed like the Albatross in *The Ancient Mariner* around the Ancient Mariner's neck. The mariner however got respite due to the slimy creature in the sea. Willie gets temporary relief due to some slippery substance which awakes him to the futility of all his efforts in a half-made society. In Africa, Willie slowly and gradually finds some solace in the realization that he is not the only one bearing the burden of Albatross, there are many like him who are infested with a sense of double exile. He discovers that he is in a half-and-half word with half-and-half friends who had reconciled themselves to their position as "people of the second rank". Willie is apparently lacking in confidence, worldly wisdom and virility. He is a sort of unheroic hero, constantly in search of a new safe guard to lengthen his shadow. Naipaul interfuses the story of king Cophetua of Africa, who fell in love with a beggar maid and married her.

Thus, V.S. Naipaul's *Half a Life* shows a surpassing emotional conflict, an agony of separation and pathos of yearning for what is lost; a futile search for El Dorado which leads nowhere. Whereas 'The Enigma of Arrival' picturizes Naipaul's own conflict, crisis and his ultimate growth as a writer, *Half a Life* must be judged as 'coming of age and wisdom to Naipaul's progressive hero figure who is desperate to carve a new respectable image in the mirror of time in limbo. This self-realization of the Protagonists in his successive novels leads us to conclude that Naipaul's fiction may be having a continuity in their progressive dramatization of the immigrants' quest for selfhood in alien existence.

Naipaul describes Willie's alienation disorientation and emptiness in the ruined and dying colony of Africa. Willie narrates his African experience in a brooding before his sister believing that there was something in the African heart beyond everybody and everything. He realises how all through the years "Africa released him into sensuality" as prior to this he had led a half life in his submission to sensual desire, to confusion of caste in India and to class in England. Willie's experience and realization of halfness in life are reflected in his transcontinental migration and multidimensional socio-cultural environment. Willie leads half-a-life through his pilgrim's progress into the another world of love in order to achieve a fullness of life. Drawing the reader's attention into the depth of the story of the novel, Naipaul describes Willie's journey to find out a place for himself in the world and his dilemma is that of a man who had to leave his background and find something else:

> *Half a Life* reads as a study in estrangement and inner exile [...]. In this strange, languor often painful new novel it is not the Africans, but the settlers whose lines seem most incomplete, who are themselves. It is they who are the true Canadian grotesques, wandering restlessly without home her hope.[15]

The crises and predicaments of the heroes of Naipaul's fictional world picturise the different stages of this epical search of the expatriates in the alien surroundings. Naipaul's confessional statement in an interview with Ronald Bryden in 1973 justifies this notion as he has proclaimed: "All my work is really one work. I'm really writing one big book."[16]

All the major protagonists of Naipaul's novels suffer the tragedy of displacement, disintegration and separation from their land and Naipaul seems to share vicariously this predicament of his struggling heroes. The first-hand experience of this novelist expresses his own enigma and heroic exploit to carve an authentic identity and to shape a relentlessly truthful writer in the same ambiance. *Half a Life* is apparently a story of Willies Chandran's quest for identity and it thus presents the problem of immigrants, the loss of identity and subsequent search for identity and the struggle for existence that mulattoes undergo.

NOTES

1. V.S. Naipaul, *Half a Life*, Penguin Books, Harmondsworth, 2001, 19.
2. *Ibid.*, 41.
3. *Ibid.*, 58.
4. *Ibid.*, 61.
5. *Ibid.*, 62.
6. *Ibid.*, 61.
7. *Ibid.*, 58.
8. *Ibid.*, 118.
9. *Ibid.*, 122.
10. *Ibid.*, 132.
11. *Ibid.*, 125.
12. *Ibid.*, 135.
13. James Wood, *Half a Life*: V.S. Naipaul, Damage, pp. $24.
14. Dr. Permanand Jha, "*Exile, Alienation and Cultural Tradition: V.S. Naipaul's Half a Life*," Souvenir: All India English Teachers' Conference, 24-26 January 2002, Dept. of English, Govt. Girls' P.G. Autonomous college Bilaspur [C.G.], 3.
15. Interview by Bryden Ronald, "The Novelist V.S. Naipaul About His Work," *Listener*, 89 [March 22, 1973], 367.
16. *Ibid.*, 369.

18

Depiction of Nature in Kiran Desai's Novel: *The Inheritance of Loss*

Mirza Sibtain Beg

Kiran Desai's *The Inheritance of Loss* is a terrific novel that addresses myriad contemporary national and international issues—alienation, cultural confrontation, exploitation, displacement, exile, fundamentalism, globalization, economic disparity, insurgency, hybridity, immigration, loneliness, multiculturalism, loss of identity and search for belongingness, She exploits the technique of social realism which adds richness and variety to the diasporic panorama in the new era. Suketu Mehta opines, "Inheritance of Loss is vast in scope, from the peaks of Himalayas to the immigrant quarters of New York; the gripping stories of people buffeted by winds of history, personal and political." Gary Shteyngart rates her novel, "If god is in the details, Ms. Desai has written a holy book. Page after page, from Harlem to the Himalayas, she captures the terror and exhilaration of being alive in this world." The novel pre-eminently explores post-colonial chaos and despair in Kalimpong and Manhattan. It also dwells upon the plight of Asian immigrants in the west and the Gorkha insurgency spearheaded by Gorkha National Front in 1980's of Kalimpong near Darjeeling. Amidst All Indian English novelists Kiran Desai is conspicuous for her sensitive use of nature in her novel *The Inheritance of Loss*. She had the poet's eye for minuteness of observation and imagination to go beyond and behind the façade that nature presented to her in a lifetime of creative effort. Nature has been constant force and dominant presence in her novel. The exposition of novel's setting, characters and scintillating portrayal of beauties and bounties of nature she sprinkles metaphors in the lap of mountains, its peaks, in shadows and around. The novel spellbinds us from beginning till the end. The novel opens with stellar description of nature and culminates in the same vein:

> The colors had been those of dusk, mist moving like a water creature across the great flanks of mountains possessed of ocean shadows and depths. Briefly visible above the vapor, Kanchenjunga was a far peak whittled out of ice, gathering the last of the light, a plume of snow blown high by the storms at its summit. (1)

The novel ends bequeathing freshness of thought and charming metaphors:

> The five peaks of Kanchenjunga turned golden light that made you feel, if briefly, that truth was apparent, all you need to do was to reach out and pluck it. (324)

The story begins with Jemubhai Popatlal Patel born at Piphit in Gujrat, sets off his journey to Cambridge to get higher education. He happens to be the first of the orthodox Patel family who goes abroad to become an I.C.S. In England, he receives ill treatment because of race and ethnicity. The color of the skin, awful different accent and stickness to native culture renders him an alien among the English. He runs from pillar to post to have dwelling and is denied home because of his different culture. Eventually the financial need of a house owner Mrs. Rice fetches him a room. When Jemubhai starts his journey for England, his father comes to see him off with tears in eyes. He observes:

> The ship moved, the water split and spilled, flying fish exploded silver above the unravelment, Tom Collinses were passed around, and the party reached a crescendo. The crowd on the shore became flotsam churning at the tide's hem: scallops and starbursts, petticoat ruffles,

> rubbishy wrappings and saliva flecks, fish tails and tears. (37)

Needless to say, Jemubhai is very studious and burns his midnight oil to achieve his goal. He, however, becomes successful and secures his admission at Fitzwilliam. The novelist gives a very graphic description of his painfully pitiable condition:

> He worked twelve hours at a stretch, late into night, and thus in withdrawing, he failed to make a courageous gesture outward at crucial moment and found, instead, that his pusillanimity and his loneliness hand found fertile soil. The solitude became a habit, the habit became the man, and it crushed him into shadow. (39)

Eventually, Jemubhai qualifies the I.C.S. examination and successfully passes the written test. Despite getting through the written examination, he is unable to clear the viva-voce examination because he becomes the victim of apartheid. He becomes nervous and almost faints down to hear that, later he regains his senses and confidence when apprised by someone that a supplementary list is in the pipeline and Indians will be dealt with leniency. Jemubhai bewilders at figuring his name at the bottom of the supplementary list. Jemu bursts into tears and goes straightaway to throw himself into bed. Desai showcases the spectacle of trauma, frustration and desperation of immigrants. He faces the identity crisis there: Europeans do not take them with esteem and consider equal. The situation is painful and pathetic for him. The humiliation and indifference he comes across there renders him rude, reticent and recluse. He is very disciplined, punctual, dedicated and strict Judge. The writer shows very accurate account of his demeanors and daily chores while he gets his first posting as a judge in Uttar Pradesh:

> 6:30: he'd bathe in water that had been heated over the fire so it was redolent with the smell of wood smoke and flecked with ash. With a dusting of powder he graced his newly washed face, with a adayb of pomade, his hair crunched up toast like charcoal from having been toasted upon the flame, with marmalade over the burn. (62)

> 8:30: he rode into the fields with the local officials and everyone else in the village going along for fun. Followed by an orderly holding an umbrella over his head to shield him from the glare, he measured the fields and checked to make sure his yield estimate matched the headman's statement. (62)
>
> 2.00: after lunch, the judge sat at his desk under a tree to try cases, usually in a cross mood, for he disliked the informality, hated the splotch of leaf shadow on him imparting an untidy mongrel look. (63)
>
> 5:30: out he went into the countryside with his fishing rod or gun. The countryside was full of game; lariats of migratory birds lassoed the sky in October; quail and partridge with lines of babies strung out behind whirred by like nursery that emit sound with movement; pheasant—far foolish creatures, made to be shot—went scurrying through the bushes. The thunder of gunshot rolled away, the leaves shivered, and he experienced the profound silence that could come only after violence. (62)
>
> 9:00: sipping Ovaltine, he filled out the registers with the day's gleanings. The Petromax lantern would be lit—what a noise it made—insects fording the black to dive-bomb him with soft flowers (moths), with iridescence (beetles). (63)
>
> 11.00: he had a hot water bottle in winter, and, in all seasons, to the sound of the wind buffering the trees and the cook's snoring, he fell asleep. (63)

After serving for many years an illustrious service, Jemubhai retires and settles in a crumbled house Cho Oyu in Kalimpong high in the north eastern Himalayas with a Nepali cook, Panna Lal, and his pet Mutt. Jemubhai has only granddaughter, Sai who is an orphan and has lost parents in an accident in Russia. Jemubhai is very eccentric and inamiable and has very indifferent attitude towards other people, he becomes least happy when his grandchild joins him. Sai is amorously attached to her tutor, Gyan, who is scion of martyred Nepali Gorkha mercenary, but later he comes out of romantic liaison with Sai, sacrifices love at the altar of some noble cause and joins Gorkha National Liberation Front and leaves Sai in the lurch.

Significantly, the description of nature and beautiful landscapes finds a good space in the novel. Himalaya's panoramic beauty, Kalimpong's wild rocks, Darjeeling's natural landscapes symbolically present the pinnacle of her vision. When Sai sets off her journey from Dehradun to join his grandfather at Cho Oyu at Kalimpong, she along with her nun enjoys pristine beauty of nature peeping out of window of the train. They feel enthralled to see Teesta river leaping between white banks of sand, sun trashing through the window, reflections magnifying and echoing the light, each adding angles and colors to the other. Sai is thrilled to sense the beauty of Cho Oyu and its surroundings when she arrives at the mansion. She becomes spellbound and dazzled:

> Kanchenjunga glowed, macabre trees stretched away on either side, trunks pale, leaves black, and beyond, between the pillars of the trees, a path led to the house. (19)

When judge had purchased the mansion Cho Oyu from a scot man, he was apprised that the land had potential-quinine, sericulture, cardamom and orchids.

The judge felt he was entering a sensibility rather than a house:

> The floor was dark, almost black, wide planked; the ceiling resembled the rib cage of a whale, marks of an axe still in the timber. A fireplace made of silvery river stone sparkled like sand. Lush ferns butted into the windows, stiff seams of foliage felted with spores, curly nubs pelted with bronze fuzz...outside, passionately colored birds swooped and whistled, and the Himalayas rose layer upon layer until those gleaming peaks proved a man to be so small that it made sense to give it all up, empty it all out. (29)

Sai comes close to her tutor Gyan while taking tuitions. Both fall in love with each other after some encounters. Kiran Desai has showed their blossoming romance with deep imaginative insight. They hug each other in rain and measure ears, shoulders and the span of their rib cages. Their love blooms as they spend time together in the romantic beautiful valleys of Himalaya. They do not feel time fleeting while playing the game of courtship, reaching, recreating, teasing and poking fun with each other. Desai's description of their romance is immaculate and goes erotic:

> "kiss me!" He pleaded.
> "No" she said, delighted and terrified.
> She would hold herself ransom.
> Oh, but she had never been able stand suspense.
> A fine drizzle spelled an ellipsis on the tin roof....
> Moments clocked by precisely, and she couldn't hear it—she closed her eyes and felt the terrified measure of his lips on hers, trying to match one shape with the other. (125)

Gyan tells her that he along with other Nepali-Indians is bereft of basic amenities by the government and cites the reasons for his resolve to join Gorkha Liberation Front and fight for their rights. The army cantonment area is shown as:

> The big rocks along thin paths that veined the mountains, the trunks of trees amid huts made of bamboo and mud, corn drying in bunches under the veranda roofs, prayer flags flying overhead, pigs snorting in pens behind. Climbing perpendicular to the sky, arriving breathless at the top of Ring king pong hill. (126)

Gyan accompanying her goes on excursion to Mong Pong, they enjoy the beauty of Teesta Delo lake. They finally reach a very fascinating spot Durpin Dara, Sai is so much overjoyed to behold the natural panorama. When Gyan stops giving tuitions to Sai, for he has joined GNLF and unlikely to return, she sets out in search of Gyan and passes of the fields, she is dazzled to see beauty of the landscape. When she arrives at Gyan's house, she becomes titillated and spellbound to see the marigolds and other flowers. Not able to meet Gyan, Sai is lost in her thoughts. The writer gives considerably a very beautiful account of her pensiveness:

> She walked home very slowly, sick. The mist was thickening, smoke adding to the dusk, and the vapor. The smell of potatoes cooking came from *basti* houses all along the way, a smell that would surely connote comfort to souls across the world, but that couldn't comfort her. She felt none of the pity she'd felt earlier while contemplating this scene; even peasants could have love and happiness, but not her, not her.... (263)

Needless to say, after Gyan's joining the GNLF, Sai is left stranded and unprovided for. Jemubhai ropes in Noni to teach Sai, Maths and Physics. Mon Ami is a magnificent dwelling of Lola and Noni who are sisters. Lola is a widow and has a very lovely daughter, Pixie who is a B.B.C. correspondent. These characters show redundant anachronism in postcolonial India. The novelist exhibits colonial neurosis and simultaneously, she keeps rejuvenating our body and soul by soul stirring description of the natural sights. The description of the garden of the house of Lola is very enchanting and allures the sensitive reader:

> The caterpillars were mottled green and white, with fake blue eye ridiculous fatty, a tail, and an elephant nose. Magnificent creatures, she thought, studying one closely, but then she threw it to waiting bird that picked and a green stuffing squiggled out of the caterpillar like tooth-paste from a punctured tube. (66)

Noni, Lola and Sai are sitting in the Mon Ami drawing room. They are delighted to behold the scenic beauty peeping through window:

> An opaque scene through the window resembled something from folk: flat gray mountain and sky, flat white row of Father Booty's cows on the crest of the hill, sky showing through their legs in squish shapes. Indoors, the lamp was on, and plate of cream horns lay in the tawny light and there were tuberoses in a vase. (128)

As we go through the novel, we come to see Desai raising riddles on post-colonialism and globalization. The judge, Sai, Pixie and others lose their identity in glamour of western culture. The author also draws our attention on the issue of multiculturalism. All her characters hail from different cultural backgrounds. She possesses a very sympathetic and respectful attitudes towards all cultures. Immigration is also a very striking problem. Most Indians face such problems and undergo humiliation in Europe and America. Biju, Saeed, Harish, Saran, Rishi, Jeev and horde of others. Biju is the son of Judge's cook, he is an immigrant in U.S. residing illegally, working for slave wagers in kitchen basement of New York city. He is struggling there for survival and identity. He faces segregation and breaks down on phone talking to his father and wishing to return. Meanwhile, Kiran Desai doesn't forget to give a very beautiful account of nature there:

> It was spring the ice was melting, the freed piss was flowing. All over, in city cafes and bistros, they took advantage of this delicate nutty Silver between the winter, cold as hell and summer, hot as hell and al-fresco on the narrow pavement under the cherry blossoms. (53)

The panoramic view of Manhattan is also very fascinating:

> The sky over Manhattan is also very messy, lots of stuff in it, branches and pigeons and choppy clouds lit with weird yellow light. The wind blow strongly and the pink pom-poms of the cherry trees in riverside park swished against the unsettled mix. (266)

After Jemubhai, it is Biju who finds special mention in the novel—his transformational journey from Kalimpong to America and his return to his native town. In America he becomes compulsive victim of ethnic and racial politics. The owner of the Italian restaurant where he gets his first job finds him smelling. However, he works at different places, but nowhere finds happiness and satisfaction; and everywhere he finds himself in the doldrums; he is overlooked, cornered and always less preferred to his European counterparts. He is very proud of his culture; but there he has to suppress this feeling. He finds his cultural identity eroded. Most of Indians living in America are subject to humiliation, forced to eat beef. He finds himself painfully unable to stop cow slaughtering in America. Biju's friend Saeed who refuses to eat pork has earned his sympathies. He reminiscences his past days spent at home and longs for to return:

> The atmosphere of Kalimpong reached Biju all the way in New York; it swelled densely on the line and he could feel the pulse of the forest, smell the humid air, the green-black lushness; he could imagine all its different textures, the plumage of banana, the stark spear of the cactus, the delicate gestures of ferns; he could hear the croak t.r.r.r.whonk, we see buttock of frogs in the spinach, the rising note welding imperceptibly with the evening.... (230)

Biju becomes nostalgic, remembers his childhood and days spent with his grandmother and beautiful landscapes:

> Fishing eagles hovered above the water, changed their horizontal glide within a single moment, plunged, rose sometimes with a thrashing muscle of silver. (103)

Over and above, we witness a complex relationship between her vision of life and her use of nature. On the whole, we find a very subtle artistic integration in the novel. The emotional life of the characters is often reverberated in natural scenes. The entire design aligns with the plot of the human drama. The descriptions are shown with immaculate intensity, sensitiveness and deep imaginative insight. The crusty judge an agnostic, always spurned his family prayers, crestfallen after the death of his wife, Nimi Patel, has now found tryst with solitude. He bawls, frowns and frets all the time. Kiran Desai compares his pensiveness to the serenity, calmness and stillness of nature:

> His pusillanimity and his loneliness had found fertile soil. He retreated into a solitude that grew in weight day by day. The solitude became a habit, the habit became the man and it crushed him into a shadow. (39)

Like Wordsworth, she instinctively unites nature and man, making the external settings a kind of sharer in the human fate. She is of the opinion that the best life is spent in undemanding harmony with the biological and geographical environment. In the case of Kiran Desai, there seems to be a passionate intuition—that the natural world is the source and repository of all the energies that control human experience.

Kiran Desai's portrayal of nature is on a vast canvas, all encompassing, and it is all done with great sympathy and imaginative insight. She is conscious not only of space but also of time. Her descriptions with the dimension of symbolic meaning are obviously having philosophical overtones. She has employed similes and metaphors elegantly in her entire novel. Watchman's wife's saying "Kangchenjunga smoking like volcano or a cigar" (23), and when Sai searches pet Mutt, her reaction "the falling lanterns of drunk plummeted like shooting stars" (289), Sai's account of Padamasambhava "with his wrathful smile ensconced in a curly mustache, his carmine cloak, diamond lotus hat vulture feature" (141), portrayal of Sai "ear lobes downy as tobacco leaves, the tender substance of her hair" (125), Biju's recalling of past days spent together with grandmother "fishing eagles hovered above the water, changed their horizontal glide within a single moment, plunged, rose sometimes with a thrashing muscle of silver" (103) are the examples, reflective of her command on language and craft of fiction. There are some other examples which testifies that she wields her facile pen with poetic heart as cook's appraisal of sales girl "a glimpse through the nightie placket of breasts so buttery that even woman who saw them were captivated" (86), Sayeed's saying "memories are like diamonds", uncle Poty's comment "dreadful legs those English girls have" (46), Sai's appraisal of grandfather "more lizard than human" and of dog Mutt "more human than dog" (32); and judge's saying "elderly ladies even the hapless blue-haired, spotted faces like collapsing pumpkins" (39).

Thus, we may say that Kiran Desai has proffered us the panoramic view of nature conscientiously and comprehensively. She dazzles us with her dazzling description of landscapes, mist, rains, clouds, cascading rivers and rivulets, Himalaya's peaks kissing sky remarkably. Nature in her novel *The Inheritance of Loss* has many dimensions: the link with the universe, the natural life as standard against human values and civilization and the symbolic expression of inscrutable forces that rule with ironical waywardness. She transforms amazingly the Kalimpong and Manhattan landscapes into a scene of vastness and echo, and she also lends it an aura of contemplativeness by virtue of coloring it with subdued tints and shadows.

WORKS CITED

Desai, Kiran. *The Inheritance of Loss*. New Delhi: Penguin Books, 2006. (All subsequent references are to this edition).

Mehta, Suketu. Quoted from the blurb of the book *The Inheritance of Loss*, The author of *The Maximum City.*

Shteyngart, Gary. Quoted from the blurb of the book *The Inheritance of Loss*, the author of *The Russian Debutante's Handbook*.

19

Diasporic Responses in the Poetry of A.K. Ramanujan

Charu Mehrotra

Diaspora is a word that signifies people of a certain racial origin that inhabit different areas and territories across that world. There heredity is rooted in a certain civilization, Indian diaspora is the case of those who are referred here though their environment differs in accordance with their chosen country of residence. This dichotomy of heredity and environment breeds in the diasporic mind, a kind of schizophrenia, a confusion of identity. This identify crisis has earned for the Indian Diaspora in America the mocking sobriquet—ABCD'S-American Born Confused Desis.

The most persistent emotion in the diasporic mind is that of nostalgia, sweet memories of a lost paradise. However, with the passage of time, nostalgia is tempered with reality. Any member of Indian Diaspora, when he revisits India, is shocked by the scene of squalor, poverty, corruption and superstition that pock mark the contemporary Indian society. The Paradisal India of his dream is juxtaposed with the internal Indian reality and the resultant culture-shock leaves an indelible impression on the diasporic mind. If the member of the diaspora happens to be a literate, his work echoes his identity crisis, cultural confusion and schizophrenia.

Undoubtedly, A.K. Ramanujan was an expatriate but the urge to protect, preserve and express a characteristic Indian sensibility remained alive in him. His poetry reflects a curious blend of irony and nostalgia. In fact, the prominent themes that we discern in many of his poems, such as "Obituary", "Love, poems for a Life: I & II", "Small-Scale Reflection On a Great House", "Of Mothers Among Other Things", "History" and "Looking For A Cousin On A Swing" are some Indian memories seen through the prism of rationalism. Despite his long stay abroad, his poems are scented with nostalgic memories of his family, but an ironic stance overhangs these recollections.

His poetry in true diasporic way, is written in contemporary spoken English, there is no attempt to impose a false sense of antiquity by finding quaint or outdated expressions. He rather incorporates modern scientific jargon and computers to give his poetry a-post-modern look. Secondly and more importantly, he does not make any efforts to imitate western poetic rhythms and prosody but seeks inspiration from classical Tamil and Kannada poets to bring a typical Indian resonance to his poems.

In the poem "Extended Family" though the poet has juxtaposed the sets of value-posited objects, his return from the peripheral perambulation to the centre of his self, rooted in his nature soil is obvious. In Ramanujan's case his past never forsakes him whether it is the individual past or historical past or cultural past. It has rather imparted richness of understanding and the texture of impression, expression to his writings. In Ramanujan's case the evocation of past is constantly associated with the social documentation of the Hindu joint or extended family in rural settling while comparing his family members and his nature cultures, Ramanujan confesses of sharing his father's attributes in a typically jocular vein, he refers to the naked bathing of his grandfather that enables him to rediscover himself in relation to other:

> Yet like grandfather
> I bath before the village crow,
> The dry chlorine water
> My only Ganges,
> The naked Chicago bulb
> A cousin of the Vedic sun (*CP*, 169) (Emphasis added)

In spite of realizing the unsophisticatedness of this way of talking both Ramanujan follows it in Chicago apartments—"slap soap on my back/like father/and think/in proverbs" (169). While his father chanted hymns and shlokas during his bath, Ramanujan is content to think of proverbs. The following lines of the poem distinguish their habits brilliantly:

> Like him
> I wipe myself dry
> With an unwashed
> Sears Turkish towel (*CP*, 169) (Emphasis added)

The son in Ramanujan's poetry, as we see mostly in India, in his usual way continues his father's old habits as discerned in his similar manner of slapping soap on his back and drying himself with an unwashed towel. However, the elements of irony, at the same time, cannot be ignored as the poet mourns that even if he bathes like his grandfather, he does not realize the sanctimony of the bath in the dry chlorine water, as the holy Ganges water is absent. Thus, in poem after poem Ramanujan ironically whirls back to the memory of his native land, of his family and of his native culture. It is the impact of Industrialization and urbanization that turns the extended family of multi-generational type into nuclear family and Ramanujan's ironic reflection on his a nuclear family, and also the extended family are quite evident as he transacts with the past. It is the rootedness in his own culture and tradition and the relatedness to his own family and people that gives a sort of emotional stability to Ramanujan and enables him to connect with an alien world. In spite of being an expatriate, he never allows his western work-orientedness subordinate his native sensibility as well as his native relationships. In fact, we get a unique representation of a typical Indian joint family in his poem: In order to overcome his rootlessness and in order to recover the sense of belonging, Ramanujan explains his extended connection to Indian past in his poetry. Indeed the recollections of Indian society have brought tranquillity to a native heart that makes connections with alien veins, beat/ and learn to miss a beat/ in a foreign body.

The most remarkable feature of A.K. Ramanujan's poetry is his firm adherence to his cultural roots. Even when living like an expatriate, he never is an exile dangling rootless like an outsider belonging nowhere. His Hindu sanskaras forever guide his sentiments and sensibility. Even though often he refers to his past in an ironic, even satiric, way he does not blindly adulate Indian culture but always look at life with the peculiar Hindu quality of detachment D. Ramkrishna comments:

He (Ramanujan) is different from the expatriates like an exotic. Ramanujan rootedness in Indian culture and involvement with American culture has resulted in his skilful articulation of both the Indian and the western ideas with ease.[1] As a poet, linguist, folklorist, translator and literary theorist he is one of the world's foremost intellectuals. He is unique in bringing together two great cultures, having been at home in both.

Though Ramanujan had stayed for a long time in the United States, his poetic corpus strongly exhibits his warm associations with land of his birth, his memorable past, his nature customs and connectives, his way of living and modes of perception. Yet his Indian past is tempered with the western scepticism; his poetry a confluence of Indian culture and Anglo-American aesthetics. And this is what we call his diasporic Indianness. His Indianness is a mean with which he regulates his behaviour, attitudes and values. It is quite satisfactory to note that Ramanujan has naturalized the Indian theme more than the western ones and it is the indianness irresistability charms us all. He has frequently made use of peculiar diasporic sensibility in all the four volumes of his poetry: *The Stridens* (1966), *Relation* (1971), *Second Sight* (1986) and *The Black Hen* (1955). In all these volumes, Ramanujan has exploited the native themes in ample measures. They deal particularly with his native environment, with his family and relations with the hindu myths and legends but his mode is ironical.

Ramanujan's identity develops from a specific Indian culture. It is this specificity of a cultural identity that often contributes to the development of a recalcitrant personality. This is why, Ramanujan's use of myths, legends and tales from

Indian affirms his instinctive access to the rich cultural heritage of India. By invoking such myths and legends, Ramanujan is not only able to ascertain their contemporary relevance but also to perpetuate a link between the past and the present. His poems illustrate Ramanujan's unique and sharp Indian diasporic sensibility as well as his perceptive critical approach to Indian society. Ramanujan's experience in his entire people corpus centres round his native land, its myths and legends, its family life, its society. His articulation of Indian ethos is really superb indeed. Ramanujan has interpreted very well the soul of India to the western world.

Living for long in the United States Ramanujan created significant poetry on his native culture and tradition. His nostalgic reflection on the land of his birth and its people remind us of R. Parthasarathy's observation in his exile:

> There is something to be said for exile.
> You learn roots are deep.[2]

In this connection it has to be said that memory plays a vital role in his poetry. It provides the poet with an emotional base for his poetic creativity. Ramanujan's poetic creation do not aim at presenting an exotic Hindu India in an alien environment but they offer a true homage to his Indian heritage. Further if we have a cursory glance at Ramanujan's life and poetical works, we shall regard him as a genuine poet and consummate translator. To quote A.N. Dwivedi in this connection:

> In his poetry confirms his position as a genuine (an attribute that he won during his own life time), his translation brings him out as a mighty interpreter of the soul of the India to the west. On both counts he has contributed his best.[3]

A.K. Ramanujan's poetry truly reflects the complexities of the diasporic responses to the multifaceted experience of the Indian people. Various themes of his poetry-nature, love, man, heritage, myth, legend, etc., on the one hand, and mysticism, metaphysical longing spirituality, philosophic concerns on the other are seen through the prism of exile. It is glorious to note that among the poets writing in English A.K. Ramanujan stands out as a unique figure for his substantial use of Indian myth and legends in his poetry. Being an expatriate with a sense of commitment Ramanujan is deeply rooted in the native ethos and tradition. He has aptly succeeded in amalgamating the critical rational outlook of the West with the rich cultural and spiritual heritage of the East. In spite of his long stay in United States, his poems are remarkable for his warm association with the East. Some factors like the religiosity of his family members, their solid groundings in Hindu mythology and the superb command over Sanskrit language and literature have contributed much to the left and handling of his charming poetry. One can easily confront numerous Hindu gods and goddesses, customs and rituals in his poem. In fact, he has brilliantly and poetically fused the experience of the outer world with the responses of the inner world.

In fact, it is his aliveness to India scene that constitutes the essence of his definition of Indianness, and through his authoritative treatment of Indology. Ramanujan has succeeded in telling the world what is truly Oriental about India.

Thus the native element as well as his personal experiences as an expatriate have sleeked into his poetry originally written in English. In fact, it is an intense awareness of alienation and a feeling for a nostalgic leap into the past, which awaken sharply the native sensibility in him more than it does in other Indian English poets.

Ramanujan's poetry centres on a variety of themes; for instance delicate family relations, Indian myths and legends, Hindu gods and goddesses and the mechanical routine of urban life are some of the prominent themes in his poetry. A close reading of Ramanujan's poetry convinces on that his vision of life, by and large, is coloured by his Hindu consciousness. Various ancient myths and legends of Hindu religion shape in his mind and to a large extent determine his attitude to life. His attempt to assimilate ancient Hindu tradition to English becomes successful as he brings myths, legends, into the texture of his poetry. By making superb use of folklore as themes in his poetry, Ramanujan has revived old forgotten myths in his poetry and made the modern generation aware of their ancient culture. In this respect his poetry very aptly confirms to the norm of post-colonial literature as he has successfully converted his expatriate condition and post-colonial situation to his advantage and brought the image of Indian alive in his poetry.

NOTES

1. D. Ramakrishna, "Ramanujan's Credo", *Millennium Perspectives on A.K. Ramanujan*, ed. Surya Nath Pandey (Delhi: Atlantic, 2001): 1 (emphasis added).
2. Premila Paul, "Roots That Roam", 115.
3. A.N. Dwivedi, "The Poetic Art of A.K. Ramanujan" (Delhi: B.R. Pub., 1995): 11.
4. *The Collected Poems of A.K. Ramanujan* (CP) Oxford University Press, New Delhi, India, 1995.

Note: Page numbers are given after every quotation.

20

Midnight's Children: Tale of a Split Self in Quest of Wholeness and an Identity

Suman Chauhan

Salman Rushdie remains a major Indian writer in English. His birth coincides with the birth of a new modern nation on August 15, 1947. He has been justly labeled by the critics as a post-colonial writer who knows his trade well. His second novel *Midnight's Children* was published in 1981 and it raised a storm in the hitherto middle class world of fiction writing both in English and in vernaculars. While the great masters of India in the English Writing, Raja Rao and R.K. Narayan tried to uphold in their fiction the mainstream politics and purity of Brahmanical order, Rushdie for the first time burst into the world of fiction with subversive themes like impurity, illegitimacy, plurality and hybridity. He understands that a civilization called India exists at many levels and that the vast landscape called India may be profitably understood as a dream, a college of many colours, a blending of cultures and nationalities, a pluralistic society and in no way unitary. In his epical novel *Midnight's Children*, he speaks of many Indians and many versions of reality. High seriousness of the elderly writers, in his fiction is replaced by playfulness, comicality and trivialization. *Midnight's Children* remains an Indian novel in the sense that the author delves deep into Indian psyche. The urge for the largeness, bigness exemplifies one typical Indian mindset, a desire for the whole. The narrator hero of the novel *Midnight's Children*, Saleem Sinai is the proponent of this Indian mind set, and proclaims, "To understand just one life, you have to swallow the world."[1] *Midnight's Children* remains an impure text because the protagonists are of illegitimate birth and Saleem has four fathers and three mothers in a fairy-tale fashion. Though a post-modern text, the hero Saleem does not suffer from alienation, nor does he feel an exile in a society of teeming millions who jostle in and around him. After Rushdie, Indian fiction is not what it was. The succeeding generation of Indian writers of fiction finds in Rushdie a guru of the post-colonial times and more and more Indian writers of English show their concern for community, nation, society and so on. It may be said, and said rightly, that with Rushdie, Indian English fiction comes of age. *Midnight's Children* remains a classic of post-colonial Indian writing, a novel of novels. "To understand just one life, you have to swallow the world"[2] (109), so observes the narrator Saleem in Salman Rushdie's epic novel *Midnight's Children* (1981). In this text, the narrator hero is philosophically obsessed with a desire, rather Indian desire, for the whole. He attempts to swallow all of India. Salman Rushdie's second novel *Midnight's Children* published in 1981 was hailed as 'Post-colonial meta-fiction, a novel about third world novels'. Saleem, the principal narrator, the most gifted of 1001 *Midnight's Children*, has been endowed with a magical power and a vision. His physical importance and deformed shape may be read as a caricature of the political map of India. In *Midnight's Children* Rushdie presents an ideological post-colonial critique of the linear, imperialist discourse of meta-history which represses rather distorts India's own account of history. India is a vast and ancient land teeming with millions of people of different races and colours. Ancient epics, myths and oral tradition inform the lives of the people even today. Entire narrative is clothed in fantasy. Myth and reality overlap boundaries. Fantasy may be seen as seriously narrating political reality when the readers are the author share certain views. Saleem's narrative is valuable precisely because it is self-conscious and invites judgment and criticism. *Midnight's Children* portrays the delirious joy of people which accompanies the formal dissolution of the empire and birth of Indian nation-state at the precise hour of the midnight in 1947 when Mountbatten hands over power to Nehru, the first Prime Minister.

Classified as a "Picaresque novel," *Midnight's Children* documents the demented wanderings of a split self in quest of wholeness and an identity. It is a political elegy delineating the disappointed hopes of the self placed in a critical juncture of history. Saleem Sinai is India and India's history between 1947 and 1975 is literally written on Saleem's body. He carries India's history between dream and nightmare. The several strata of the novel symbolise Saleem's gradual amputation and loss of freedom, sanity and individuality. *Midnight's Children* becomes a symbol of man's fundamental human conditions, that of the alienation of the self. Saleem Sinai, the narrator-protagonist defines himself by identifying his lot with the fate of his country. Born at midnight on August 15, 1947, the date on which India emerged as an independent state, Saleem from birth has greatness prophesied for him because of this nexus. He discovers that he is not the centre of India's history but only a small and an insignificant factor in larger forces of history. A native alien and a hopeless and helpless victim of history, he leads a life of anguish and isolation. Saleem seeks to resolve his agonizing problems of identity by withdrawing himself into the realm of fantasy. After news of my grandfather's death and the arrival of Reverend Mother in Pakistan, I began to dream repeatedly of Kashmir, although I had never walked in Shalimar Bagh, I did so at night; I floated in Shikaras and climbed Sankara Acharya's hill as my grandfather had.

Saleem sees the isolated facts of history only as they relate to him as an individual, only a fragment of the societal self and not to society as a whole. Rushdie himself writes in *Midnight's Children*:

> Reality is a question of Perspective; the further you get from the past, the more concrete and plausible it seems—but as you approach the present, it inevitably seems more and more incredible.[3]

Saleem Sinai sustains so many simultaneous identities. He is by turns defiant, modest strident subtle, fatalistic, recalcitrant, fastidious, baddy, flippant and solemn but seldom composed and never in tune with his inner self. Ashutosh Banerjee observes: "Now Saleem is maddening, keeping his interlocutrix Padma, on the tenterhooks, being dilatory in revealing his parentage. And again he is pouring a long narrative out all at one at one go in breathless haste in large paragraphs without any full stops."[4] Saleem the narrator protagonist himself, whose concentre is a part of the societal centre dispersed to many individuals in a collective. Everything leaks into everything else in *Midnight's Children* and more things have to be portrayed, because a human being, inside himself, is anything but a whole, anything but homogenous, all kinds of everything are jumbled up inside him, and he is one person one minute and another the next.

Rushdie does not see a human being as "a unified whole" but as a fragment of his spatio-temporal existence. Saleem is a part of history reduced to this partitioned state by the Indo-Pak war of 1985. He and his family are restate fragments and almost ruined by this war. Saleem's family and its historical past have ceased to exist as tangible and perceptible objects. They have simply been reduced to figments of his memory, rather his fancy, by the devastating war. He sees himself schizophrenically, in both the first and third person. Hence, the reality of the character as a "unified whole" and "a separate entity" is married. The unities of time and place are not uniformly adhered to throughout the novel. The wavering and shaky nature of Saleem's chimes with the unstable and sloppy narrative technique of the novel. Saleem adopts various narrative modes to convey experience. He is yet to attain adequacy and wholeness, stability and equipoise. Saleem, the self-conscious narrator, oscillates between the past and the present, the historical and the personal, the apocalyptic and the expensive. He has no stable identity but he assumes many identities. Throughout the novel, Saleem inner life is a function of the historical forces affecting his state. He is, in his own mind, the latent, elusive centre of India's history. His hold upon reality comes from a view that the reality of the state is fragmented and dispersed in the consciousness of all individuals and not in the consciousness of any one individual. *Midnight's Children* belongs to the "Look-back in-anger" or "Protest" type of fiction written by one who is alienated by option or compelled expatriation haunted by "an upsurge to look back even at the risk of being mutated into pillars of salt".[5] Saleem is doomed to lead the life of a social out cast, an exile. Reduced to the fragments by forces beyond his control, he is conscious of the loss of his historical centrality which is dispersed to many individuals. Saleem's is a fragmented and frustrated quest for meaning in life.

I became afraid that everything was wrong—that my much trumpeted existence might turn out to be utterly useless, void and without the shred of a purpose.

His variegated experiences simultaneously make him "confused about being good". Alienated, he admits: "I am so far gone, in my desperate need for meaning, that I am prepared to distort everything...in my confusion I can not judge". "An unfortunate fellow with a face like a cartoon", he is fatally "gripped by some deep malaise".[6] Saleem's fragmentation of self occurs partly due to his abnormally morbid nature and partly due to his nurture and inheritance. Saleem's father was "unnerved, adrift, unmanned", and his mother became the victim of the "sprit of detached fatigue" and, eventually "feel apart".

He is fully aware of his problems and plights, misfortunes and discordances, so typical of a rootless person. At the height of self-estrangement, Saleem looks at himself as only the broken bits and fragments of his former self.

I am tearing myself apart, cannot even agree with myself talking and arguing like a wild fellow cracking up, memory going.

"Saleem Sinai", observes Kathleen Flanagan "sees himself as a part of society, not a detached mind-reader at its centre, but socio-historical forces crush him down and his private self is reduced "to speak of voiceless dust".[7] Saleem now begins to see himself as a vulnerable part of society. His struggle to tell his story and India's is an attempt to achieve self-consummation or rather to make whole his fragmentary private existence. Rushdie remarks: "Our physical alienation from India almost inevitably means that we will not be capable of reclaiming precisely the thing actual cities or villages, but invisible ones, imaginary homelands, India's of the mind."[8] O.P. Mathur maintains: "Saleem Sinai who is the embodiment of a supreme moment of history, a crystallization an evolving mood, a distillation of a vision nostalgic, critical and philosophical, is a camera eye, which is itself cracked and fragmented with, as the novelist remarks, some of its fragments missing. Saleem's "literally disintegrating" and "fissured" body from which history pours out is a possible allusion to the underlying political fragmentation and fissiparous tendencies of Indian politics, past and present, which have contributed to the making of its history. He has also portrayed the feel of those times through the fertile but rambling imagination and the fragmented but meaningful vision of an ironical narrator with a representatively multiple identity. There is something of incarceration in the personality and career of the picaresque hero Saleem Sinai but he is not away from society. Saleem's mind is the parliament of various viewpoints and hence a whole, unifying various fragment into the episode of history. He is a paradigm of an alienated human soul, "sucked into the annihilating whirlpool of the multitudes, and unable to live or die in peace".[9] He is at the centre of things instead of a victim at the periphery and he realises his centripetal role in recreating history in the phantasm of his psyche when he rhetorically question himself. "Am I so far gone, in my desperate need for meaning, that I am prepared to distort everything".[10]

Midnight's Children is an expression of the despair of Saleem Sinai, a broken self, living on the edges, in fragments. In his interview with Kumkum Sangari, Rushdie admits:

> Instead of being an insignificant dot in this multitude, Saleem Sinai actually contains the multitude. It is an aspect of him rather than he an aspect of it.[11]

In fact, Saleem has no real self-image. He exists only on the metafictional canvas of historiography. The theme of fragmentation runs throughout. Even it is perceptible in Saleem's personal appearance specially his grotesque face: Fragmentation of identity in an alien world is pursued through motifs of compartmentalization of the self pertaining to each generation Saleem's family which relegates him to the margins of history.

Nehru's famous midnight speech coined in the finest English language sounds metaphoric and ironic.

> ...years ago we made a tryst with destiny.... A moment comes, which comes but rarely when the soul of a nation long suppressed finds utterance....[12]

"India had been divided anew. But the boundaries of these states were not formed by rivers or mountains or any natural features of the terrain: they were instead wall of words. Language divided us." This epic novel was conceived in a dream about the large Indian city of Bombay, an industrial city, a city of film, and also of a young man's dream. The city as a metaphor defines the authorial self and in a way informs the novel. In his collection of essays "Imaginary Homelands", Rushdie observes, "to be a Bombayite and afterwards a Londoner was also to fall in love with the metropolis".[13] The narrative of *Midnight's Children* parodies Bombay cinema's fantasy operations.... "This melodramatic device...was a genuine kind of Bombay Talkie, B-movie nation and I thought that a book which grew out of the movie city ought to contain such nations. These are children not so much of their parents but children of time, children of history." On the realistic level, such conventions suggest the plurality of post-colonial identities. Saleem represents, the multiple and complex identities of the post-colonial Indian because he is born of British father and Hindu mother, exchanged at birth by Christian nurse and brought up by Muslim businessman as his son.

This comic-epic novel is a blend of literary genres and is coined in a mood of irony, satire and fantasy but the author has serious purpose in mind.

But in the case of Rushdie, the classic myth only explains the contemporary situation. Theroor trivializes the epical heroes in a mood of hilarity. Just a position of trivial and serious, elitism and mass culture of Bombay film. Centrally and marginality of position and vice versa, purity and hybridity of racial and national identities and post-coloniality of history are the major themes and issues which the epic novel *Midnight's Children* successfully addresses.

In short, *Midnight's Children* is the greatest novel from the pen of Rushdie. It is solidly built of facts and figures, dates and events.

NOTES

1. Salman Rushdie (ed.), "Imaginary Homelands", *Essays & Criticism*, Harmondsworth Penguin, 1981-1991.
2. Aruna Srivastava, "The Empire Writes Back: Language and History in *Midnight's Children*", *Ariel*: 20 (4) (1989): 62-78.
3. Salman Rushdie, "Interview with Salman Rushdie" by C. Pattanayak, *The Literary Criticism*, XVIII, 1983.
4. Ashutosh Banarjee, "Narrative Technique in *Midnight's Children*", *The Common Wealth Review*, Vol. 1, No. 21, 1990: 24-25.
5. Salman Rushdie, *The Indian Express*, March 11, 1984: 8.
6. Kumkum Sangari, "Interview with Salman Rushdie", *The Book Review*, March-April, 1984, Vol. 3, No. 5: 247.
7. Flanagan, Kathleen on fragmented self in *Midnight's Children,* 165.
8. This is reported by Salman Rushdie himself Introduction to the 2006, 25th Anniversary Special edition, Vintage Books, 25 December, 2006.
9. *Midnight's Children*, by Salman Rushdie, publisher Jonathan Cape, 1981, *Magic Realism*, London: 20.
10. Dr. O.P. Mathur, "Salman Rushdie's *Midnight's Children*: The Emergency as Another Midnight", 2004: 21.
11. Kumkum Sangari, "Interview with Salman Rushdie, *The Book Review*, March-April, 1984, Vol. 3, No. 5: 251.
12. *Midnight's Children*, by Salman Rushdie publisher Jonathan Cape, 1981, *Magic Realism*, London: 21.
13. "Imaginary Homelands", Salman Rushdie, 1991. Penguin Books, Australia (43).

21

A Diasporic Glance on Vikram Seth's *A Suitable Boy*

Parul Rastogi

Indian English literature has reasonably long period of growth. It began in early nineteenth century and has continued ever since, acquiring much newer and much larger dimensions. After Independence, and particularly in the last two decades of the 20th century, it got integrated with the development of "Indian Bhasha Languages" and came to be considered as one of the major Indian language/literature for all purposes. We take an example of Vikram Seth's novel *A Suitable Boy* and study it through a Diasporic glance.

A Suitable Boy is an outstanding achievement for any Indian English writer today. It is both comprehensive and compact and an able account of many forces that operate in the Indian society in the years immediately after independence and a scintillating analysis of clash of personalities, convictions and cultures. When India gained independence from Great Britain in 1947 some stalwart nationalists predicted that the imperial languages would vanish from the subcontinent. At that time only a handful of novels in English by Indians had appeared so those who foresaw the demise of this foreign language assumed that such a hybrid form will fade as well since 1947. Several Indian writers of English language fiction have gained international stature moreover, the astounding reception throughout the English speaking world to Vikram Seth's *A Suitable Boy* should help to set aside any doubts concerning the effectiveness and staying quality of English as a literary medium for Indian writers not only is *A Suitable Boy* written in a western language about an eastern culture. It is also more reminiscent of nineteenth century British fiction than to the fashionable dictates of postmodernism relating a straightforward, fairly ordinary story of four families and their acquaintances. It offers no flight of fancy, no experimentation with language no questioning of the narrator's role, or any of the other staples that characterize much contemporary internation fiction.

One of the characters in *A Suitable Boy*, who is writing a long novel, compares his book's structure to a banyan tree. "It sprouts, and grows and spreads, and drops down branches that become trunks or intertwine with other branches". That analogy applies to Seth's novel as well.[1]

The fictional tree's main trunk is the family, and its inter-winning branches consists of out side matters that affect the family in one way or another as politics or corruption, business and industry, the law, religion, enmity between hindu and muslim, and universal life.

The narrative centers on the Mehra family, headed by the widowed Mrs. Rupa Mehra who sets the plot into motion once she has successfully married her elder daughter to "A Suitable Boy" and launches a search for other such husband for her younger daughter Lata.

A Suitable Boy is both a reflection of the contemporary social nebulosity and a study attempt to probe in to that and determine now but that can be shaped and controlled. Jonathan Yardley so aptly put it as her "Three and a Half Pounds of perfection".[2] Seth views the Indian edition with pride, as marking "A watershed in Indian efforts to be part of main stream of world publishing."[3]

It was a distinctly Indian novel and is set wholly in India. The title of the book suggests that an "Indian sensibility" is at work. This term suitable boy is actively used in the Indian market of arranged marriages where the search is always on for suitable boys and girls.

The suitable boy by Vikram Seth is the story of four families in India in the early 1950's after British occupation has ended and the India/Pakistan partition has taken place. It is not an epic novel but in the usual sense of the word it is certainly epic in scale over 1400 pages in length it was published in 1993. To understand the novel, the reader must also understand to a certain extent the Indian culture of social castes and arranged marriage that is implied. A great deal of effort put forth on the part of a family to find a suitable boy for their unmarried daughters. As Indian girls gain more independence like going out shopping in small group of friends and attending university classes over the idea of an arranged marriage arguably, the central character of the novel Lata Mehra questions how a woman could marry and live with a man she could not love because she knew nothing about him.

The novel begins with the arranged marriage of Lata's sister Savita to Pran Kapoor, a young man who is Professor in Brahampur University and from a prominent family. He is therefore a suitable boy. Lata's widowed mother who made the arrangements of Savita's marriage is intent on marrying of her youngest daughter Lata with him. Although the novel is not political in nature, there is enough conflict between Hindu and the Muslim. To explain certain prejudices that Lata rushes head long as she meets and eventually falls in love with Kabir Durrani, a Muslim and a son of prominent mathematician at the university. To further complicate the plot Maan Kapoor, Pran's younger brother, become infatuated with the notorious Muslim Saeeda Bai. Lata's situation became complicated when some seen her out walking with Kabir and reports it to her mother. Mrs. Rupa Mehra thinks that Lata has ruined her reputation and no suitable boy's family will have her marry their son. When she learns that Kabir is Muslim, she hastily packs herself and Lata off to Calcutta.

The plot contains a great many political intrigues that are difficult to follow and would be uninteresting were it not for the fact that various family members are involved in the action. Begum Adeeba Khan narrowly manages to retain the family residence after a run in with L.N. Agarwal over the handling of a near riot. The mela was caused by the intention to erect a Hindu temple adjacent to a mosque which incidentally, had once been a Hindu temple. The sticking point was a phallus of Lord Shiva in the temple directly between the mosque and Mecca, towards which Muslims pray. The political maneuvering comes ahead with the passage of the zamindari abolition bill which will effectively cause large landholders to lose much of their property.

The plot continues throughout the novel centering mostly on the suitable boy theme played out in sub-plots involving Maan Kapoor and Saeeda Bai Ishaq and Tanseen and most especially Lata and Kabir and suitable boys to whom she is introduced in Calcutta. In the end, Lata resolves to give up Kabir and marry a suitable boy she likes but does not love. Aside from Lata's heart breaking decision not to marry Kabir, there is little real ugliness in the novel outside of inter and intra family intrigues which Seth somehow manages to make readers interested.

The plot complications involve human differences beginning with the religious conflicts between Hindu and Muslim Vikram Seth sets up the major conflicts in the novel with his opening chapter. Beside from the cultural tradition of making arranged marriages for Indian children of higher castes, he manages to insert the sense of disenfranchisement between Hindu and Muslim in reference to political intrigues at the time. Due to being orthodox elements, no free relationship is allowed in India. Mostly the married people have to lead their life under social pressure. Indian marriages are arranged according to social and traditional values. All the rites related to the custom are performed orthodox elements support the Indian marriages. Indian married life entirely depends on compromise. In this novel, Lata submits to her mother Mrs. Mehra's arrangement that means she is defying not only her mother but also barriers of caste and religion. D.C.R.A. Goonetillke says "Lata finally settles for Hareesh, not implausible because unromantic, an index of Seth's own pragmatism and of the direction in which India is, probably, heading."[4]

There is a hint at the social caste system in the friends of Maan's who do not really fit in with the upper classes. The antagonism between Muslims and Hindus is depicted graphically when the Raja of March tears a page out of Saeeda Bai's book sent to her by Maan. Perhaps the attitudes of Maan and Lata towards Muslims indicate a much more tolerant position within the younger generation. It is an absolute wholesome picture of a secular India, giving an experience to the reader what it is to be an Indian as Thomas Blom Hansen says "The secular state in India, in other words, not merely produced public spheres full of reason and science, as is some times suggested. On the contrary, the public spheres in secular India remained full of religious signs and practices, packaged and represented as culture realm represented as a political pure a sublime now a Friday prayer, a mosque, or a Hindu procession and temple were no longer manifestations of community and sectarian strength but picturesque and awesome manifestations of Indian culture and the Indian nation."[5]

The details of the political conflicts going on in India after the partition which separated India and Pakistan, Seth's point of view is both wry and affectionate. Woven in to the main plot he shows the story of troubled times of 1950s, the rift in the congress, the abolition of zamindari system, arduous efforts by a country trying to stand on its own feet, religious strife, communal riots strands of cultural life. In other words, it is an absolute wholesome picture of secular India. In this novel, the political maneuvering of L.N. Agarwal, which almost causes the government confiscation of baiters' house, is the prime example of the effects of the Bihar Zamindari Act.

The theme of caste differences is covered heavily. The attitudes of the haves versus the have nots are clearly defined. Rasheed is fair and honest man who wants to do what is right by the people like Kechhery, but his father and grandfather want to keep them suppressed and not to give up any land by the Zamindari Bill. Conflict is foreshadowed in Rasheed's wanting to see the Kutchery, is taken as a case of aftermath of the Zamindari Bill. Key to the whole issue is Mahesh Kapoor's pushing of the Zamindari Act and Rasheed tries to use it to good effect, but his family opposes and censors him for his action part.

There is the political conflict over the Zamindari Act that comes ahead in the court. There is the conflict between Muslim and Hindu in the aftermath of the tragedy at the Ganga. There is the conflict between Veena and Mahesh over visiting Bhaskar in the hospital. An interesting irony is that it is the "Unsuitable Muslim Boy" Kabir who locates Bhaskar and notifies his family the fact that Lata and her mother are in Lucknow while all of this is going on mitigates the impact of Kabir's actions that might have influenced Lata a great deal.

Malati represents the liberated modern Indian girl who has affairs with boys as she desires. She is, however, discrete in her meeting with boys. Religious conflict and model principles are stressed as Maan continues his infatuation with Saeeda Bai. Seth's commentary on Hinduism includes Mrs. Rupa's not knowing much about her "Particular brand of Hinduism" Kakoli or Kuku also represents the younger generation's ideas about love and romance when she visits a rehearsal of Lata's play and declares Kabir to be "delicious". Seth also refers to the Muslim practice of sacrificing animals as something repugnant to Hindus. Politics is the theme and how they can become affected by isolated incidents.

The irony of the situation for Mahesh Kapoor is that he cannot bring pressure on the police investigations while attempting the limit, the ability of the landowners to pressurize local officials in order to retain their lands, in danger from the Zamindari Abolition and Land Reforms Act.

By involving so many characters in various complicated twists of plot—social, economic, and political the theme of *A Suitable Boy*, Seth wraps things up in something of a jumble of endings and beginning subjects with which he appears to be uncomfortable, he glosses over quickly, like Rasheed's suicide. Seth offers a huge thick and multi layered slice of Indian life that in its veracity serves to counter the widespread false views of India and improve the world's understanding. The structure of the novel is chronologically divided into 19 parts with enumerated sections. With each part the structure of the novel seems to stumble over, it lies in the effort to weave the theme of social change into the political conflicts in the early stage of post-colonialism and post-partition. Certain assumptions by Seth also complicate the structure of the work e.g. an assumption of universal understanding of Hindu and Muslim holidays as tradition.

The setting of the novel is mainly in Purva Pradesh, a fictitious province in India. The capital city of the province or state, is Brahmpur where the main political India occurs at the state level. Brahmpur is situated on the holy river Ganga and up river is the attraction called the Barsaat Mahal. The city is home to a major university, very urban shopping areas with movie theaters, parks, fields for athletics, cricket and polo. From Brahmpur, the action of the novel includes the real location of Calcutta, Delhi, Banaras. Much of the political campaigning took place in the Salempur-cum-Baitar region, an agricultural land, populated largely by Muslims.

The fictional Barsaat Mahal is based on the famous Taj Mahal in Agra. Its use in the novel represents romance. The industrial revolution affected the England of Austen, Nehru's socialist and industrial revolution affected the India of the fifties. Vikram Seth basically an English Brown Shahib, sits away from the growing and unfulfilling aspiration and consequent frustration of this middle class. The political conditions, Vikram Seth uses fall into three categories. In the first group, there are Indian national figures like Jawaharlal Nehru, Rafi Ahmed Kidwai and Rajrishi Purushotam Das Tandon who appears in their real name. Seth ministry assesses their role in Indian politics and points and their feet of clay. In the second category, there are some leaders who appear with changed names but their characters are identifiable. There is Purva Pradesh, Uttar Pradesh chief minister called S.S. Sharma who seems to be the sitting image of G.B. Pant, there are two state ministers, the secular Mahesh Kapoor who seems to be the dramatized version of Damoder

Swaroop Seth and L.N. Agarwal who echoes the personality of L.B. Gupta, the last group are fictional characters that represent the emergent forces in the Indian politics. In that regard, the theme of *A Suitable Boy* stands as a hallmark of traditional Indian customs and culture. The theme of religious intolerance runs heavily throughout the novel. The Raja of Marh becomes the arch symbol of religious militancy with his erecting the temple of shrine adjacent to a mosque. The phallic symbol of Shiva the centerpiece of the temple is an act of spite designed to insult muslims. On both sides the riots and attacks occur in the name of religion. Arranged marriages are not the only cultural custom but also there is an emerging shift in the role of women in the culture. Other women in the novel represent the post-partition modern Indian women, although the theme of politics in the novel is secondary to *A Suitable Boy* theme. It nevertheless lends credence to the social upheaval of post independent India. Anita Desai suggests that "If Seth's novel is to have an artistic equivalent, then it is the folk painting on village wall, a mural in a cave, or a stitched and embroidered quilt patiently patched together and embellished by that multiplicity of detail that gives it diversity and richness."[6]

NOTES

1. <www.enotescom.http//www.e.notes.com> Topic in depth.
2. Roopali Gupta, *Vikram Seth's Art an Appraisal*, Atlantic Publishers and Distributors, New Delhi, 60.
3. Seemita Mohanty, *A Critical Analysis of Vikram Seth's Poetry & Fiction*, Atlantic Publishers and Distributors, New Delhi, 159.
4. *Ibid.*, 160-61.
5. *Ibid.*, 165.
6. *Ibid.*, 200.